COPING WITH CAPITAL SURGES

COPING WITH CAPITAL SURGES

The Return of Finance to Latin America

edited by

Ricardo Ffrench-Davis

Stephany Griffith-Jones

Lynne Rienner Publishers ■ Boulder
International Development Research Centre ■ Ottawa

Published in the United States of America in 1995 by
Lynne Rienner Publishers, Inc.
1800 30th Street, Boulder, Colorado 80301

and in the United Kingdom by
Lynne Rienner Publishers, Inc.
3 Henrietta Street, Covent Garden, London WC2E 8LU

Published in Canada by the International Development Research Centre
PO Box 8500
Ottawa K1G 3H9 Canada
   Canadian ISBN 0-88936-602-0
   Canadian ISBN 0-88936-750-7 (pbk.)

Library of Congress Cataloging-in-Publication Data
Coping with capital surges: the return of finance to Latin America/
   edited by Ricardo Ffrench-Davis and Stephany Griffith-Jones.
      p.   cm.
   "IDRC-ECLAC project."
   Includes bibliographical references and index.
   ISBN 1-55587-562-9 (alk. paper) ISBN 1-55587-581-5 (pbk.) (alk. paper)
   1. Capital movements—Latin America. 2. Capital movements—
Government policy—Latin America. 3. Investments, Foreign—Latin
America. 4. Latin America—Economic policy. I. Ffrench-Davis,
Ricardo. II. Griffith-Jones, Stephany. III. International
Development Research Centre (Canada). IV. United Nations. Economic
Commission for Latin America and the Caribbean.
HG3891.C68   1995
332'.042—dc20   94-38888
                                                            CIP

British Cataloguing in Publication Data
A Cataloguing in Publication record for this book
is available from the British Library.

Printed and bound in the United States of America

     The paper used in this publication meets the requirements
 ∞ of the American National Standard for Permanence of
     Paper for Printed Library Materials Z39.48-1984.

 5 4 3 2 1

Contents

Preface

This book is based on a research project initially conceived at a brain-storming meeting called by the president of the International Development Research Centre of Canada (IDRC), Keith Bezanson. At this meeting, Roy Culpeper and Stephany Griffith-Jones defined the return of massive private capital flows to Latin America as a key emerging issue both in international finance and for the Latin American region. Soon after, these ideas were further developed in discussions among Ricardo Ffrench-Davis, David Glover, and Stephany Griffith-Jones.

We are very grateful to IDRC for rapidly responding to the need for research on this new, important topic, and for providing both substantive insights and financial support for the project. We thank IDRC's David Glover for helping develop the idea, Gary McMahon for supporting the initial phase of the project, and Rohinton Medhora for very important contributions during the rest of the project. We also wish to express our gratitude to the Economic Commission for Latin America and the Caribbean (ECLAC, or CEPAL) for providing intellectual and financial backing to this project as well as hosting two workshops, and to the World Bank for contributing a paper written by its staff members.

This research project is the fourth in a series of policy-oriented research studies funded by IDRC on key issues for Latin America and developing countries in general. The first, led by Stephany Griffith-Jones, dealt with negotiation of external debt; the second, led by Ennio Rodríguez, dealt with negotiation on adjustment; the third, led by Diana Tussie, dealt with trade negotiations. All the previous projects also resulted in books.

This project—like the previous ones funded by IDRC—has certain unique features. One is the interaction of senior academics and policy-makers, of specialists from developing and developed countries. This project benefited additionally from the participation of colleagues from international organizations, particularly ECLAC, the World Bank, the International Monetary Fund (IMF), and the Inter-American Development Bank (IDB).

A second characteristic of IDRC projects that this study shares is the use of several meetings among authors, with invited commentators, to enrich the results and share experiences. A first meeting was held in March 1993 in Santiago at ECLAC to discuss a framework paper for the project prepared by Roy Culpeper and Stephany Griffith-Jones and outlines of papers on case studies. A second meeting was held at the same location in December 1993 to discuss the drafts of papers contained in this book. In the latter meeting, we benefited from valuable contributions from commentators, which included representatives of the Chilean Central Bank and Ministry of Finance, the Federal Reserve Bank of Dallas, the World Bank, IDB, IMF, and private financial institutions (British, U.S., and Chilean), as well as academics.

A final set of meetings in which we presented the results of our project to senior academics, private financiers, central bankers, and journalists was held in London (at the Institute of Latin American Studies of London University), Washington, D.C. (at the Brookings Institute and IDB), and New York (at the United Nations). We are very grateful to Victor Bulmer-Thomas in London, Nora Lustig and Robert Devlin in Washington, and Cristián Ossa in New York for their crucial help in organizing such high-level meetings. We are also particularly grateful to Enrique Iglesias, president of the IDB, and Jean Claude Milleron, Undersecretary-General of the United Nations, for very stimulating and insightful comments.

The chapters in this volume are divided into three groups. The first group (Chapters 1, 2, and 3) deals with sources of flows, distinguishing between North American lending and investing (the main source of private flows to Latin America in the 1990s), European lending and investing (although second to the United States in importance, European flows are more significant than is generally perceived in the Latin American region), and Japanese funding (characterized until now by their rather low level). The first two chapters are written by academics and the third is written by two World Bank colleagues, Punam Chuhan and Kwang Jun. Although our book differentiates among the scale, features, and motivations of investors and lenders based in North America, Europe, and Japan (a distinction that we believe is valuable for a deeper understanding of the different markets), it is worth mentioning the limits of such a distinction, because of the trend toward globalization of financial markets. Each of the chapters on sources of financial flows analyzes separately foreign direct investment, securities (both bonds and shares), and bank lending, as well as examining the motivations of lenders and investors and existing regulations that affect such flows.

The second group of chapters (Chapters 4, 5, and 6) deals in depth with the features of capital flows and their macroeconomic impact, as well as the policy response of the economic authorities, in three Latin American countries: Chile, Argentina, and Mexico. All three countries are among those that have experienced particularly large increases in their capital inflows in the early 1990s, with a specially dramatic increase in the case of Mexico. Emphasis is placed on the variety of policy responses of the economic authorities to the massive inflows in the three countries; these policy responses fundamentally relate to attempts (1) to moderate the impact of capital inflows on appreciating the exchange rate (especially in the Chilean case); (2) to reduce the monetary impact of foreign exchange operations; and (3) to moderate capital inflows, particularly of a short-term nature (as was done especially in Chile and Colombia).

The authors of the case studies include senior policymakers, such as the former president of the Central Bank of Argentina, José Luis Machinea; the former deputy minister of finance of Mexico, José Angel Gurría; and the former research director of the Chilean Central Bank, Ricardo Ffrench-Davis; as well as other well-known Latin American economists such as Manuel Agosin, José María Fanelli, and Andras Uthoff.

The third section of the book (the concluding chapter, written by Robert Devlin and the two editors of the book) draws out the policy implications for recipient countries and lessons from the capital markets case studies. An important theme of this chapter is that the return of private capital flows to Latin America is to be welcomed, due both to their potential positive contribution to the recovery of economic activity and development in the region, and to the increased potential profitability for industrial countries' investors and lenders; however, to make the mutual benefits from these flows sustainable, governments, both in source and recipient countries, should take appropriate measures. Among the measures discussed are better monitoring of the flows and appropriate, as well as coordinated, supervision of such flows. Regulatory gaps are identified, such as the global regulation of securities, which urgently need to be filled. Of equal importance, in recipient countries adequate macroeconomic measures need to be taken to make the benefits of the private capital flows sustainable in the long term and to avoid, for example, excessive overvaluation of the currency and bubbles in the stock exchange.

The chapters in this book were written mainly in a time of abundance (and indeed overabundance) of capital flows to Latin America, and the issues of managing such abundance were dominant. At the time of finishing this book, there are uncertainties about the sustainability of those flows at the recent levels. These new trends reflect the volatility of such flows and the significance of policy implications that we have examined throughout this book.

Finally, it should be mentioned that, although this book focuses basically on the return of private flows to Latin America, many of the lessons and issues raised are relevant to other developing countries and to countries—

such as those of Eastern Europe—that are in transition to market economies. Furthermore, several of the monitoring and regulatory issues raised are relevant not just for flows to Latin America, nor just for flows to the even larger category of so-called emerging markets, but are of more global relevance.

We wish to thank Alvaro Calderón and Daniel Titelman for their valuable research assistance and Lenka Arriagada for her most efficient processing of the text.

Ricardo Ffrench-Davis
Stephany Griffith-Jones
Santiago, Chile
June 1994

1

Resurgence of Private Flows to Latin America: The Role of North American Investors

ROY CULPEPER

The 1980s were a "lost decade" to the people of Latin America because external debt and economic decline combined to reduce living standards and undermine regional aspirations toward a better future. Although no Latin countries formally repudiated their debt, a series of de facto defaults manifested by mounting arrears, even on rescheduled obligations, made external creditors extremely leery about increasing their exposure in the region. Instead, the principal private creditors, commercial banks, reduced their exposure by liquidating their loans, refusing to roll over credit lines, or denying fresh credit as old obligations were amortized. The severity of the debt crisis, when juxtaposed with its historical antecedents, left most observers pessimistic by the end of the decade as to the possibilities of a renewal of private capital flows into the region. Instead, the prevailing expectation was that heavily indebted regions must rely, for the foreseeable future, primarily on official flows, for example those provided by the multilateral development banks. Yet by the end of the decade, a resurgence of external private capital flows toward the Latin American region was under way that surprised even observers in recipient countries, in both its overall volume and composition of flows.

This chapter examines one of the primary source regions of the renewed capital flows, North America (primarily the United States). It addresses such questions as: What is the identifiable magnitude of the flows

1

between the regions? What is the composition of these flows, as between bond issuance, net equity purchases, foreign direct investment, and bank lending? What accounts for the sudden change in attitude of North American investors/creditors toward a region they so recently eschewed? What role does the tax and regulatory framework in North America play in either inhibiting or stimulating these flows? and finally, What is the outlook for future flows between North and Latin America?

North America in World Capital Markets Historically

There is nothing new about international capital flows; indeed, these have been considerably larger in the past relative to the size of the world economy.[1] One estimate states that, in relative terms, international flows during 1880–1914 were perhaps three times larger than in the 1980s (Eichengreen, 1991).

An interesting finding of the historical research is that international lenders seem to suffer from amnesia. For example, in the 1970s bank lenders to Latin American countries appeared to overlook the fact that many previous episodes of active lending (as during the 1920s) turned sour with widespread default (as during the 1930s)—by many of the same borrowers in Latin America and elsewhere. Moreover, there are few indications that there were penalties imposed by creditors upon defaulters (or rewards for nondefaulters) in the form of lesser (or greater) access to the creditors' capital markets. Instead, the evidence indicates that all borrowers (both defaulters and nondefaulters, such as Argentina) suffered loss of access to the private capital markets from the 1930s until the late 1960s (Eichengreen, 1991). This suggests that, other things being equal, it makes more sense for a borrower to default or to declare a conciliatory moratorium during difficult times than to endure the additional hardships of maintaining full debt service.

Over time, the shape and composition of the international capital markets, as well as the direction of capital flows, have all changed profoundly. Some borrowers became lenders in their own right. North America—here connoting only Canada and the United States—was a net debtor to the rest of the world prior to 1914. The United States accounted for 8.0 percent of world gross creditor positions but 15.5 percent of world gross debtor positions in 1914.

The situation changed dramatically, at least in the case of the United States, in the interwar years. In the 1920s, the United States became a net creditor on a massive scale, and New York became the center of international lending, before the 1929 crash (Canada remained a net debtor).

It was in the pessimistic aftermath of the depression that the postwar global economic order was established at Bretton Woods, primarily by the

United States and the United Kingdom. The new order was based on the premise that private international capital flows were not just unlikely—in large volumes they were also downright undesirable, bringing in their wake instability and loss of control over domestic economic policy (Bryant, 1987).[2] Thus, the International Monetary Fund (IMF) and the World Bank were both designed to increase stability, predictability, and the public-sector role in international capital markets. As the IMF Articles of Agreement still indicate, the world in 1945 was not unfriendly to restraints by nation-states on international capital flows.

In order to ascertain why and how private flows to the rest of the world resuscitated during and after the 1960s, it is necessary to appreciate the way in which domestic capital markets evolved within North America and Europe. The postwar foundations of North American capital markets were laid during the Great Depression. Widespread failures in the banking system created financial havoc by undermining the confidence ordinary citizens had regarding banks.

The collapse of the banking system, in turn, contributed to the depth and duration of the economic downturn. Pervasive default by international borrowers in Latin America and in other developing countries added to the financial turmoil by inflicting uncertainty and capital losses on bond-holders. These events gave a large impetus to the U.S. administration and the Congress to enact reforms (part of the "New Deal") to shore up the banking and financial systems.

To begin with, the Federal Securities Acts of the 1930s attempted to create a "firewall" between banking and the rest of the financial sector. The securities legislation had two objectives: first, to provide a safety net for banks to help protect against widespread insolvency during future downturns. Accordingly, government-backed insurance schemes were created for depositors; in addition, limits were imposed on the interest rates banks could offer depositors (via "Regulation Q").

Earlier, the McFadden Act of 1928 had prohibited interstate branch banking to protect smaller state and single-branch banks against competition from the large city-based banks. Such measures helped to increase the profitability of smaller banks. In addition, the Federal Reserve system (which had been created two decades earlier as a loose conglomeration of regional clearing banks) was transformed into an effective central bank with powers to control reserves, create liquidity, and act as a lender of last resort.

However, the securities legislation had a second objective—to put an end to the insider dealings that had so inflated stock prices in the run-up to the 1929 crash. It thus attempted to put an end to market manipulation of stock and bond prices by taking banks out of the business of underwriting, dealing, and brokering in corporate securities. Legislation in 1934 (the Securities Exchange Act) created the federal Securities and Exchange

Commission (SEC), which sets standards for the public disclosure of information concerning the financial condition and management of firms whose securities are offered on the nation's exchanges. In addition, the SEC initiated regulation of trading behavior on the exchanges, with enforcement powers to apprehend those involved in abuses such as conflicts of interest, price manipulation, and use of insider information (Pierce, 1991).

The shape and structure of the U.S. domestic capital market emerging from the depression set the context for the relationship between the United States as a capital exporter and developing-country capital importers in the postwar period out to 1990. To begin with, the bond market was more or less closed to developing-country borrowers. Bond-holders were chastened by the defaults of the depression, and settlement of outstanding claims lingered in some cases into the 1960s. Moreover, until recently, SEC registration requirements that were put in place to protect investors against high-risk bonds acted as a "barrier to entry" against developing-country bond issuers.[3]

The task of providing external capital to developing countries in the first two postwar decades was thus left largely to official lenders such as the World Bank and the Inter-American Development Bank, which was established in 1959. Private lenders and investors avoided developing-country markets. Eventually, the hiatus in private flows was ended—first, by a resumption of foreign direct investment, and second, through lending from the banking system. The story of why banking came to play such a prominent role in international capital flows is a curious one, and needs to be related to the evolution of banking after the depression.

The New Deal reforms and an unusually long period of economic growth and stability for two decades after World War II created the impression that banks had been rendered permanently safe and immune to failure (Pierce, 1991). But several developments were occurring in U.S. financial markets that threatened the profitability of the banking sector and forced it into high-risk lending activities (including lending to developing countries) not traditionally the preserve of commercial banks.

Precipitating these changes from the mid-1960s was a more inflationary environment due to the funding (via deficit financing) of the Vietnam War. Interest rates were eventually raised by the Federal Reserve in 1966 to curb excess demand. Because of the ceiling on deposit interest rates, however, some depositors withdrew funds to take advantage of higher rates on treasury bills (TBs) and other market instruments. Consequently, it became difficult for banks to meet loan demand from their commercial customers, leading to a "credit crunch." Partly as a result of this, business borrowers began to tap the market directly by selling highly liquid, short-term notes that offered competitive interest rates to investors and to state and local governments. This so-called commercial paper market grew by 50 percent in 1966, and in 1969 had expanded by 250 percent over 1965 levels. So began the trend to "disintermediation," in which borrowers access savers directly without the intermediation of deposit-taking banks (Pierce, 1991).

To stem the loss of deposits, the banks themselves resorted in the late 1960s to the short-term financial markets by developing negotiable certificates of deposit (CDs) in competition with commercial paper. However, banks were still constrained by interest rate ceilings so that they could not offer competitive rates on CDs when market levels rose above these ceilings. But this development marked the inception of "liability management": instead of being passively dependent on deposits for their loanable funds, banks now began to actively seek out the funds they needed by borrowing them in the market.

The "firewall" between banking and financial markets in the United States had begun to melt. U.S. regulators tried during the 1970s to keep these two markets apart through interest rate ceilings on bank deposits, on the assumption that these would constrain the banks' costs, maintain profitability, and obviate the need for high-risk lending. But, as depositors defected to higher-yielding instruments, this turned out to be more of a disadvantage than an advantage, and banks sought to circumvent the ceilings.

Interest rate ceilings could not be imposed on offshore markets, so by the end of the 1960s banks sought the funds they needed by offering CDs in the burgeoning Eurodollar markets centered in London. Moreover, domestically, large banks formed "holding companies," technically not banks, which could issue CDs not subject to the interest rate ceilings. All of these developments were accelerated by large-scale computerization, which made it easier for all operators in the financial markets, banks and nonbanks alike, to standardize their borrowing and lending procedures and to cut costs.

Hence, by the time of the first oil price shock (1973–1974), banks were well positioned to mop up excess international liquidity in the form of petrodollars, which flowed in large quantities from oil-exporting countries to the Euromarkets. In the new era of liability management, banks could float CDs in the Euromarkets, offering savers highly liquid and safe financial investments. The banks used the proceeds to make loans to developing-country borrowers, many of whom were plunged into acute balance-of-payments deficits by the oil price shock.

As is now well known, the banks were encouraged in this behavior by government officials throughout the world and by international organizations such as the IMF. It seemed urgent to remedy the international payments disequilibria caused by the two oil price shocks of the 1970s by recycling the petrodollar surpluses to deficit countries. The commercial banks rose to the task. What was peculiar, as far as banking was concerned, was the nature of most of the lending: unsecured general-purpose sovereign loans provided for balance-of-payments support, far removed from the usual custom of commercially tied and collateralized bank credit.

Another critical development, which broke down the barriers between banking and the rest of the U.S. financial sector, was the advent in the 1970s of money-market mutual funds (MMFs) as deposit-taking intermediaries. Technically, MMFs offer shares to the public in a fund that invests in high-yielding and low-risk securities, such as TBs, CDs, and commercial paper. In practice, the shares are used as checking accounts, very similar to interest-bearing demand deposits. The intense competition for deposits from the MMFs ultimately led banks to pressure for the introduction of interest-bearing checking accounts and the effective termination of Regulation Q in 1982 (Litan, 1991).

But the resulting competition for deposits simply intensified during the late 1970s and early 1980s. Added to escalating liability management, the result was a spectacular growth in assets and growing competition for borrowers. So banks found themselves faced with competition on both sides of their balance sheets, with regard to liabilities (borrowed funds, including deposits) as well as assets (loans). Competition for clients led to a binge in lending domestically to energy, agriculture (because of booming commodity and energy prices), and real estate. Internationally, there was another surge in lending to Latin American and other developing countries after 1979, associated with the second oil price shock. International lending was regarded by the banks as part of a portfolio diversification strategy. The lack of any international regulation, however, led to excessive bank lending to some countries and insufficient concern with risk. Both factors were to be abruptly reversed in the 1980s, as banks abruptly ceased lending and became acutely risk averse (Devlin, 1989).

Developments in Financial Markets Since 1980

The story of the subsequent debt crisis after 1982, precipitated by high interest rates and recession in the countries of the Organization for Economic Cooperation and Development (OECD), is now well known. The debt crisis, especially in its initial stages, appeared to threaten the solvency of the U.S. banking system, although it did not at any point lead to the insolvency of any particular U.S. bank.

Indeed, the rapidly rising failure rate of U.S. banks in the 1980s was due more to their exposure to domestic borrowers in crisis—in agriculture, energy, and real estate development—all victims of price deflation in the latter half of the 1980s. By 1989, the fraction of U.S. bank assets devoted to real estate loans had climbed to 37 percent (IMF, 1991). Moreover, a growing portion of the lending portfolios of larger banks was concentrated in risky domestic transactions such as leveraged buyouts (LBOs); by 1990, more than 35 percent of the domestic commercial loans of money-center banks supported LBOs (IMF, 1993a). Total losses from failed banks over the next several years are estimated at between U.S.$15 billion and U.S.$88 billion, centering around U.S.$30 billion. These losses are concentrated in the larger banks, which tend to have riskier loan portfolios and are less well capitalized than the smaller banks (IMF 1993a: 19).[4]

In contrast, the banks were never as vulnerable to default by their Third World borrowers as by their domestic borrowers. When the debt crisis broke out in 1982, the exposure of U.S. banks to developing countries was around 11 percent of total assets; this proportion fell continuously thereafter, due to liquidation of developing-country loans and a rapid buildup of lending to the domestic sectors. Problems in the banks' developing-country portfolios surfaced a few years before their loans to domestic borrowers ran into trouble. It was thus easier for banks to take remedial measures to protect themselves (e.g., through loan-loss reserves) during the boom years of the mid- to late 1980s and to reduce foreign exposure in favor of domestic clients.

Rapid and profound changes continued to shake U.S. financial markets during the 1980s. The postwar financial order, created out of the shambles of the depression by the New Deal reforms, more or less disappeared. The privileged position of banks had been eroded by technology and the forces of competition. The turmoil that engulfed all the deposit-taking institutions (banks and the savings and loan associations, or "thrifts") illustrated the quandary facing these intermediaries, formerly the bedrock of the financial sector. Despite liability management, banks and thrifts are in part still passively dependent for their funding on deposits; and their main assets—custom-made commercial loans and mortgages—are illiquid. Bank loans, by their very nature, are assets held to term, and unlike other financial assets are not generally tradable on secondary markets. This imbues the banks' asset portfolios with considerable inflexibility.

Technology and market forces conspired to undercut the banks and thrifts at their own business through the innovation of standardized borrowing and lending, and via the process of "securitization." As the term suggests, the end product of such financial innovation is generally a financial asset that can be traded on secondary markets. Investors who buy tradable securities enjoy a degree of liquidity that banks, investing in loans, cannot. Securitization originated in U.S. financial markets when mortgages were pooled by federal agencies and sold to investors in the form of certificates collateralized by the underlying loans. This practice was later extended to consumer credit by private creditors such as General

Motors Acceptance Corporation (GMAC) and G.E. Capital. The ability to sell such assets to investors enables the creditor to extend credit to a much wider pool of borrowers, substantially enhancing lending capacity. Consequently, finance companies such as GMAC had more equity capital than any U.S. bank except for Citicorp. Indeed, in 1990, GMAC's assets exceeded those of all the banks except the two largest (Litan, 1991).

Banks eventually rose to the challenge of securitization during the Third World debt crisis. A secondary market in bank loans to developing countries, was, in fact, organized after about 1985 by investment dealers who found purchasers (often speculators or agents for debt-equity swaps) for banks wishing to unload or swap portions of their Third World debt portfolios. Although bid and offer prices eventually were published, this was largely a "distress" market heavily influenced by large individual transactions. This market was initially thin and lacked liquidity; nonetheless, the fact that bank loans could be bought and sold by third parties marked an important transition toward the securitization of bank assets.

Eventually, a part of the overhang of bank lending to the developing countries became "securitized" via debt conversions and the Brady Plan. The latter involved a negotiated conversion, under the auspices of official agencies including the IMF, the World Bank, and the U.S. Treasury, of bank debt into bonds. By mid-1993, eight debtor countries had reached agreements with their creditor banks, resulting in the conversion of their bank debts into bonds, which either reduced the principal outstanding or reduced interest costs. Six were Latin American debtors: Argentina, Bolivia, Costa Rica, Mexico, Uruguay, and Venezuela.

Other debt conversions did not take place under official sponsorship but utilized the secondary market for bank loans. These featured purchasers of discounted bank debt who negotiated with debtor countries to transform their claims into portfolio equity, local debt, or the purchase of real assets. Privatization of state-owned enterprises became a major vehicle for the conversion of bank debt into claims on real assets in Mexico, Chile, and Argentina. When the purchasers were foreign investors, as they were to a great extent, such debt-equity swaps also constituted one of the main channels of foreign direct investment. The secondary market grew substantially: turnover (including "Brady bonds" and new instruments) was estimated at U.S.$200 billion in 1991 and as much as U.S.$500 billion in 1992 (IMF, 1993b).

But in the final analysis, the Brady Plan and the conversion of bank claims into other assets represented variations of options whereby banks could "exit" from their positions in developing countries. The real significance of securitization and the conversion of bank debt is that they paved the way back for developing-country borrowers into the international bond and other markets. Brady bonds enabled them to establish an international market presence without having to go through the conventional process of public offerings. Once this financial beachhead was attained, all that remained was for borrowers to access capital markets in more conventional ways.

The acute debt-servicing problems of the 1980s brought to an end the willingness and the ability of the banks to continue to lend to developing countries. Heavy loan-loss provisioning from 1987 formally recognized the doubtful nature of much Third World lending. The disincentive to lend was heightened by the Basle accords on bank capital adequacy in 1989, which required that banks maintain a capital-asset ratio of 8 percent against their Third World assets, a much higher ratio than prevalent at most banks. With the withdrawal of the banks, which had been by far the leading sources of external capital, it was widely believed at the end of the 1980s (as in the early postwar period) that developing-country borrowers would likely be heavily dependent on official creditors such as the multilateral banks in the foreseeable future (World Bank, 1991).

Recent Flows to Latin America: The Role of the U.S. Capital Market

We have already alluded to the rise during the 1970s of money-market mutual funds in the United States. During the 1980s the trend continued toward the institutionalization of investment, under the management of mutual funds, pension funds, and life insurance companies. Because of demographic shifts (the aging of the "baby boom" generation, leading to a buildup of pension funds and life insurance) and because of investor preferences for professional management of their portfolios, an increasing portion of household financial assets came to be managed in such "collective investment institutions" (see Table 1.1).

Table 1.1   Growth of Institutional Investors
(collective financial assets as a percentage of household assets)

	1980	1985	1990
United States	20.0	26.0	31.2
Japan	15.6	20.2	26.4
Germany	22.6	29.0	35.1
France	10.6	23.6	36.3
United Kingdom	41.5	53.1	58.6
Canada	20.4	24.9	29.7

Source: OECD (1993), p. 22.

Mutual fund assets alone have enjoyed spectacular growth since 1980. By 1987 some 2,000 funds were available in the United States; this doubled to more than 4,200 in June 1993. At that point there were twice as many funds as shares listed on the New York Stock Exchange, and mutual-fund assets, at U.S.$1.8 trillion, were almost as large as commercial-bank deposits.

Another important development took place in the structure of pension plans. Throughout North America there has been a pronounced shift away from "defined-benefit" pension schemes, which stipulate the level of pension benefits to be paid out of cumulative pension assets, toward "defined-contribution" schemes. The latter, which stipulate only the value of cumulative contributions (including capital gains and reinvested income), have been given preferred tax status in the United States and Canada. Beneficiaries are often given a choice of investment vehicles, so these pension plans have also supported the growth of mutual funds and other portfolio investments offering diversification. As such funds proliferated, many began to offer investors special "niches," for example, investing in international securities. The number of international funds increased by 80 percent from 1990 to 1993 (*Economist*, August 14, 1993).

Yet other important developments took place during the 1980s that transformed the economic prospects of many Latin American borrowers and permitted them to access the evolving capital markets in North America and elsewhere. These changes occurred partly under economic reforms introduced by the multilateral institutions during the 1980s and partly through negotiations with banks and official creditors in the Paris Club. Reforms led to large-scale divestiture by governments of productive enterprises.

Economic reforms brought about a complete change in the climate for foreign investment. By 1990, a new breed of U.S. portfolio investors, examining the risks and returns inherent in Latin American markets, found them vastly more appealing than did the commercial banks a few years earlier, when the principal borrowers in Latin America were governments experiencing debt-servicing problems. Moreover, a deepening recession and falling interest rates in the United States and other industrial countries made investment in those markets less appealing relative to opportunities in the emerging markets of Latin America (Culpeper and Griffith-Jones, 1992; Calvo, Leiderman, and Reinhart, 1993).

Since 1989, the resurgence of capital flows has taken three principal forms: foreign direct investment (FDI), bond purchases, and portfolio equity flows, in that order (see Table 1.2). The flows to Latin America show a similar pattern (see Table 1.3). The portfolio portions (bonds and equity) are considered next.

Table 1.2   Capital Inflows to Developing Countries, 1989–1992
(millions of U.S.$)

	1989	1990	1991	1992
FDI flows	28,644	31,345	38,768	40,000[a]
Bonds	5,487	6,164	12,527	23,574
Portfolio equity[b]	—	1,262	5,442	9,391

Source: FDI—UN (1993a); bonds and equity—IMF (1993b).
Notes: [a]Estimate.
[b]New issues only; secondary purchases are additional.

Table 1.3   Capital Inflows to Latin America, 1989–1992
(millions of U.S.$)

	1989	1990	1991	1992
FDI flows	8,326	9,950	15,235	16,000[a]
Bonds	833	2,589	6,832	12,272
Portfolio equity[b]	—	98	4,120	4,195

Source: FDI—UN (1993a); bonds and equity—IMF (1993b).
Notes: [a]Estimate.
[b]New issues only.

Bond Issuance

A strong recovery for developing-country borrowers took hold in the international bond markets after 1989, particularly for countries in the Western Hemisphere. Mexico and, to a lesser degree, Brazil led this re-entry (see Table 1.4).

Table 1.4   International Bond Issues by Developing Countries
(millions of U.S.$)

	1989	1990	1991	1992	First half 1993
Developing countries	5,487	6,164	12,527	23,574	21,218
Asia	1,601	1,630	3,099	6,014	4,930
Western Hemisphere	833	2,589	6,832	12,272	11,167
Argentina		21	795	1,570	941
Brazil			1,837	3,655	2,962
Chile			200		333
Mexico	570	2,306	3,373	5,916	5,932

Source: IMF (1993b), table 7.

Why did the bond markets recover so dramatically, and why has the resurgence particularly benefited the Latin American borrowers? Part of the reason—certainly in the cases of Mexico and Argentina—was the Brady Plan, which helped to pave the re-entry of those two borrowers into the bond markets. This does not, however, explain the re-entry of Brazil into the bond markets because that country by October 1993 still had not reached a debt-restructuring agreement (a "Brady package") with its creditor banks.

One may try to explain the revival of bond flows by examining the behavior of bond investors. However, the source or ultimate origin of bond financing is not simple to discern using "demand-side" data (i.e., data on countries issuing bonds and markets of issuance). In particular, the share of U.S. investors or residents in the flows of bond financing is not easy to extract from these data. The reason is that it is difficult to disaggregate sources of financing, especially in the international (or Euro-) markets, which are much larger than the domestic markets. Since 1990, these markets have absorbed from three to five times the volume of foreign bond issues offered in the major domestic markets of the United States, Japan, Europe, and elsewhere (see Table 1.5). Moreover, the currency denomination of offerings in the international market does not reveal much about the nationality of the bond purchaser. Most investors purchasing U.S. dollar Eurobonds are not necessarily U.S. residents or nationals; instead, they are likely to be international investors who maintain diversified portfolios in assets denominated in various currencies.

Thus, although more than a third of the international issues in recent years have been denominated in U.S. dollars, this does not necessarily correspond to the proportion of U.S. investors. Indeed, one source estimates that only 15 percent of a U.S. dollar Eurobond issued for Latin American borrowers is taken up by U.S. investors, whereas 55 percent is bought by

Table 1.5   International and Foreign Bond Offerings, 1990–1992
(billions of U.S.$)

	1990	1991	1992
International (Euromarket) issues	180.1	248.5	276.1
U.S. dollar	70.0	76.9	103.2
Deutsche Mark	18.3	19.9	33.8
Yen	22.8	35.7	33.7
Foreign issues (in domestic markets)	49.8	49.1	57.6
United States	9.9	12.9	23.2
Switzerland	23.2	20.2	18.1
Japan	7.9	5.2	7.4

Source: OECD (1993), table 1, p. 113.

Europeans, 20 percent by Latin Americans, and the remaining 10 percent by Japanese and other investors (Fedder and Mukherjee, 1992). These estimates most likely understate the share of U.S. investors; nonetheless, much of the bond financing flows to Latin America does appear to originate in Europe, and from flight capital of Latin American investors.

Most investors in the domestic bond markets, on the other hand, can be presumed to be residents; thus, U.S. residents are the predominant investors in the U.S. bond market. This market was estimated to raise up to U.S.$150 billion for bond issuers by 1990. Most of the bond issuers in the U.S. market are, in turn, domestic issuers. Foreign bond issues in this market (the so-called Yankee market), accounted for about 10 percent of the total; and developing-country borrowers have traditionally accounted for a small fraction—at most 10 percent of foreign issues, or 1 percent of the total—until the 1990s (Fedder and Mukherjee, 1992). As mentioned above, stringent SEC registration requirements severely restricted this market for developing-country issuers until 1989, when the SEC introduced Rule 144-A. The latter liberalized access only to the private placement segment of the U.S. market, however, and did not exempt issuers from the stringent financial disclosure requirements for listings in the larger publicly traded market.

Data on the "demand" side are not helpful in ascertaining the ultimate origin of (and the share of U.S. investors in) financing for bond offerings, but some indications of the sources of funding can be found from supply-side data. Recent surveys of U.S. portfolio investors indicate that a major institutional source of investment in bonds in the United States was the insurance industry (bonds comprised 60 percent of these institutions' assets in 1992). In 1992, foreign bonds were said to have accounted for 3.7 percent of their U.S.$1,624 billion in assets. U.S. insurance companies are subject to restrictions on the composition of their investment portfolios by the state in which they are domiciled. In New York State, there is a ceiling of 6 percent on the proportion of foreign assets. Moreover, there are further restrictions on investing in foreign securities that are rated below investment grade by the industry association (Chuan, 1993). Because very few Latin American issuers to date have been given an investment-grade rating, this limits investment in Latin bonds to a small share of the insurance companies' portfolios.

Further evidence on the relative share of U.S. investors is provided by U.S. Treasury data (see Table 1.6). However, the data include both new issues and secondary market purchases as well as sales of foreign securities. Moreover, the data refer to transactions in the U.S. market and do not refer to the nationality of the transactors. Thus, the ultimate purchasers of Latin American bonds issued in the U.S. market could include Latin American, European, and Japanese investors.

Table 1.6   Sales of Long-Term Bonds by Foreigners in the United States
(millions of U.S.$)

	1991	1992
Total	340,294	504,129
Latin America/Caribbean[a]	19,575	33,716
Argentina	373	791
Brazil	415	412
Chile	58	90
Mexico	1,108	3,522

Source: Computed from U.S. Treasury (1992, 1993), table CM-V-5.
Note: [a]Includes Netherlands Antilles and British West Indies.

The data for Latin America and the Caribbean are further skewed by the inclusion of the Netherlands Antilles, Cayman Islands, Bermuda, and Bahamas offshore banking centers, through which U.S. and international transactions are effected.[5] To the extent that these data reflect transactions undertaken by U.S. investors (and not simply by U.S. brokers on behalf of both U.S. and non-U.S. residents), they suggest that U.S. investors play a significant, but not necessarily preponderant, role in financing bond flows to the region. Bearing in mind that the gross flows of Table 1.6 include secondary market purchases whereas the figures in Table 1.4 represent new bond issues, it can be surmised that in 1991 and 1992, U.S. residents were significant investors in Argentine and Mexican bonds, but less so in Brazilian bonds. Overall, Latin American bonds accounted for about 6 percent of gross foreign bonds (including those issued in offshore banking centers) purchased by U.S. investors.

Bond flows to Mexico include purchases of Cetes, which are peso-denominated obligations of the Mexican Treasury. The IMF estimates that foreigners purchased U.S.$5.9 billion worth of Cetes in 1991–1992 (IMF, 1993b). This is a dramatic and virtually unprecedented development; few observers would have predicted in 1989 that foreign investors would purchase peso-denominated paper in such large volumes. It demonstrates the "bullishness" with which some investors have regarded the Mexican market in the early 1990s.

Despite the fact that U.S. insurance companies and pension companies still take a very cautious approach to investing in emerging market bonds (Chuan, 1993), the surge in bond investment that has taken place in 1993 is attributable to life insurance companies as well as to mutual funds and other institutional investors with an "appetite" for lower-rated (and therefore higher-yielding) debt, such as that issued by Latin American sovereigns and private firms. This segment, particularly of the Yankee bond market, has been considerably widened because of the relative decline of domestic U.S. interest rates and bond yields (*Financial Times,* April 5, 1993).[6]

Portfolio Equity Flows

Since 1990, international equity issues, particularly of Latin American countries, have grown extremely rapidly to the point where they now account for a significant volume of capital inflows (Table 1.7). In addition to the purchase of new issues, portfolio equity flows to developing countries have also taken place through secondary market purchases by foreign investors. These were estimated at U.S.$12 billion in 1991 and U.S.$14 billion in 1992, when emerging market transactions were said to account for 28 percent of all international equity flows (IMF, 1993b). Available data indicate that secondary market inflows, which amounted to almost U.S.$46 billion from 1989 to 1992, were considerably larger than primary inflows over the same period (Howell, 1993).

There has been much analysis recently of the phenomenal rise of international equity flows to emerging markets since 1990.[7] As to developing-country capital importers, this recent literature suggests that equity markets in the industrial countries represent a huge and largely untapped source of capital. Only 0.1 to 0.2 percent of the assets of institutional funds are placed in emerging market securities, well below the emerging markets' 7 percent share of world stock market capitalization (Agtmael, 1993; Chuan, 1993). In 1991, total assets of pension funds and life and casualty insurance companies in five major industrial nations (Canada, Germany, Japan, the United Kingdom, and the United States) were estimated at U.S.$8.3 trillion (World Bank, 1993a); in the United States alone these assets were estimated at U.S.$5.6 trillion in 1992 (Chuan, 1993). Thus, considerable additional annual equity investment in emerging market securities

Table 1.7   International Equity Issues by Developing Countries
              (millions of U.S.$)

	1990	1991	1992	First half 1993
Developing countries	1,262	5,442	9,391	4,179
Asia	1,040	1,028	4,732	1,478
Western Hemisphere	98	4,120	4,195	2,611
Argentina		356	504	2,095
Brazil			133	
Chile	98		129	114
Mexico		3,764	3,058	375

Source: IMF (1993b), table 13.

is projected over the next decade—some estimates are around U.S.$15–30 billion per year. The funding will come from growth in institutional investors' assets (pension funds, insurance companies, and mutual funds) fed by additional savings in the industrial countries, and from "rebalancing" of portfolios to invest a larger share in emerging markets (Chuan, 1993; Howell, 1993).

From the viewpoint of industrial-country investors, emerging market equities represent a new opportunity to increase portfolio returns. In the long run, returns in emerging markets are likely to be higher than in the industrial countries because economic growth will be higher, particularly once the economic policy environment is conducive. In the late 1980s, market-friendly economic reforms were implemented in many Latin American countries. Moreover, the reforms included liberalization of access to local stock markets, which traditionally had been restricted.

The recent surge of equity inflows has itself helped to bid up stock prices substantially. According to the International Finance Corporation, total returns in U.S. stockmarkets (as measured by the Standard and Poor's 500) from 1987 to 1992 were 119 percent; in contrast, total returns for 20 emerging markets in the same period were 148 percent. Returns in Latin America in the same period were a spectacular 321 percent (World Bank, 1993a). Moreover, returns on "investible" portfolios available to foreign investors show how superior performance in Latin American countries was compared to developed-country equities (Table 1.8). There are, however, risks that if large equity outflows occur, stock prices can fall sharply.

At the same time as increasing their returns, industrial-country investors stood to decrease their risks (as measured by the variability of returns) by diversifying their portfolios into emerging market equities—a rather counterintuitive result because increasing returns are usually obtained only with increasing risk. Indeed, analysis by the World Bank suggests that if U.S. investors had held 20 percent of their portfolios in emerging markets (compared with actual holdings of around 0.2 percent) they would have increased their returns by 1 percent and reduced their risk by some two to three percentage points. This finding is based on the low previous correlations between the developed and emerging market indices: returns in these two markets have tended, especially until recently, not to move in the same direction at the same time, indicating that a certain amount of diversification lowers the overall volatility (and hence risk) of the portfolio. However, the same analysis suggests that increasing the share of emerging markets beyond 20 percent increases risk, even though total returns would continue to increase (i.e., the normal risk-return relationship occurs) (World Bank, 1993a).

The statistical basis of this relationship has recently been challenged. Correlations between developed and emerging market indices are low for

Table 1.8   Annualized Investible Total Returns, 1988–1992
(percent returns, measured in U.S.$)

Argentina	115.1
Brazil	60.5
Chile	46.9
Mexico	55.2
Venezuela	90.6
United States	15.6
EAFE[a]	–2.2

Source: IFC (1993), p. 74.
Note: [a]Europe, Australia, and Far East (developed countries).

short periods of time (monthly observations) but much higher over longer periods (yearly observations). Thus, over the long run, the benefits of diversification in the form of lower risks may be significantly reduced. Underlying this statistical debate are contesting hypotheses on the degree of integration of world capital markets. Low correlation coefficients support a hypothesis of low integration: markets respond to local, not global, economic forces. Conversely, high correlation coefficients provide evidence of a greater degree of global market integration. Most observers agree that, over time, market correlation coefficients will increase as real (goods) markets also become increasingly integrated on a global scale (see Mullin, 1993).

In contrast to the "rational" motivation of global portfolio diversification, there is also a "herd mentality" among some investors who do not necessarily discriminate within regions. The two motivations are not necessarily inconsistent. Latin America could be considered "hot" by foreign investors who wish to diversify away from, say, East Asia, but who do not differentiate between countries in the region. This might explain why Brazil (despite its macroeconomic problems) has been a beneficiary of portfolio inflows, along with Mexico and Chile (countries that have resolved their macroeconomic problems to a greater extent). This lack of differentiation does not reflect irrationality as much as the fact that information is costly. At the same time, a "stampede" toward Latin America as a whole represents portfolio diversification at the global level, since hitherto the "emerging markets" were concentrated in East and Southeast Asia. Unfortunately, such "bandwagon" effects can be dynamically unstable, as new inflows bid up prices in a self-fulfilling cycle until prices reach unsustainable levels. This appears to have happened in 1992.

As with bond markets, a question is what percentage of equity flows originate with investors resident in the United States. And as with bond flows, the answer is difficult to extract from the demand-side data. It is worth noting that the portfolios of U.S. equity investors are strongly biased toward domestic equities, which account for about 96 percent of their investments. If U.S. investors were internationally diversified, they would hold a much lower share in U.S. equities because U.S. equity markets account for only about one-third of total world market capitalization (Tesar and Werner, 1993).

Moreover, even though U.S. investors are no doubt relatively important, they have until recently not been the leading foreign investors in emerging markets. Some evidence on recent flows is provided by Howell (1993), according to whom U.K. residents were the largest providers of equity capital on the secondary markets, with net purchases from 1989 to 1992 of U.S.$10.4 billion out of a total of U.S.$45.9 billion. U.S. investors were in second place with a total of U.S.$9.6 billion, or about one-fifth of the total. Other significant sources of investment were Hong Kong, Japan, Switzerland, and other European countries.

However, the share of U.S. investors likely increased during 1991–1992. Data are available from the U.S. Treasury on foreign equity purchases in the United States (Table 1.9). As with the Treasury data on bond purchases, these figures include both initial offerings and secondary market transactions. And as with the bond data, the figures reflect the locus of transaction in the United States and do not necessarily pertain to transactions exclusively by U.S. investors.

Comparing the data of Table 1.9 on gross sales of equity by foreigners (i.e., purchases by U.S. investors) with the data of Table 1.7 on equity issues by Latin American countries, one can infer that, in contrast to bond finance, U.S. investors appear to have provided a significant proportion of equity financing for Mexico, Brazil, and Argentina. The huge figures for Mexico reflect the U.S.$2 billion flotation of Telmex shares in the U.S. markets in 1991–1992 as part of the privatization of the telecommunications utility. Particularly in 1992, gross equity sales exceeded new equity issues by a considerable margin, indicating a high level of secondary market purchases (in Brazil new issues were relatively low).[8]

The strong interest of U.S. investors in Latin American equity is partly due to the presence of Latin flight capital in the U.S. market, as well as growing business and trade links with the region. The Enterprise for the Americas initiative and the negotiation of the North American Free Trade Agreement (NAFTA) with Mexico have both enhanced the potential of economic integration in the region. This in turn has increased the degree of interest by U.S. investors in obtaining a stake in rapidly growing companies in the region.

Recent empirical work suggests that falling U.S. interest rates and the slowdown in the U.S. economy explain about one-half of the equity outflows to Latin America (Calvo, Leiderman, and Reinhart, 1993; Chuan, Claessens, and Mamingi, 1993). Country or local factors such as the

Table 1.9   Sales of Portfolio Equity by Foreigners to U.S. Residents
(millions of U.S.$)

	1991	1992
Total	151,190	182,173
Latin America/Caribbean[a]	12,703	19,673
Argentina	149	749
Brazil	626	1,968
Chile	43	171
Mexico	7,031	8,391

Source: Computed from U.S. Treasury (1992, 1993), table CM-V-5.
Note: [a]Includes Netherlands Antilles and British West Indies.

performance of the local stock market explain the remaining variation in flows. Other work, however, has found a much weaker relationship between these variables (Tesar and Werner, 1993).

Such empirical work may be important in predicting the behavior of equity investors if conditions were to change—for example, if interest rates were to rise in the United States or if the rate of growth in industrial countries were to pick up. The implication of the work of those who emphasize global rather than local factors is that the inflows to Latin America in 1989 to 1992 could easily be reversed once economic conditions in the industrial countries improve and interest rates begin to rise sufficiently.

It is worth noting that a dramatic shift took place in the latter half of 1992 and the first half of 1993 because of a stock market "correction" emanating from Mexico to the rest of Latin America. Overvalued stock prices declined by some 25 percent on average from June to October. The extent of the fall varied between countries, from about 20 percent in Chile to well over 50 percent in Argentina and Brazil. Given the magnitude of this correction, it seems important that foreign investors did not abandon the region altogether when the bull market in equities stalled. Instead, preliminary reports indicate that portfolio investment continued to increase in 1993, but the increase has been largely in the form of bond financing.

Finally, the rapid expansion of the "derivatives"[9] market may be grounds for some concern. According to some estimates, the face amount of derivative products is now around U.S.$14 trillion (Wall Street Journal, October 28, 1993). Most of the concern expressed so far (e.g., by Federal Reserve Chairman Alan Greenspan or Board member Gerald Corrigan) is for the potential systemic instability that might be triggered by the failure of key operators in the market. Analysis by the Group of Thirty has called for greater transparency in dealer operations (by adopting daily market-to-market valuations of their daily positions), but by and large their July 1993 report suggested that threats to global systemic stability were small and could be contained. In any case, even if derivatives posed threats to systemic stability, it is not clear how regulators could remedy the problem because most trades occur in the over-the-counter market (i.e., they take place privately between dealers and their customers) and are not listed on exchanges. Indeed, for this reason basic information on the volume and nature of transactions is difficult to collect.

It can be surmised that most derivatives transactions take place between domestic parties in the same industrial country. Increasingly, however, the nature of these transactions is international; for example, the underlying assets are frequently foreign assets. Again, data are extremely scarce. At least one informed observer (a U.S. official) claims that trading of derivatives based on Mexican securities has grown very rapidly and is extremely brisk, and that the potential exists for great volatility in the market. The same observer claimed that some U.S.$6 billion in paper losses were sustained due to derivatives trades in Mexico in 1992. The implication of all this is that there is a need for greater transparency and information on the volume and nature of derivatives transactions, as well as a need for further discussion and analysis of the requirements for prudential oversight.

The Regulatory Environment, Taxation, and U.S. Portfolio Flows

To what extent do regulations governing domestic capital market transactions in the United States impede access to developing-country issuers of securities wishing to access the U.S. capital market? Two kinds of regulations are pertinent: those governing all transactions in the market and those governing the behavior of particular actors. In the first category are the regulations of the U.S. Securities and Exchange Commission; in the second is legislation or even self-imposed rules affecting the activity of institutional investors such as life insurance companies and pension funds. Both categories of regulations currently inhibit the volume and nature of securities issued in the U.S. market.

With regard to marketwide regulations, the greatest "barrier to entry" of Latin American entities (particularly corporations) to the public domestic market (including the Yankee market for bonds and public listings of equity issues on stock exchanges) are the registration requirements by the SEC for full financial disclosure. Such requirements include adherence to U.S. generally accepted accounting principles (GAAP). Very few, if any, non-U.S. corporate entities have until now been able to meet this standard. A great many Latin American enterprises are either state-owned or closely held (privately owned) firms managed by majority stockholders. In either case management is typically reluctant to be as transparent and forthright as publicly held private firms in OECD countries.[10] For this reason, initial entry into the U.S. market has typically begun with private placement of securities, which obviates the need for full SEC-mandated registration and disclosure.

However, entry into the private placement market was also constrained until the adoption of Rule 144-A by the SEC in April 1990, by which private placements are restricted to eligible investors (referred to historically as "sophisticated investors"). Before the adoption of Rule 144-A, the problem with such private placements was that buyers had to hold the securities for at least two years before reselling them to other eligible investors, and even then the process implied a cumbersome, costly procedure involving case-by-case decisions by the SEC. The resulting loss of market liquidity, administrative uncertainty, and transactions costs inhibited issuers of securities as well as investors. Rule 144-A (and "Regulation S," which clarifies its implementation) enables "qualified institutional buyers" (some 3,300 institutions and broker-dealers that meet certain minimum size or net worth requirements) to buy and resell privately placed securities before the two-year restricted period (Bank of New York, 1992). Many Latin American companies entered the U.S. equity market by issuing American Depositary Receipts (ADRs)[11] under Rule 144-A in the private placement market. Rule 144-A has reduced both the time and the cost of accessing the U.S. equity market. A Rule 144-A ADR issue typically costs about U.S.$500,000 in fees and takes six weeks to process, compared to several million dollars and six to eight months for publicly listed ADRs (Chuan, 1993, p. 33).

Another marketwide regulation that may constrain entry into the U.S. capital market is Rule 17f-5 of the Investment Company Act of 1940. This rule requires that custody of foreign securities can be provided only by institutions with a minimum of U.S.$200 million in shareholder equity. This rule affects smaller mutual funds, which have been among the more aggressive investors in emerging markets. The SEC is currently reviewing the rule and may reduce the U.S.$200 million requirement (IMF, 1993b).

With regard to the behavior of U.S. institutional investors, both legislation and self-imposed regulation limit the foreign content of investment portfolios. The regulatory environment is complicated by the involvement of both federal and state legislative authorities. For example, the life insurance industry is regulated by states, and regulations vary from state to state.

In the case of the life insurance industry there are regulations that govern both the foreign content and the asset quality of investment portfolios. Such regulations come under the authority of state governments. New York State, the most influential state on these issues, limits the foreign investments of insurance companies to 6 percent of assets—a ceiling that has only recently been raised from 3 percent. Because "foreign investments" include securities of other developed countries (except for Canada, which is exempt), the effect of this ceiling is to limit emerging market investments to a very small share. Moreover, there are state regulations governing the quality of investments. Typically, these restrict securities rated below investment grade. The rating system used is that of an industry association, the National Association of Insurance Commissioners; the system tends to differ from those of the national rating agencies such as Standard and Poor's or Moody's. Because of recent problems in the industry, NAIC has downgraded some securities previously considered investment grade (Chuan, 1993). The implication of such regulations would seem to rule out developing-country securities, almost all of which are below investment grade. However, a recent investment survey indicated that insurance companies were second only to mutual funds in participation in emerging markets (Greenwich Associates, 1993).

In contrast, U.S. pension funds—particularly private funds—are much less constrained by domestic regulations in their foreign investment behavior. Federal legislation (the Employee Retirement Income Security Act of 1974, or ERISA) requires private pension plan managers to exercise prudence in investment, but also to diversify investment to reduce risk. There are no quantitative restrictions on foreign investment. As for public pension funds, these are regulated at the state level, with varying degrees of restriction on foreign investment (World Bank, 1993a; Chuan, 1993).

Regulatory standards are imposed on pension funds and the life insurance industry for prudential reasons: fund managers are constrained by law in order to limit the risk to which beneficiaries may be exposed. However, the issue is the consistency of such regulations across the United States, and standardization among investor groups (World Bank, 1993c).[12]

It should be added that the regulatory environment and the paucity of information in the Latin American countries themselves are important factors affecting U.S. investors' behavior. Private sector representatives as well as public sector officials remarked in interviews that insider trading is rife in many markets. Moreover, the markets are thin, and large swings in stock prices are possible on the basis of a few transactions. Finally, U.S. investors would benefit from more objective research on companies whose shares are listed or being offered.

The lack of transparency and of information on investment prospects may be a cause for concern. There is no reason to believe that professional investment managers in charge of mutual funds and the portfolios of pension funds and insurance companies have any better knowledge or access to information regarding the risks of their clients' investments than is generally available. Moreover, these "professional investors" are a different group from the commercial banks—the "professional creditors" to developing countries in the 1970s—and have not faced the consequences of overlending experienced by the banks. Thus, professional investors may be "overinvesting" without due regard for risk, much as the banks did two decades ago. The circumstances are disturbingly similar: low returns and excess liquidity in industrial-country markets, coupled with a conviction that returns in Latin America and other emerging markets are bound to be higher.

The same lack of information may, in fact, limit the wisdom of other parties involved in assessing investment risks, notably the rating agencies. A case could be made in either direction: the rating agencies are excessively conservative (as evidenced by their reluctance to award investment-grade ratings), or they are too liberal (in ignoring recent history and the scope of downside risks). In the first case, U.S. institutional investment is unduly restricted; in the second, it is given a false sense of security.

Bank Lending

Between 1985 and 1991, claims by U.S. banks on less-developed countries (LDCs), including those in Latin America, fell by 50 percent (Table 1.10). In 1992, there was evidence of a gradual resumption of bank lending, as exposures recovered from their low levels of 1991. Moreover, a trend of increased bank lending to the region continued in 1993, according to the Bank for International Settlements (BIS, 1993).

However, the bulk of new bank credit commitments in the 1990s appear to be going to Asian rather than Latin American countries. Asian developing countries attracted about U.S.$36 billion in new bank commitments from 1990 to 1992, compared to U.S.$5.2 billion in the case of Western Hemisphere borrowers. Some loan facilities have been established for Latin American corporations in the private and public sectors in Chile, Mexico, Colombia, and Venezuela (IMF, 1993b). Given the domestic problems of the U.S. banking sector, the recent experience of the debt

Table 1.10 U.S. Commercial Bank Claims on Developing Countries
             (billions of U.S.$)

	1985	1987	1989	1990	1991	1992
All LDCs	134.2	110.8	82.2	71.8	67.0	73.0
Latin America/Caribbean	82.4	74.7	53.2	44.3	41.1	45.7
Argentina	8.4	8.8	4.5	3.5	3.8	5.8
Brazil	22.8	22.7	16.3	11.4	6.9	7.4
Chile	6.6	6.0	5.0	3.9	2.7	3.2
Mexico	24.9	22.7	16.1	15.2	16.5	17.3

Source: World Bank (1993c), table 7a, p. 30.

crisis, and the resolution of the crisis via securitization and conversions, it does not seem likely that banks will constitute a major source of private capital to the region in the foreseeable future.

U.S. Direct Investment Abroad

The literature on foreign direct investment has recognized for some time that FDI is better understood via theories of industrial organization, the product-cycle, and international trade, and in terms of the behavior of the firm (particularly the multinational enterprise), rather than in terms of theories of portfolio capital movements.[13] Thus, in trying to understand foreign direct investment flows from North America to Latin America, it is necessary to employ a somewhat different frame of reference than portfolio flows of equity and debt finance. The latter can better be understood in the context of world capital markets, whereas FDI needs to be situated in the context of trade relationships and the strategic market behavior of transnational corporations. However, both kinds of flows respond to profitable opportunities and depend on the climate for investment in recipient countries.

Foreign direct investment has been a form of international investment used more, perhaps, by U.S.-based corporations than by firms headquartered in other developed countries. Historically, it has dominated all other forms of U.S. private international investment, including portfolio flows (bonds and equity) and claims by U.S. banks on foreign borrowers (Table 1.11), except for a short period in the 1920s when portfolio claims briefly stood above FDI, in the 1970s when bank flows grew faster, and very recently when portfolio flows again seem to be predominant (U.S. Department of Commerce, 1988).

It is noteworthy that the worldwide distribution of U.S. FDI changed markedly after World War II. In 1950, the stock of U.S. direct investment abroad (USDIA) was evenly divided between developing and developed countries. A large portion (almost 39 percent) of the stock of USDIA was in Latin America in 1950, compared to 30 percent in Canada and less than 15 percent in Europe. By 1966, Latin America's share dropped to less than 19 percent, whereas Europe's doubled to 32 percent and Canada's remained at 30 percent. These trends continued into the 1980s, except that Canada's share also declined (Table 1.12).

Essentially, before World War II USDIA was strongly concentrated in the primary sectors (particularly petroleum and mining, but also agriculture). Direct investment in Latin America and other developing countries sought to obtain primary products and raw materials for the rapidly expanding U.S. manufacturing sector.

Table 1.11   International Investment Position of the United States
(billions of U.S.$)

	1914	1929	1950	1960	1970	1980
FDI	2.65	7.52	11.8	31.9	75.5	215
Portfolio	0.86	7.84	5.31	9.6	20.9	62.7
Bank claims	—	—	—	.3	13.8	204

Source: U.S. Department of Commerce (1988), tables 31–32, pp. 129–130.

Table 1.12   U.S. Direct Investment Abroad (Stocks), by Destination

	Investment (billions of U.S.$)			Percentage Distribution		
	1950	1966	1986	1950	1966	1986
All countries	11.8	51.8	259.9	100.0	100.0	100.0
Canada	3.6	15.7	50.2	30.4	30.3	19.3
Europe	1.7	16.4	123.2	14.7	31.6	47.4
Latin America	4.6	9.8	35.0	38.8	18.8	13.5
Argentina	0.4	0.8	3.0	3.0	1.5	1.1
Brazil	0.6	0.9	9.1	5.5	1.7	3.5
Chile	0.5	0.8	0.2	4.6	1.5	0.1
Mexico	0.4	1.3	4.8	3.5	2.6	1.9
Venezuela	1.0	2.1	1.8	8.4	4.1	0.7

Source: U.S. Department of Commerce (1988), p. 100.

After the war, however, U.S. corporations established branch plants in Europe and Canada more than in developing countries. Furthermore, during the 1950s and 1960s, most of this investment was concentrated in the manufacturing sector to increase or establish the presence of U.S. firms in rapidly growing consumer markets in the developed countries, typically behind national or regional tariff barriers. Meanwhile, in the first three decades of the postwar period, developing countries became increasingly cautious about foreign direct investment, erecting barriers to entry in the form of regulations, unfriendly tax regimes, and so forth. In some cases, host governments expropriated or nationalized the local facilities of transnational corporations (TNCs) to try to exert greater control or sovereignty over resources within their own boundaries.

In the 1980s, the debt crisis slowed down, and in some instances reversed, U.S. direct investment in developing countries. The debt overhang drastically reduced the earnings performance of foreign-owned affiliates by limiting the availability of foreign exchange. More generally, earnings were depressed by the serious economic downturn prevalent in the debt-distressed countries. Thus, USDIA peaked in Mexico in 1981 but then declined. After 1986, however, investment in maquiladora operations was strong. Similarly, USDIA in Argentina and Brazil declined after 1980 but recovered in and after 1986 (U.S. Department of Commerce, 1988). Moreover, after 1986, market-based "microsolutions" to the debt crisis began to emerge on an ad hoc, case-by-case basis. One such solution was the debt-equity swap, which became the major vehicle in many Latin American countries for a revival of FDI.

During the 1980s, then, the stock of USDIA increased in Latin America and the Caribbean (LAC), but the region did not hold its share of U.S. worldwide FDI, which declined from about 20 percent to 17.5 percent (Table 1.13). By 1991, the LAC region accounted for 11.2 percent of the assets of worldwide U.S. FDI,[14] 13.6 percent of total net income, and 19.4 percent of total employment (see Appendix 1.1).

Table 1.13   Distribution of U.S. FDI Stock, 1980 and 1990
(millions of U.S.$)

	1980	1990
Western Europe	96,065	203,613
Canada	45,119	68,431
Latin America/Caribbean	43,564	74,156
Argentina	2,540	2,889
Brazil	7,704	15,416
Chile	536	1,341
Mexico	5,986	9,360
Venezuela	1,908	1,581
World	220,178	423,183

Source: UN (1993a), pp. 494–496.

In the 1980s and 1990s, foreign direct investment has increasingly flowed into the service sectors rather than into primary or manufacturing industries. Such investment went into telecommunications, transportation, banking, and public utilities (UN, 1993a). Transnational corporations are now adopting strategies of "deep" and "complex" integration, whereby the entire production process is unbundled and distributed worldwide. Intermediate goods and services (including rapidly growing information services) are produced or sourced at a range of locations by the TNC, its affiliates, or unrelated firms. The locus of intermediate production, final assembly, and distribution is determined by relative costs, the local economic policy environment, and the configuration of ultimate markets.[15]

Although the United States is still the major home country for FDI, its position relative to other major industrial countries has declined since

1987, when it accounted for about one-third of the stock of foreign investment abroad; by 1992, this proportion had fallen below one-quarter (UN,
1993b, table I.1). The decline of the United States relative to the other
G-5 industrial countries is apparent from data on flows of FDI for the
same period. Only in 1992 was the United States the largest source of FDI
(Table 1.14).

In terms of its worldwide distribution, it is clear that a small proportion of USDIA has flowed to developing countries. But of that part, a significant proportion has flowed to Latin America and the Caribbean (Table
1.15).

It is becoming clear that in the 1990s TNCs headquartered in the
United States, Europe, and Japan (the so-called triad) are pursuing regional
strategies whereby FDI from one of these three groups of investor countries dominates FDI from the other two (as measured by recent FDI flows
and/or ownership of cumulative stocks). However, the division of the
world into three parts is not without competition or rivalry. For example,
U.S. TNCs dominate most, but not all, of Latin America; TNCs from the

Table 1.14 Outflows of Foreign Investment, 1987–1992
             (billions of U.S.$)

	1987	1988	1989	1990	1991	1992
France	9	14	19	35	24	17
Germany	9	13	18	28	21	17
Japan	20	34	44	48	31	16
United Kingdom	31	37	35	18	18	15
United States	26	14	26	29	29	36

Source: UN (1993b), table I.3.

Table 1.15 Distribution of Outward U.S. FDI Flows, 1987–1990
             (millions of U.S.$)

	1987	1988	1989	1990
Developed countries	21,269	13,307	21,833	21,318
Developing countries	6,769	975	6,893	7,639
Latin America/Caribbean	5,115	287	4,578	4,797
Argentina	−125	−82	43	164
Brazil	800	1,676	1,892	1,054
Chile	78	223	368	293
Mexico	328	608	1,455	1,949
Venezuela	−85	−188	−96	39

Source: UN (1993a), pp. 487–489.

European Community are also active in this market. Three Latin American countries in which FDI from Europe (as measured by stocks or recent flows) exceeds that of the United States are Brazil, Paraguay, and Uruguay. "Intensity ratios" confirm that Latin America is receiving a greater share of worldwide U.S. FDI flows than its share of total FDI, although, curiously, U.S. FDI is not as strongly skewed toward Latin America as is U.S. foreign trade (UN, 1993b).

It is interesting to note that the recent sectoral composition of U.S. FDI in Latin America and the Caribbean has been strongly oriented toward secondary industries (manufacturing), compared to its bias toward tertiary activities (services) in its major destination area, Western Europe (Table 1.16).

Despite the recent trends in U.S. FDI flows, its cumulative stock of foreign investment in Latin America and the Caribbean is heavily oriented toward the tertiary sector, more so than U.S. FDI in Western Europe or the world as a whole (Table 1.17). This is likely because of heavy past U.S. investment in financial services and utilities.[16]

Two interrelated sets of factors explain recent trends in U.S. FDI to the LAC region: (1) the regional strategy of U.S. TNCs, and (2) the evolving policy environment at the national and international levels. At the national level, economic reforms by many Latin American countries have led to real depreciation (particularly during the 1980s) and the elimination of antiexport bias in the manufacturing sector. These developments were

Table 1.16 Sectoral Distribution of Average U.S. FDI Flows, 1988–1990
(millions of U.S.$)

	Primary	Secondary	Tertiary
Western Europe	199	3,413	9,701
Latin America/Caribbean	−371	2,530	813

Source: UN (1993a), p. 490.

Table 1.17 Sectoral Distribution of U.S. FDI Stock, 1990
(millions of U.S.$)

	Primary	Secondary	Tertiary	Total
Western Europe	24,183	83,875	91,730	203,613
Latin America/Caribbean	5,275	23,802	41,162	74,156
World	35,053	187,403	200,727	423,183

Source: UN (1993a), p. 497.

buttressed by deregulation and easier repatriation of earnings. As a result, manufacturing of tradables became more competitive.

With regard to TNC regional strategy, it is clear that even prior to the 1992 negotiation of NAFTA, U.S. firms were investing in the maquiladora sector in Mexico to obtain a low-cost source of intermediate and final production for the U.S. market (see Table 1.15). Much of this investment was in the manufacturing sector, particularly automobiles and parts. This investment was induced by the liberalization of the trade and foreign investment regimes in Mexico in the second half of the 1980s and by exchange-rate depreciation. The advent of NAFTA then served to formalize trade and investment relations[17] between the United States, Mexico, and Canada, and to accelerate the pace of U.S. foreign investment in anticipation of the more integrated market NAFTA would create.

As to NAFTA itself, the agreement has extensive provisions (in Part 5) for the regulation of investment, services, and related matters—in this respect (and in other ways) going far beyond its predecessor, the Free Trade Agreement (FTA) between Canada and the United States. For example, beside the FTA's prohibition of export requirements, and controls on local content and profit repatriation, there are additional prohibitions on trade balancing, world/regional product mandates, and technology transfer requirements. The importance of the provisions on investment are a reflection of its centrality in economic relations between countries. The provisions call for "national treatment" of foreign investors, that is, no less favorable treatment than accorded to domestic investors. The agreement prohibits performance requirements (e.g., export requirements, local content), which often have been imposed by developing countries on foreign investors in the past. Other noteworthy provisions relate to the repatriation of profit, dividend, interest, royalty, and other payments; prescribe rules to be followed in the event of expropriation; and contain measures for the settlement of disputes between investors and host governments (UN, 1993b). Such measures give foreign investors a considerable margin of comfort regarding the "rules of the game" in comparison with the environment of uncertainty and unpredictability that has traditionally prevailed in developing countries.

The implementation of NAFTA is likely to stimulate FDI across the region in anticipation of a widening of the economic zone. Several other countries in the region (most notably, Chile) have expressed an interest in joining NAFTA, foreshadowing the eventual creation of a unified hemispheric economic area. The countries most able and willing to join such an economic area are likely to be those that have considerably liberalized their trade and investment regimes (e.g., Chile and Argentina). It is uncertain whether the foreign investment dynamics will follow the Mexican example. If so, much FDI in the manufacturing and service sectors may be anticipated, as TNCs integrate their goods and services production throughout the hemisphere.

If the nations of the Western Hemisphere move collectively toward regional integration at the political level, it is likely that "deep" integration[18] will take place economically through the investment strategies of TNCs. The investment behavior of TNCs in the already integrated regions Europe and North America (Canada and the United States) serves as a precedent leading to rationalization of production through investments in new facilities, increased specialization, and concentration of production in order to serve the new markets more competitively. Furthermore, continued economic growth in the demographically younger Latin American countries would likely shift the locus of market opportunities for TNCs away from the slower growth and aging populations in the United States and Canada to these "southern" members.

Regulatory and Other Policies Affecting U.S. FDI

Domestic "framework" policies. There is little, if any, regulation per se governing U.S. foreign direct investment. However, regulatory policies affecting domestic investment may indirectly influence the volume or direction of FDI by U.S. firms. In particular, regulations governing health, safety, working conditions, and the environmental impact of the operations of U.S. firms have all become more stringent in the last decade. Such regulations increase the cost of domestic operations over foreign operations in countries where such regulations are either less stringent or nonexistent, as in most of Latin America. Hence, firms contemplating new investment in a U.S. or Latin American location, and otherwise indifferent between the two, might choose the Latin American location for the above reasons (Dreyer et al., 1991).

There is some anecdotal evidence to support the hypothesis of investment diversion. For example, Canadian firms in the natural resources sector (mining and forest products) have reportedly opted for Chilean over Canadian sites because of the longer and stricter environmental assessment procedures in Canada. Perhaps the strongest evidence is provided by the negotiation by the Clinton administration of the so-called NAFTA side agreements with Mexico, pertaining to labor and environmental standards. These agreements were motivated as much by concerns over job losses due to U.S. firms seeking to invest in Mexico because of its lower-cost regulatory climate, as by desires to improve working conditions and the environmental impact of Mexican industry.

Thus, as the economies of the Western Hemisphere become more integrated, it is likely that the regulatory environment within the industrial countries will increasingly have international overtones. Although it is possible that regulations in the United States and Canada might become more lax in order to make investment there more competitive, it seems more likely that labor and public interest groups will press to elevate regulatory standards throughout the region to make them more compatible with North American standards.

Tax policy. Among other policies affecting U.S. FDI, the potentially most important is the tax policy.[19] Tax provisions implemented before 1981, which accelerated depreciation schedules and increased the limits for eligible capital expenditures, had the effect of raising the after-tax return expected from domestic investment relative to foreign investment. Between 1981 and 1987, these provisions were gradually eliminated, and the U.S. tax system became relatively neutral with respect to the location of investment. However, paradoxically, when the incentives to invest domestically were in place, U.S. FDI in developing countries grew rapidly; and when the incentives were being eliminated, FDI from the United States kept falling (Dreyer et al., 1991). Thus, although the U.S. tax system may have had an impact on FDI, clearly other factors were more important.

More recent empirical work suggests that home-country tax rates affect FDI considerably, and negatively, and that these rates are more important than host-country rates (Jun, 1992). However, this analysis is based on FDI flows among industrial countries. Further work is required to test the relationship between taxation levels and FDI flows between developed and developing countries.

Promotional policies. Finally, the United States, along with other industrial countries, supports FDI in developing countries via certain promotional policies. For example, the Overseas Private Investment Corporation (OPIC) was established in 1971 to encourage U.S. FDI in developing countries by providing insurance against the risks of currency inconvertibility, expropriation, and political violence. To the extent that this insurance reduces the risks on developing-country FDI, it improves the risk-return calculus and stimulates additional FDI at the margin. However, insurance cover is provided for a very small proportion of U.S. developing-country FDI. As of the end of 1988, OPIC's insurance liability was U.S.$3.1 billion, corresponding to 3.5 percent of the stock of U.S. FDI in developing countries (Dreyer et al., 1991).

In addition to OPIC, other agencies (primarily the U.S. Agency for International Development—USAID—through its Trade and Investment Program) support U.S. FDI by capacity or institution-building programs in developing countries so that they may more effectively attract foreign investment. Supported activities include technical assistance to establish export and investment promotion agencies. In addition, the program funds feasibility studies and training programs related to major projects. Funds must be awarded to U.S. companies and must help position U.S. firms for subsequent investment, but the projects are chosen by the host country and reflect its development priorities. The missions of USAID in the Latin America/Caribbean region—for example, in Costa Rica, El Salvador, Jamaica and Haiti—have been particularly active in assisting such agencies. About U.S.$30–40 million a year is estimated to be allocated to these activities (Bélot and Weigel, 1992; Dreyer et al., 1991).

Bilateral investment treaties. The United States established a program for bilateral investment treaties in 1981 to reduce barriers to FDI as well as to protect it. Such treaties typically include provisions for national or most-favored-nation treatment (whichever is better) for foreign investors; prompt, adequate, and effective compensation for expropriation; unrestricted profit and other financial transfers related to an investment; and intracountry and international dispute settlement procedures. As of January 1993, the United States had concluded 22 treaties, predominantly with countries in Eastern Europe, the former Soviet Union, and developing countries.

It is worth noting, however, that Argentina is the only Latin American country with which the United States has negotiated a treaty (in November 1991).[20] This suggests that U.S. commercial policy toward the region may be on a somewhat different plane, a notion buttressed by the Enterprise for the Americas initiative launched by President Bush. Of course, the provisions of NAFTA include, among other things, all the elements of a bilateral investment treaty, so that a treaty with Mexico would be redundant. Hence, further investment treaties with Latin American countries may well come under the aegis of a widening economic community created by bringing additional members of the region into NAFTA.

Conclusions

Rather than to recapitulate the major findings presented in this chapter, it may be more useful to summarize what factors appear to be underlying the main trends, and what are the implications, if any, for policy in the United States.

Portfolio Flows

First of all, it is useful to note that the data on portfolio flows leave much to be desired. This is especially the case for secondary market transactions as opposed to new issues or initial public or private offerings, data about which are usually required by the need to meet regulatory requirements (e.g., by the SEC). It is even more the case for derivatives trading, most of which takes place in over-the-counter markets. More complete, consistent, and prompt reporting of secondary market and derivative transactions would be beneficial to all participants (source and recipient countries, savers, investors, and borrowers alike). Securities and exchange authorities in the Americas are already attempting to coordinate their activities and work toward a harmonization of standards (Schapiro, 1993), but there may be a role for regional organizations such as the Economic Commission for Latin America and the Caribbean (ECLAC/CEPAL) or the Inter-American Development Bank (IDB) to develop a standardized reporting and information system for the region.

Secondly, the fact that bank lending to the region has declined and has been replaced by portfolio flows is as much a reflection of the transformation of financial markets in North America and other industrial countries as it is a reaction to the debt problems in the 1980s. International lending by commercial banks was an anomaly brought about by the expansion of the banking system spurred on by competition from nonbanking institutions and by assumptions about the relative "safety" of banks. The withdrawal of banks from international lending was accompanied by disintermediation and securitization in the industrial countries' own financial markets, and eventually by the securitization of much developing-country bank debt. Once bank loans began to be converted into bonds, the way was paved for developing-country markets to access the industrial bond markets directly.

As for portfolio equity flows, these are a new phenomenon historically, which reflect the secular rise of professionally managed collective investment institutions (pension funds, life insurance companies, and especially mutual funds). The aging of industrial-country populations is partly responsible for this trend, but so is a shift in the preferences and behavior of savers, away from deposit-taking interest-earning debt vehicles and toward channels geared to capital appreciation and long-term growth. U.S. savers/investors are—at the margin—likely to perceive such long-term opportunities to be increasingly greater in Latin America and the Caribbean than at home. These perceptions are based on the younger populations of the region, but also on the emergence of a more stable economic and political environment. Greater integration via NAFTA and its extensions southward, by underpinning growth prospects in the region, will deepen confidence by portfolio investors in making long-term commitments. Diversification is also likely to be an increasingly significant strategic consideration as investors internationalize their portfolios to increase their returns and hedge their risks. Given the size of U.S. asset portfolios and the still remarkably tiny proportion of U.S. portfolio investment allocated to emerging markets, even small reallocations may provide the region with significant additional inflows of equity capital. Thus, even if interest rates and financial returns in the United States and other industrial countries rise (modestly, at any rate) from their current low levels, there are reasons to expect U.S. investors to increasingly look for portfolio investment opportunities in Latin America and the Caribbean (*Financial Times*, February 7, 1994). The stability of these flows is by no means assured, however. Recent history is sobering. International "diversification" was also a strategy pursued by the commercial banks in the 1970s, but in the 1980s the banks' developing-country portfolios appeared much less sound. When they stopped lending, the banks deepened the very debt-servicing crisis they sought to avoid. A particular source of instability requiring further research is the role of derivatives, for which investment is increasing considerably.

Access to U.S. portfolio markets and investors—both debt and equity—is now as open as it is likely to get. The chief constraints on issuers of equity or bonds now appear to be the transparency of financial reporting by issuing firms or entities. The development and implementation across the region of standardized generally accepted accounting principles would be the single most powerful initiative to give regional entities greater access to the U.S. market. It would also be easier to secure an "investment-grade" rating if companies were to adopt GAAP. There may be scope for technical assistance by regional agencies such as the Inter-American Development Bank in this regard. Complementary initiatives, which depend more on the private sector, might include a deepening of market research on the capabilities and prospects of local firms better to inform U.S. investors in making portfolio choices.

In the meantime, further research into the behavior of the principal market agents might yield some useful insights. Given limited information, how do the professional investors make choices? On what basis of information do they allocate their portfolios to the emerging markets? Are these decisions comparable to portfolio choices for domestic investments, where the information base is more sound? Similarly, questions may be posed regarding the rating agencies: How do these agencies award their grades for emerging markets in the absence of information as complete as for industrial-country risks? Should the agencies themselves be subject to the same standards of accountability and transparency, so that both borrowers and investors are more aware of the basis for their grading decisions?

Finally, perhaps the most powerful lever available to the United States and other industrial countries is that of their domestic interest rates. Given the strong evidence that the upsurge in portfolio flows to emerging markets has been in part due to the substantial decline in U.S. interest rates after 1990 (Calvo, Leiderman, and Reinhart, 1993), it would follow that a substantial increase would eliminate the yield differential enjoyed by foreign investors and possibly trigger a mass exodus of portfolio capital. While the impact might not be as "systemic" as the debt crisis in the 1980s, which threatened the integrity of the financial and banking systems, it might nonetheless be serious both for developing countries faced by capital flight and for portfolio investors. The latter would include large numbers of older investors who might face capital losses and whose pension assets and retirement incomes are undermined as a result. Thus, as the global financial system extends its reach into portfolio markets, the consequences of domestic interest rate policy in the United States and other industrial countries for global macroeconomic stability should not be underestimated. Again, the experience of the 1980s is sobering—the debt crisis was, in part, precipitated by the dramatic interest rate escalation of 1980–1981 in the United States and elsewhere. Although domestic imperatives will, no doubt, continue to dominate interest rate policy formation in the industrial countries, there are more global reasons than ever to suggest that interest rates be kept relatively low and stable.

Foreign Direct Investment

Foreign direct investment is clearly driven by the prospect of increasing economic integration throughout the region. At the political level, the implementation of NAFTA is clearly a significant step in this direction. NAFTA provides a context within which transnational firms may embark on investments throughout the region and move them toward "deep" integration structures of production, just as in the European Community and in the Canada/U.S. context at present.

Hence, a southward extension of NAFTA would likely stimulate significant increments of U.S. FDI in the region, much as it has for Mexico over the last six years. In the next two decades, however, it is also likely that the ultimate market orientation of investment will progressively turn toward the region itself rather than toward the United States or Canada.

The regulatory framework within which economic integration takes place is likely to be a growing political issue throughout the region. A foretaste of this debate emerged with the "side-deals" between the United States and Mexico with regard to NAFTA; concurrently, the new Liberal government in Canada has expressed its intent to discuss a subsidy code with the United States. Discussions on social and environmental regulation affecting investment and trade in the region, with a view to harmonization of standards, will reduce uncertainty among investors as well as political opposition in the United States and Canada.

**Appendix 1.1   U.S. Direct Investment Abroad: Basic Data
(1991 preliminary estimates)**

Nonbank foreign affiliates of nonbank U.S. parents

	Number of Affiliates	Total assets (millions of U.S.$)	Net income (millions of U.S.$)	Number of Employees (thousands)
All countries	17,877	1,690,161	77,096	6,898.1
Canada	1,932	203,493	3,171	911.6
Europe	8,707	919,186	44,986	2,973.3
Latin America/Caribbean	2,839	189,490	10,477	1,338.8
Argentina	148	5,809	343	58.5
Brazil	456	31,433	516	394.8
Chile	109	5,118	152	24.6
Venezuela	200	6,060	362	86.7
Mexico	589	28,772	2,958	577.3

Source: U.S. Department of Commerce (July 1993), table II.A.1.

Notes

An earlier version of this chapter was presented at a workshop held at UN-CEPAL headquarters in Santiago, Chile, on December 6–7, 1993. Many useful comments were provided by participants at the workshop, including (inter alia) William Gruben of the Federal Reserve Bank of Dallas, Vittorio Corbo of the Universidad Católica de Chile, Stephany Griffith-Jones of the Institute of Development Studies in Sussex, and Robert Devlin of UN-CEPAL. Helpful suggestions were also received from Charles Collyns of the International Monetary Fund. The author is also grateful for comments from his colleagues Ann Weston and Andrew Clark, and for discussions with officials of the U.S. Treasury Department, the Securities and Exchange Commission, the Federal Reserve Bank of New York, and Wall Street–based securities firms. However, the views expressed in this chapter are those of the author and not necessarily of those consulted in its preparation. The author would like to thank Sarah Matthews for preparing the final text.

1. See Stallings (1987) for an excellent discussion of debt and international lending in historical perspective.

2. Bryant quotes a 1944 speech in which Keynes said: "We intend to retain control of our domestic rate of interest, so that we can keep it as low as suits our own purposes, without interference from the ebb and flow of international capital movements or flights of hot money."

3. However, the existence of SEC rules concerning bond issues in the United States served in the 1960s to stimulate the expansion of the Euromarket, at first in London but subsequently in other offshore financial markets in which U.S. dollars were borrowed and loaned without U.S. regulatory constraints. Latin American countries had some access to the Eurobond markets.

4. Similar weaknesses beset the ill-fated savings and loan (S&L) institutions, which invested heavily in real estate and got caught in a web of interest-rate risk, asset deflation, and occasional fraud. All of this was exacerbated by initiatives to deregulate the industry as well as to increase insurance coverage provided to

depositors. By 1993, the total cost of protecting insured depositors from loss was estimated to be up to U.S.$175 billion, or 3 percent of U.S. gross domestic product (GDP) (National Commission on Financial Institution Reform, Recovery and Enforcement, July 1993, p. 4).

5. In 1992, of the $33.7 billion (U.S. dollars) in gross bond sales to the region, $27.5 billion originated from the Netherlands Antilles ($11.7 billion), Bermuda ($7.6 billion), British West Indies (Cayman Islands, $4.5 billion), and the Bahamas ($2.7 billion).

6. According to a recent industry survey, 16 percent of mutual funds surveyed already included emerging market bonds in their portfolios, and another 16 percent planned to include these in the future. Insurance companies were a close second: 14 percent included them at present and another 3 percent planned to participate in the future (Greenwich Associates, 1993).

7. In September 1993 the World Bank held a symposium in Washington, D.C., "Portfolio Investment in Developing Countries," which gathered together many leading analysts, including representatives of leading securities firms.

8. The offshore centers are far less important for equity than for bond transactions; hence they skew the data far less. Still, the Netherlands Antilles, British West Indies, Bermuda, and Bahamas accounted for U.S.$8 billion out of the U.S.$19.7 billion in gross equity sales by Latin Americans in 1992.

9. Derivatives are hedging instruments including swaps, options, forwards, and futures. They are "derived" from the value of an underlying asset, and typically hedge against a particular feature of the asset—its interest rate, its price, or its currency denomination.

10. Pemex, the Mexican state oil company, is reportedly adopting GAAP in order to list its shares in the U.S. market (World Bank, 1993c).

11. ADRs are U.S. dollar–denominated, equity-based instruments backed by a trust containing stocks of a foreign company. ADRs are traded on major exchanges or in the over-the-counter market (IMF, 1993b).

12. According to Chuan (1993), the NAIC is attempting to reconcile state laws governing the insurance industry.

13. See Dunning (1993), chapter 4, for a summary of the theoretical literature.

14. Nonbank affiliates of nonbank U.S. parents only.

15. See UN (1993b), part 2, for a discussion on integrated international production.

16. However, FDI stock data are skewed because they are based on historical cost rather than on current value. Thus, the real value of U.S. FDI in Latin American primary sectors might be understated relative to secondary and tertiary sector FDI to the extent that most primary FDI was undertaken many years ago, whereas secondary or tertiary investment might be more recent.

17. NAFTA is a misnomer because the agreement pertains to a range of issues, including investment behavior, outside the ambit of "trade" relations.

18. "Shallow" integration takes place at the level of trade, whereas "deep" integration occurs in the production process, i.e., within TNCs and between TNCs and unaffiliated firms. The precedents are the European Community and the U.S./Canada case (even before the FTA). In both cases, TNCs have rationalized their production facilities among countries of the group in order to reap cost, location, technological, and other advantages. For example, in the European Community, Unilever reduced and concentrated its 13 toilet soap production facilities into four key units, and its cleaning/hygiene business into one facility in Italy. In the case of Canada and the United States, the Auto Pact created a free-trade zone for

the "big three" auto makers in 1965; subsequently, they rationalized production so that particular models and parts were made in Canada and others in the United States (UN, 1993b).

19. However, the monetary policy has perhaps had the most dramatic impact on net FDI flows from the United States. Restrictive monetary policies during the 1980s had the effect of increasing the rate of return of capital in the United States. The effect of increasing the returns on capital relative to other countries was to attract net inflows of capital—including net inflows of FDI, which were unprecedented in the 1980s. However, other factors relating to ownership, location, and the international integration of production among TNCs were probably at least as important as the rate of interest.

20. However, two Caribbean nations—Haiti and Grenada—have also signed bilateral investment treaties with the United States.

References

Agtmael, A. van (1993), "Portfolio investment in emerging markets: The view of a practitioner," paper presented to World Bank Symposium on Portfolio Investment in Developing Countries, September.

Bank for International Settlements (BIS) (1993), *63rd Annual Report*, Basle, June.

Bank of New York (1992), "Rule 144A and Regulation S: Regulatory developments impacting depositary receipts," *Bulletin*, New York, June.

Bélot, T., and D. Weigel (1992), "Programs in industrial countries to promote foreign direct investment in developing countries," IFC, Washington, D.C.

Bryant, R. C. (1987), "International financial intermediation," The Brookings Institution, Washington, D.C.

Calvo, G., L. Leiderman, and C. Reinhart (1993), "Capital inflows and the real exchange rate appreciation in Latin America: The role of external factors," *IMF Staff Papers*, vol. 40, no. 1, March.

Chenery, H., and T. N. Srinivasan, eds. (1989), *Handbook of Development Economics*, vol. 2, including E. A. Cardoso and R. Dornbusch, "Foreign private capital flows" (ch. 26) and G. K. Helleiner, "Transnational corporations and direct foreign investment" (ch. 27).

Culpeper, R., and S. Griffith-Jones (1992), "Rapid return of private flows to Latin America: New trends and new policy issues," paper presented to a workshop in Santiago, October.

Chuan, P., with S. Claessens and N. Mamingi (1993), "Equity and bond flows to Asia and Latin America: The role of global and country factors," *Policy Research Working Papers*, WPS1160, The World Bank, International Economics Department, Washington, D.C., July.

Chuan, P. (1993), "Source of portfolio investment in emerging markets," mimeo, The World Bank, Washington, D.C., September.

Devlin, R. (1989), *Debt and crisis in Latin America: The supply side of the story*, Princeton University Press, Princeton, N.J.

Devries, M. G. (1986), "The IMF in a changing world, 1945–85," IMF, Washington, D.C.

Dreyer, J. S., with A. Singer, K. A. Froot, A. Gubitz, and J. Prasad Singh (1991), "Industrialized countries' policies affecting foreign direct investment in developing countries," vol. 2, *Country Studies*, The World Bank/MIGA, Washington, D.C.

Dunning, J. H. (1993), *Multinational enterprises and the global economy*, Addison-Wesley, Wokingham.

Economist (1993), "Up and up until it popped," August 14.

Eichengreen, B. (1991), "Historical research on international lending and debt," *Journal of Economic Perspectives*, vol. 2, pp. 149–169, Spring.

Fedder, M.J.J., and M. Mukherjee (1992), "The reemergence of developing countries in the international bond markets," in J. D. Shilling (ed.), *Beyond syndicated loans: Sources of credit for developing countries*, World Bank, Washington, D.C.

Fischer, B., and H. Reisen (1993), "Liberalising capital flows in developing countries," OECD Development Centre, Paris.

Fishlow, A. (1985), "Lessons from the past: Capital markets during the 19th century and the interwar period," *International Organization*, vol. 39, Summer.

Global Derivatives Study Group (1993), *Derivatives: Practices and principles*, Group of Thirty, Washington, D.C., July.

Greenwich Associates (1993), *Institutional fixed-income investors 1993*, Greenwich.

Howell, M. (1993), "Institutional investors as a source of portfolio investment in developing countries," paper presented to World Bank Symposium on Portfolio Investment in LDCs, September 9–10.

International Finance Corporation (1993), *Emerging stock markets factbook, 1993*, Washington, D.C.

International Monetary Fund (IMF) (1991), *International capital markets: Developments and prospects*, Washington, D.C., May.

——— (1993a), *International capital markets. Part II: Systemic issues in international finance*, Washington, D.C., August.

——— (1993b), *Private market financing for developing countries*, Washington, D.C., December.

Jun, J. (1992), "The effects of taxation on foreign direct investment: Evidence from country specific data," The World Bank, Washington, D.C., September.

Litan, R. E. (1991), *The revolution in U.S. finance*, The Brookings Institution, Washington, D.C.

Mullin, J. (1993), "Emerging equity markets in the global economy," *Federal Reserve Bank of New York, Quarterly Review*, Summer.

National Commission on Financial Institution Reform, Recovery and Enforcement (1993), "Origins and causes of the S&L debacle: A blueprint for reform," report to the President and Congress of the United States, Washington, D.C., July.

O'Brien, R. (1992), "Global financial integration: The end of geography," Council on Foreign Relations Press for the Royal Institute of International Affairs, New York.

O'Brien, R., and S. Hewin, eds. (1991), "Finance and the international economy," vol. 4, Oxford University Press for the AMEX Bank Review, New York; especially R. C. Smith and I. Walter, "Reconfiguration of global financial markets in the 1990s."

Organization for Economic Cooperation and Development (OECD) (1993), *Financial Market Trends*, vol. 55, Paris, June.

Pierce, J. L. (1991), "The future of banking," Yale University Press, New Haven and London.

Salomon Brothers, Sovereign Assessment Group (1992), "Private capital flows to Latin America: Volume triples to U.S.$40 billion in 1991," New York, February.

Schadler, S., M. Carkovic, A. Bennett, and R. Kalin (1993), "Recent experiences with surges in capital inflows," *Occasional Paper* 108, IMF, Washington, D.C., December.

Schapiro, M. L. (1993), "Remarks before the Council of Securities Regulators for the Americas," Buenos Aires, June.

Shilling, J. D., ed. (1992), "Beyond syndicated loans: Sources of credit for developing countries," *World Bank Technical Paper*, no. 463, World Bank, Washington, D.C.

Stallings, B. (1987), *Banker to the Third World*, University of California Press, Berkeley.

Tesar, L., and I. Werner (1993), "U.S. equity investment in emerging stock markets," paper presented to World Bank Symposium on Portfolio Investment in Developing Countries, September.

United Nations (1993a), *World Investment Directory, Volume III: Developed Countries*, New York.

———— (1993b), *World Investment Report 1993*, New York.

United States Department of Commerce, International Trade Administration (1993), *International direct investment: Global trends and the U.S. role*, Washington, D.C., July.

United States Department of the Treasury (1991, 1992, and 1993), *Treasury Bulletin* (quarterly), Washington, D.C., June.

White, L. J. (1992), "Why now? Change and turmoil in U.S. banking," *Occasional Paper*, no. 38, Group of Thirty, Washington, D.C.

The World Bank (1991), *World Development Report 1991: The challenge of development*, Oxford University Press, New York.

———— (1993a), *Global economic prospects and the developing countries 1993*, Washington, D.C.

———— (1993b), Economics and Statistics Administration, Bureau of Economic Analysis, "U.S. direct investment abroad: Operations of U.S. parent companies and their foreign affiliates," preliminary 1991 estimates, Washington, D.C.

———— (1993c), *Financial flows to developing countries quarterly review*, Washington, D.C., July.

2

European Private Flows to Latin America: The Facts and the Issues

STEPHANY GRIFFITH-JONES

The statistical analysis in this chapter starts at a global level because markets are increasingly integrated and globalized, and therefore the trends (such as securitization) and forces that operate at a global level are very relevant to understand what happens in specific flows, such as European flows going to Latin America. Indeed, particularly in some markets, it is impossible to establish clearly what a "European" flow is. For example, for a U.S. pension fund that buys Latin American bonds in Luxembourg, the flow is registered as originating in Europe, but the actual source of funds comes from the United States. Similarly, a U.S. pension fund can hire an investment manager in London or Edinburgh to manage money going to emerging markets, mainly destined to Pacific Rim countries.

Based largely on interview material, this chapter explores the extent to which securities' investors in different types of instruments have different motivations, the factors that encourage such flows to go to Latin America, the extent to which such flows are likely to be sustainable, and the regulations that affect different types of European investors, as regards investing in so-called emerging markets.

The terms on which European private flows come in, their suitability to the needs of Latin American countries, and the risk associated with such flows will also be assessed in this chapter.

41

Recent Trends in Global Private Financial Markets, Inflows to LDCs and to Latin America

Globally, in 1993 borrowing on international capital markets continued its rapid increase for the third year in a row: in 1991 there had been an important increase (21 percent) in the aggregate volume of international capital flows; in 1992 there was a further increase of 16 percent; for 1993, the overall volume of borrowing facilities exceeded U.S.$810 billion, with an even faster rate of growth of 33 percent, on a year-to-year basis, than in the previous years (see Table 2.1). In the last six years, 1987–1993, global borrowing increased by 82 percent.

Table 2.1   Borrowing on International Capital Markets by Country
(billions of U.S.$)

Borrower Composition	1989	1990	1991	1992	1993
OECD countries	426.5	384.4	457.9	535.7	690.6
Developing countries	21.8	28.6	46.2	47.3	84.4
Central Eastern Europe	4.7	4.6	1.8	1.5	6.2
Others	13.5	17.3	19.0	25.2	29.3
Total	466.5	434.9	524.9	609.7	810.5
Year-to-year percentage change	+2.8	−6.8	+20.7	+16.2	+33.0

Source: OECD, Financial Market Trends, vols. 54, 55, and 57, February 1993, June 1993, and February 1994.

In 1993, continuing the trend of the 1990–1992 period, when borrowing on international capital markets by developing countries increased very significantly (by 31 percent in 1990, by a massive 62 percent in 1991, but slowing down to 2 percent in 1992), borrowing increased even more rapidly, by 78 percent (see Table 2.2). As a result, the share of LDC total borrowing had increased from 4.7 percent in 1989, to 6.6 percent in 1990, and to about 9 percent in 1991, then declined in 1992, but grew in 1993 to more than 10 percent. In particular, issues of bonds by developing countries accelerated the very sharp increase that had started in 1990 (see Table 2.2).

Indeed, issues of bonds by developing countries in 1993, at more than U.S.$45 billion, were around three times their 1992 level! A similarly dramatic increase in bond issues was registered by Latin American borrowers (see Table 2.3).

Other sources, such as the 1993 World Bank Study, Global Economic Prospects and the Developing Countries, which makes a major effort to

Table 2.2   Borrowing by Developing Countries (billions of U.S.$)

Instruments	1989	1990	1991	1992	1993
Bonds	2.6	4.5	8.3	14.0	45.6
Equities	0.1	1.0	5.0	7.2	10.7
Syndicated loans	16.2	19.8	26.7	16.5	18.4
Committed borrowing facilities	0.9	2.1	4.5	1.7	1.2
Non-underwritten facilities[a]	2.0	1.2	1.7	7.9	8.5
Total	21.8	28.6	46.2	47.3	84.4
Percent increase over previous year		31	62	2	78

Source: OECD, Financial Market Trends, vols. 54, 55, and 57, February 1993, June 1993, and February 1994; elaborated on the basis of the statistical annexes.
Note: [a]Including Euro-commercial paper and medium-term note programs.

Table 2.3   Borrowing by Latin American Countries (billions of U.S.$)

Instruments	1989	1990	1991	1992	1993
Bonds	—	1.0	4.6	8.2	23.7
Equities[a]	—	—	4.4	4.5	5.5
Syndicated loans	1.9	3.3	0.9	1.0	2.2
Committed borrowing facilities	0.1	—	2.8	0.3	—
Non-underwritten facilities[b]	—	—	1.2	6.1	6.8
Total of Latin American countries	2.0	4.3	13.9	20.1	38.2
Percent of Latin American countries of total borrowing of LDCs	9.2	15.0	30.1	42.5	45.3

Source: OECD, Financial Market Trends, vols. 54, 55, and 57, February 1993, June 1993, and February 1994; elaborated on the basis of the statistical annexes.
Notes: [a]New issues and initial public offerings of common and preferred shares.
[b]Including Euro-commercial paper and medium-term note programs.

have complete coverage of these new flows to LDCs, report somewhat higher figures for Latin America. They estimate, for example, a U.S.$11.7 billion issue of Latin American bonds in 1992 (as opposed to the U.S.$8.2 billion reported by the OECD), and a U.S.$5.5 billion equity investment in Latin America in 1992 (as opposed to the U.S.$4.5 billion reported by the OECD). However, the trends reported are similar for both sources, particularly the continued rapid growth for bonds (with the OECD also forecasting a further increase in Latin American bond offerings as several countries approach investment-grade ratings).

Returning to global trends, in 1993 the main dynamism did not come from syndicated credits (although these grew slightly) but from securities, which increased by 46 percent (see Table 2.4). As can be seen by comparing Tables 2.2 and 2.4, borrowing by developing countries seems to follow overall trends similar to global ones, particularly regarding the declining importance of syndicated loans and the rapid rise of securities (both bonds and equities).

The data in Table 2.5 show the relative importance of different types of private flows to Latin America and the Caribbean and their evolution through time, and allow a comparison with Asian countries.

Table 2.4   Borrowing on International Capital Markets by Type of Flow
(billions of U.S.$)

	1989	1990	1991	1992	1993
Securities	263.8	237.2	321.0	357.2	521.7
Loans	121.1	124.5	116.0	117.9	130.1
Committed backup facilities	8.4	7.0	7.7	6.7	8.2
Non-underwritten facilities[a]	73.2	66.2	80.2	127.9	150.5
Total	466.5	434.9	524.9	609.7	810.5
Year-to-year percentage change	+2.8	−6.8	+20.7	+16.2	+32.9

Source: OECD, Financial Market Trends, vols. 54, 55, and 57, February 1993, June 1993, and February 1994.
Note: [a]Including Euro-commercial paper and medium-term note programs.

Table 2.5   Developing Countries: Capital Flows[a]
(as a % of total, unless otherwise stated)

	1971–1976	1977–1981	1982–1988	1989–1992
Western Hemisphere	11.8	10.6	14.2	24.0
Foreign direct investment	—	—	—	6.3
Portfolio equity	2.6	4.5	2.3	6.3
Bonds	60.0	66.9	36.2	14.7
Commercial bank loans	8.9	6.2	8.8	7.7
Suppliers and export credits	15.9	11.2	35.1	35.9
Official loans	0.8	0.6	3.4	5.1
Grants	17.5	49.5	36.8	42.8
Total in billions of U.S. dollars	36.2	57.8	35.8	34.8
Total in billions of constant dollars[b]				
Asia				
Foreign direct investment	7.1	6.1	9.8	18.4
Portfolio equity	—	—	—	3.6
Bonds	0.8	1.4	5.6	4.4
Commercial bank loans	23.5	32.1	32.5	23.5
Supplies and export credits	12.5	14.8	11.8	13.3
Official loans	44.8	35.5	33.3	30.9
Grants	11.4	10.1	7.0	5.9
Total in billions of U.S. dollars	9.6	23.2	39.8	66.5
Total in billions of constant dollars[b]	17.8	24.3	37.5	53.4

Source: IMF (1993).
Notes: [a]Gross long-term flows.
[b]Deflated using unit value of total imports in U.S.$ (1985 = 100).

As can be seen in Table 2.5 for Latin America and the Caribbean, the 1977–1981 and the 1989–1992 periods show a very sharp increase in FDI flows (from 10.6 to 24.0 percent of total capital flows), the rapid emergence of portfolio equity (from 0 to 6.3 percent), some increase in the share of bonds (from 4.5 to 6.3 percent), and a sharp decline in commercial bank lending (from 66.9 to 14.7 percent). Similar, but somewhat less dramatic changes occur for the Asian countries. For example, for the Asian countries the share of commercial bank loans declines, but far less drastically than for the LAC region, and the share of portfolio equity increases to only 3.6 percent of total capital flows. According to the IMF data, there are more drastic changes in the Asian countries than in the LAC countries in the very rapid increase in the share of FDI and in the increase in the share of bonds.

European Private Flows to Latin America

Foreign Direct Investment

In the 1987–1990 period, direct investment originating in Europe represented about 25 percent of total world investment in Latin America (see Table 2.6). It is noteworthy that the European country from which the highest flow came was the United Kingdom (U.S.$2.5 billion), followed by Germany (U.S.$1.4 billion), Spain (U.S.$0.7 billion), and France (U.S.$0.6 billion). The European country of origin distribution in the 1987–1990 period differs from that in earlier periods: in 1979–1982, Germany was the largest source, followed by France, with the United Kingdom in the third place (Table 2.6).

Since 1985, and particularly since 1988, the share of FDI going to LAC that originates in the United States has increased sharply, and the share of flows originating in Europe has declined somewhat. Indeed, in 1989 the nominal value (in U.S.$) of European FDI to LAC actually fell, although in 1990 it recovered its 1988 level. It is interesting to note that European investors were "bad weather friends"; in 1983–1988, when FDI flows from Japan fell sharply, and U.S. flows became negative due to the Latin American economic and debt crisis, European FDI to the region fell far less than that of Japan, and Europe became the largest source of FDI flows to LAC.

The increased share of FDI investment in LAC originating in the United States in 1987–1990 can be attributed to closer integration within the Americas, with the prospect of NAFTA playing an important role. On the other hand, the decline in the share of European FDI going to LAC in the 1987–1990 period can partly be attributed to the effects of the 1992

Table 2.6 FDI Flows from Europe, the United States, and Japan to Latin America and the Caribbean (millions of U.S.$)

	1979–1982	1983–1986	1987–1990	1987	1988	1989	1990	1991
Belgium	69	24	136	26	57	–5	58	34
France	1,161	394	588	84	111	112	281	–12
Germany	1,458	721	1,366	377	398	302	289	373
Italy	322	473	477	97	210	114	56	123
Netherlands	204	350	480	48	17	122	293	314
Spain	722	303	706	89	148	187	282	580
Switzerland	n.a.	n.a.	n.a.	n.a.	n.a.	n.a.	n.a.	n.a.
United Kingdom	1,141	1,241	2,561	805	842	437	477	n.a.
Europe total	5,097	3,506	6,314	1,526	1,783	1,269	1,736	n.a.
United States	8,542	–415	8,412	708	943	3,544	3,217	n.a.
Japan	2,058	555	1,364	–23	471	343	573	560
World total	23,870	13,259	25,652	5,356	7,553	6,266	6,477	10,939

Source: Table (except for world total) is reproduced from IDB/IRELA (1992). Data sources: OECD, Paris; Overseas Development Administration, Statistics Department, (unpublished data), London; and Secretaría de Estado de Comercio, Ministerio de Industria, Comercio y Turismo, *Sector Exterior, 1990*, Madrid; IMF, balance-of-payments tapes.

Notes: Spanish FDI figures are not strictly comparable with FDI data published by the OECD. The IMF (source of total world data) reports FDI outflow and inflow data whereas the OECD (source of the country breakdowns) reports only outflows. IMF and OECD coverage and reporting practices also differ. For further information, see IDB/IRELA (1992). n.a. = not available.

start of the single European market, as its prospects have tended to increase intra–European Community investment flows (IRELA, 1993).

The sectoral distribution of FDI flows varies according to regions of origin. It is reported (IRELA, 1993) that European FDI in Latin America is particularly active in the manufacturing sector, in contrast with that of the United States and Japan, which are reported to be particularly active in primary sectors. More specifically, European FDI is concentrated in the following sectors: automotives, chemicals, minerals, petrochemicals, electronics, aircraft, and food products (Beetz and van Ryckeghem, 1993).

Finally, Table 2.7 shows the intercountry distribution of European FDI flows to Latin America for the 1987–1990 period; Brazil is by far the largest recipient of European flows (U.S.$3.2 billion) with Argentina coming second (U.S.$0.9 billion), Mexico third (U.S.$0.8 billion), and Chile fourth (U.S.$0.6 billion). In the case of Brazil, Argentina, and Chile, the main European source was the United Kingdom; for Mexico, the main European source was Germany.

Bonds

As pointed out above, it is practically impossible to distinguish bond sources by geographical region, as international and Eurobonds are traded globally, and as information is not available regarding the purchaser. However, valuable hints can be extracted from available information.

Indeed, as can be seen in Table 2.8, when Latin America returned in a significant way to the bond market in 1989, the bonds it issued were denominated only in U.S. dollars; the share in dollars fell somewhat (to 87 percent in 1991), but rose again (to 96 percent) in the first half of 1993. There are no Latin American bonds issued in yen. The rest are all issued in European currencies, and especially in deutsche Marks (DM), in European currency units (ECU), and other European currencies. The concentration of bond issues in dollars also exists for the total of LDCs, but is significantly less marked than for Latin America (again, see Table 2.8); globally, for all borrowers, the distribution of currencies is quite different, with the U.S. dollar accounting for around 30 percent in the 18 months starting in January 1991; the deutsche Mark, 8 percent; the European currency unit, 10 percent; and other currencies (mainly European), 37 percent (Collyns et al., 1992).

The high share of dollar-denominated bonds reflected both the currency preferences of investors (for example, much of Latin American flight capital is believed to be in U.S. dollars) and the currency composition of Latin American companies' receipts. Furthermore, the sharp fall in U.S. short-term interest rates made U.S.-based investors more willing to purchase Latin American securities. In this context, Latin American

Table 2.7 FDI Flows from European Countries to Latin America and the Caribbean, 1987–1990 (millions of U.S.$)

	Belgium	France	Germany	Italy	Netherlands	Spain	Switzerland	United Kingdom	Europe
Argentina	−35	97	338	61	51	162	n.a.	204	878
Barbados	0	1	0	2	1	—	n.a.	−10	−6
Bolivia	−1	0	−3	—	—	—	n.a.	—	−3
Brazil	143	102	482	337	410	73	n.a.	1,706	3,253
Chile	5	62	16	5	39	215	n.a.	285	626
Colombia	0	29	17	4	31	14	n.a.	81	175
Costa Rica	−1	0	3	6	3	2	n.a.	—	13
Dominican Republic	—	0	1	1	2	23	n.a.	—	27
Ecuador	12	36	−2	0	3	4	n.a.	0	53
El Salvador	0	—	−6	0	—	—	n.a.	—	−6
Guatemala	−1	—	−17	1	0	3	n.a.	—	−15
Guyana	0	8	0	—	1	—	n.a.	4	13
Haiti	0	0	0	—	—	—	n.a.	—	0
Honduras	2	—	—	0	0	—	n.a.	—	2
Jamaica	0	3	1	1	1	—	n.a.	53	59
Mexico	−20	113	431	30	14	109	n.a.	74	752
Nicaragua	1	0	−6	0	2	—	n.a.	—	−3
Paraguay	1	1	5	4	—	7	n.a.	—	18
Peru	5	0	30	8	1	11	n.a.	13	68
Suriname	2	1	—	0	−81	—	n.a.	—	−78
Trinidad & Tobago	—	4	0	−17	1	—	n.a.	9	−3
Uruguay	−1	73	12	1	1	34	n.a.	8	127
Venezuela	24	58	64	33	−1	51	n.a.	134	363
Total	136	588	1,366	477	480	706	n.a.	2,561	6,314

Source: Table reproduced from IDB/IRELA (1992). Data sources: OECD, Paris; Overseas Development Administration, Statistics Department (unpublished data), London; Secretaría de Estado de Comercio, Ministerio de Industria, Comercio y Turismo, *Sector Exterior 1990*, Madrid.

Note: Spanish FDI figures are included into the table, but are not strictly comparable with FDI data published by the OECD. For further information see IDB/IRELA (1992). n.a. = not available.

**Table 2.8   International Bond Issues by Currency of Denomination
(% share)**

	1989	1991	1993 (First Half)
Latin American borrowers			
U.S. dollar	100	87	96
Deutsche Mark	—	5	2
Yen	—	—	—
Ecu	—	2	—
Other currencies	—	5	2
Total	100	100	100
All developing countries			
U.S. dollar	56	65	75
Deutsche Mark	22	17	8
Yen	17	9	14
Ecu	2	5	0
Other currencies	3	5	3
Total	100	100	100

Source: Author's calculations and data, originating from C. Collyns et al., "Private Market Financing for Developing Countries," *World Economic and Financial Survey,* IMF, December 1992, Washington, D.C.; and C. Collyns et al., "Private Market Financing for Developing Countries," *World Economic and Financial Survey,* IMF, December 1993, Washington, D.C.

borrowers have been able to tap also the rapidly growing "Yankee" market, whereas they have not tapped the equivalent market in European currencies, such as sterling.

It is noteworthy that although Latin American international bonds are denominated mainly in U.S. dollars, they are practically all listed in Europe, with a very heavy concentration of listing in Luxembourg. It is also important to stress that within European currencies, the deutsche Mark bonds are by far the largest. This is because European investor interest in Latin American bonds is mainly still restricted to the deutsche Mark sector; in Germany, banks (and particularly savings banks, many of which operate at a municipal level) play a key role in distributing bond issues to domestic retail customers. Thus, retail customers in Germany rely on their banks to apply quality control, and banks try to maintain the confidence of their customers by avoiding bond defaults. As a consequence, German banks tend to avoid issuing or marketing bonds from countries where bank debt packages have not yet been finalized. It is reported that there is also beginning to be some interest from German institutional investors in Latin American bonds.[1]

In the United Kingdom, both institutional and retail investors are not very keen on bonds, in general, partly because they experienced severe losses on fixed-income instruments in the high inflation years of the 1970s. Indeed, it is interesting to note the sharp contrast between the general preferences for bonds versus equities in different European countries.

This is illustrated in Table 2.9 for pension fund investors, for different European countries for which comparative data are available. There is a particularly sharp contrast between the United Kingdom, where pension funds distribute their foreign assets by putting only 6 percent into foreign bonds and as much as 94 percent into foreign equities, and Germany, where pension funds distribute their foreign assets by putting as much as 93 percent into foreign bonds and as little as 7 percent into foreign equities. (There is also the important difference between the United Kingdom and Germany in that in the former a far higher proportion of total assets is invested in foreign assets; see Table 2.9.) The other European country that has a strong preference for bonds is Switzerland (again, see Table 2.9). This is consistent with reports that a growing (although still small) share of Latin American Eurobonds is being placed via Switzerland. It is also interesting that Dutch pension funds have a fairly high share of their foreign assets as bonds. The preferences of Dutch, Swiss, and British pension funds are particularly relevant in the short term, given their high level of foreign assets. However, for the medium term, it is particularly important to understand the preferences of those institutions—particularly the German pension funds—that have a very small share of total assets in foreign investments and might therefore increase them substantially.

Table 2.9   Foreign Assets of Pension Funds (End of 1988)

	Foreign Assets (billions of U.S.$)	Percent of Total Assets	Foreign Bonds as Percentage of Foreign Assets	Foreign Equities as Percentage of Foreign Assets
United Kingdom	53.8	14.0	6	94
Germany	0.2	0.4	93	7
Netherlands	15.0	14.0	41	59
Switzerland	9.0	4.0	70	30
France	1.2	4.0	15	85
United States[a]	62.8	4.0	14	86

Source: E. P. Davies, "The Structure, Regulation and Performance of Pension Funds in Nine Industrial Countries," Policy Research Working Paper, No. 1229, World Bank, Washington, D.C., 1993.

Note: [a]Figures for the United States included for comparison.

Equities

Comparative estimates of global secondary flows into emerging stock markets of Latin America, the Pacific Rim, and Europe show that investors have diverted a very rapidly increasing portion of their total allocation to Latin America through the late 1980s and early 1990s.

The level of secondary flows to Latin America is estimated to have fallen in 1992, after having increased sharply before. The bulk of net inflows to emerging markets in 1986–1987 went into the Pacific Rim, with only 17 percent to Latin America; this share increased systematically and rapidly until 1991, when more than 85 percent of flows were going into Latin America; in 1992, the share declined somewhat, but was still reportedly very high, at almost 60 percent. Preliminary estimates for the first six months in 1993 show that around 25 percent of secondary flows went to Latin America, with a major share (around 60 percent) going to the Pacific Rim, although it is estimated there was some increase in the LAC share in late 1993.

It should, however, be emphasized that it is estimated that in 1993, Latin America was dominant in primary issues within emerging markets. Around 50 percent of total issues in emerging markets came from Latin America, of which around half (30 percent of the total) were estimated to have originated in Mexico. These figures seemed to indicate that there was no problem of saturation of Latin American equities and that investor appetite for Latin American paper continued high.

As regards European flows investing in Latin American equities, there are no published data available.

However, as shown in Table 2.10, it is estimated that European purchases of Latin American equities started at very low levels in 1986–1988 (although gradually rising), increased substantially in 1989, continued growing in 1990–1991, but declined somewhat in 1992. In this respect, European flows reflect a pattern similar to total flows going to Latin American equities with, however, a certain lag. Indeed, it seems that interest in purchasing Latin American equities originated initially more from U.S.-based sources (including returning Latin American flight capital and European investors, particularly U.K. ones). The focus was first far more on the emerging markets of the Pacific Basin; European investors started somewhat later in the emerging markets of Latin America than their U.S. counterparts. However, by 1991, European investors are estimated to reach a peak of 40 percent of total secondary flows going to Latin American emerging markets (see Table 2.10), with their share declining somewhat in 1992, to around 30 percent.

It can be argued that this type of behavior is to an important extent dictated by geographical proximity. Thus, U.S. investors have in general shown a preference for Latin America, while Japanese investors have tended toward South East Asian markets. European investors (particularly from the United Kingdom) have straddled both markets, preferring South East Asia in the early stages and then more recently diverting funds to Latin America.[2]

As pointed out above, there are no detailed published figures that show the sources of funds for different regions in emerging markets. However, there is information, by investor, on funds going to the emerging markets (excluding Pacific Rim), which includes Latin America, the Indian subcontinent, the Middle East, Eastern Europe, and others (the bulk of these are likely to go to Latin America). As can be seen in Table 2.11, for the 1986–1992 period, funds originating in Europe represented 40 percent of flows going to emerging markets, with the largest portion originating in the United Kingdom (23 percent) and the second most important European source being Switzerland (with 9 percent of total flows to emerging markets).

Clearly the main source for European investment in emerging markets (including mainly those of Latin America) originates in the United Kingdom. U.K. foreign equity assets are concentrated in the hands of pension funds, life insurance companies, and unit trusts.

The accumulation of foreign assets in U.K. pension funds has been a key feature in their development. In 1975, foreign assets (all equity) represented only 5 percent of total portfolios. After the abolition of foreign

Table 2.10   Estimated European Secondary Market Flows to Latin America
(billions of U.S.$)

	1986	1987	1988	1989	1990	1991	1992[a]
Amount	0.04	0.17	0.33	1.7	3.3	4.5	2–3

Source: Estimates prepared by Angela Cozzini on the basis of the Baring Securities (1993) data base.
Note: [a]Estimate.

Table 2.11   Net Cross-Border Equity Flows (Secondary Purchases)
into the Emerging Markets by Investor
(cumulative, 1986–1992[a])

	Flows to Emerging Markets (billions of U.S.$)	Percent of Flows to Emerging Markets
Sources:		
North America	10.21	23
Europe	17.85	40
United Kingdom	10.35	23
Switzerland	4.26	9
Pacific Rim	13.57	30
Emerging markets	1.55	3
Other	2.70	6
Total	45.88	100[b]

Source: Calculations based on Howell (1993).
Notes: [a]Estimate.
[b]Totals may not equal 100 percent due to rounding.

exchange controls in 1979, there was a sharp increase in foreign assets held by U.K. pension funds, whose share more than tripled, to 18 percent, by 1990. As can be seen in Table 2.12, this is the highest share of foreign assets held by pension funds in any developed country. According to data provided by Baring Securities (1993) by end 1991, 26 percent of overall U.K. pension funds were held in foreign assets.

Table 2.12   European Pension Funds Foreign Assets
             (as a % of assets)

	1975	1980	1985	1990
United Kingdom	5	9	15	18
Germany	0	0	1	1
Netherlands	8	4	9	15
Switzerland	—	—	3	5
United States[a]	0	1	2	4
Japan[a]	0	1	5	7

Source: Based on national flow-of-funds tables (Davies, 1993).
Note: [a]Figures for the United States and Japan are included for comparison.

The increasing exposure by U.K. pension funds to foreign stocks is particularly striking. Foreign stocks accounted for only 6 percent of total assets in 1979, but are estimated by Baring Securities to have increased to over 20 percent in 1991. This is consistent with the information provided in Table 2.9 (and with interview material), which shows that by the late 1980s a very high share of U.K. pension funds foreign assets was held in foreign equities. This trend is confirmed clearly in the early 1990s.

This may have important implications for future trends. Indeed, in the United Kingdom, pension funds already have such a high proportion of their assets in foreign equities that they probably will not wish to increase this share much further. As a result, investments into emerging markets' shares (e.g., in Latin America) could come mainly from a reallocation of U.K. pension funds international assets to emerging markets, and not so much from an increase in their investment share in foreign equities. However, the reallocation of funds from developed to developing markets should not be underestimated.

Growth of investment in emerging markets by U.K. pension funds can be expected to be somewhat more limited than, for example, that of U.S. pension funds, where only around 4 percent of total assets were in foreign assets (see Table 2.12), and within this only around 3.5 percent of total assets were in foreign equities.[3] The experts (called consultants) who advise U.S. pension funds are as a result suggesting that these U.S. funds rapidly increase their share of foreign equities in total assets to around 15 percent, of which around 10 percent (that is, 1.5 percent of total) should go to emerging markets. Should these trends materialize, then U.S. pension funds investment in emerging market equities would increase both because the share of foreign equities in their total assets is rising sharply and because of reallocation of assets to emerging markets.

The situation in the Netherlands is somewhat in-between, although closer to that of the United Kingdom. The share of foreign assets held by private pension funds is already quite high, but that of public funds foreign holdings is fairly low (at only around 3 percent). As a result, there is some space for a further expansion in the share of foreign assets in Dutch pension funds, which could be reflected in a potentially fairly large increase in investment in equities in emerging markets (particularly because the Dutch pension funds have a strong preference for equities as a form of foreign asset investment).

Pension funds and life insurers have been "in the vanguard" of foreign equity investment in the United Kingdom and the Netherlands, within Europe. Both countries share a high ratio of institutional assets to GDP. In both countries, there is a relatively low level of pension benefits provided by governments, which forces individuals to save for their old age.

Within Europe, however, the United Kingdom and the Netherlands are the exception rather than the rule. For example, more generous state pensions are found in France, Italy, and Switzerland; in Germany there is a special retirement system. These countries have as a consequence low institutional assets to GDP. However, informed observers[4] believe that this is set to change as generous government pension benefits become inviable in those countries, due both to an aging population structure and the need to reduce budget deficits. As a result of these and other trends, an important increase in the pension fund assets of France, Germany, Italy, and Switzerland is estimated for the coming years. Indeed, Baring Securities[5] estimates that such assets will grow 50 percent from 1991 to 1996 and reach almost $500 billion in the latter year. Furthermore, the currently low proportion of their assets held in foreign assets is projected to also increase quite significantly in the next years. As a result, there is a large potential for higher investment by French, German, Italian, and Swiss pension funds in equities (and bonds) issued by Latin American borrowers. It may therefore be worthwhile for LA borrowers to make special efforts to attract the interest of these potentially large investors, as well as that of the more established pension funds, such as those of the United Kingdom and the Netherlands.

The U.K. pension funds are by far the most important European investors in emerging markets equities (see Table 2.11). What is the proportion of their emerging market investment going to Latin America, and how has it evolved? This is an important question, because it can be argued that investment from institutions such as pension funds implies a more long-term commitment and is therefore potentially less volatile than investment from other sources.

It is at present impossible to obtain data separating only Latin America, but information was obtained that separates Pacific Rim emerging markets from other emerging markets (which is mainly Latin American, but also include the Indian subcontinent and the Middle East). Table 2.13 provides data that refer to £185 billion of U.K. pension fund total investment made by 3,000 different investors. The information provided in this table shows that (1) Latin American equities still (in September 1993) represent an extremely low share of U.K. total assets (below 0.6 percent), although there has been a systematic and sustained increase since December 1990; and (2) Pacific Rim (excluding Japan) equities represented a ten times higher share of U.K. total assets than Latin American equities in December 1990. The level of Pacific Rim equities continued to increase in the last three years, although at a somewhat slower pace than Latin American equities. Indeed, by late 1993 Pacific Rim (excluding Japan) equities reportedly represented as high a share of U.K. pension funds assets as Japanese equities or U.S. equities.

Table 2.13 Percent Shares of Investment, in U.K. Total Pension Fund Investment, Excluding Property

	Dec. 1990	Mar. 1991	June 1991	Sep. 1991	Dec. 1991	Mar. 1992	June 1992	Sept. 1992	Dec. 1992	Mar. 1993	June 1993
Other equities (including Latin America)	0.2	0.3	0.4	0.4	0.4	0.5	0.5	0.6	0.6	0.6	0.6
Pacific Basin equities (excluding Japan)	2.1	2.6	3.0	2.8	2.9	3.3	3.5	3.4	3.7	4.2	4.6

Source: CAPS Ltd. Several issues, Quarterly Bulletin, London.
Note: Refers to £185 billion of total assets (excluding property) of 3,000 portfolios of U.K. pension funds.

The above figures would seem to confirm that there may be a very large potential for the share of Latin American equities in U.K. pension funds to rise. This was confirmed in interviews with pension fund representatives and fund investment managers. For example, a representative of Mercury, the largest pension fund manager in Europe, expressed the view that U.K. pension funds (as well as retail investors) will further increase their share going to Latin America, but this will not reach as high a level as that going to the Pacific Rim. Robert Fleming, a representative of another very·large investment manager, confirmed a similar trend and emphasized that there is increased interest in Latin America by U.K. institutional investors in late 1993; this is reflected in the fact that many U.K. brokers are now creating separate "expertise" and "desks" for Latin American securities, whereas until recently Latin American securities were covered by the U.S. analysts. This trend was further confirmed by a representative from the largest U.K. pension fund, British Rail Pension Fund (BRPF). It is interesting that this important pension fund has its assets totally externally managed by five managers on global remit, who work in an approved list of countries. All five managers had asked BRPF particularly strongly in the last year (and more informally in the previous two years) to let them invest BRPF money in Latin America, as well as in Eastern Europe. Reportedly, a decision to allow some small investment in Latin America has been made.

The interviews also showed a reported interesting difference between U.K. and U.S. investment in Latin American equities. In the United States, most brokers dealing in Latin American shares trade large volumes, so they can make enough money on commissions on secondary business. In the United Kingdom, the scale of Latin American business is still small, so brokers prefer to focus more on primary business, where far higher fees can be earned (reportedly up to 6 or 7 percent). This requires them to have good relations with primary borrowers.

For the country distribution (within Latin America) of U.K. investors, an important distinction needs to be made between general investors (such as pension funds) and more specialized investors (such as those investing in regional funds). For example, one investment manager offered its general investors what it called a "conservative portfolio" in Latin America, with around 60 percent in Mexico and around 15 percent each in Brazil, Chile, and Argentina. This same investment manager offered its specialized Latin American investors a mix with 50 percent exposure in Mexico, more than 20 percent in Brazil, around 10 percent each in Argentina and Chile, and some exposure in the less well known and/or "riskier" markets of Peru, Colombia, and Venezuela. Furthermore, Foreign and Colonial, reportedly the largest portfolio investor of Europe in Latin America, had even a more diversified portfolio in its Latin American fund, with only 32 percent in Mexico, a similar proportion in Brazil, 14 percent in Argentina, around 5 percent each in Colombia, Venezuela, Chile, and Peru, and smaller amounts (less than 1 percent) in countries such as Ecuador and Bolivia. European (particularly U.K.) investors are believed to have a broader understanding of Latin America, and are therefore more willing to have a wider range of exposure in terms of countries within Latin America, than the more "conservative" U.S.-based investors, who concentrate far more on investment in Mexican equities.

More recent (1993) trends show an increased attractiveness of Brazilian equities for U.K. investors. This is encouraged by large increases of the prices in Brazilian stock exchange.

The process of increasing country diversification within Latin America is not restricted to investment in equities in the region. Indeed, it was reported (West Merchant Bank, 1993) that there has recently been significant geographical diversification in the number of Latin American countries accessing the international bond market with the entry of Uruguay and Trinidad in 1992, and with that of Chile, Colombia, and Guatemala in 1993. It is interesting that the Guatemalan bond is collateralized by coffee export receivables; this follows a pattern first set by Mexican borrowers on the bond markets whereby the initial bond offerings made were collateralized by export receivables, with later issues often not having that characteristic, as the market became more familiar with those countries and borrowers.

Bank Lending

In contrast to the buoyant activity in the international bond and equity market, total bank lending commitments to Latin American countries declined quite sharply in the 1987–1991 period. This was because, as discussed above, there was a global fall in international bank lending. Also, access to such lending remained severely restricted for Latin American and other developing countries that had recently experienced debt-servicing difficulties. However, it is interesting that during 1992 net aggregate bank lending to Latin American countries that were not members of the Organization of Petroleum Exporting Countries (OPEC) was positive for the first time in six years, at U.S.$12.1 billion—a level not seen for a decade (Table 2.14). Furthermore, in the first three quarters of 1993, lending to that region was positive (at U.S.$0.2 billion) but far smaller than in the previous year (BIS, 1994). There is therefore possibly a new important trend emerging, of increased bank lending to Latin America.

There is no published information available regarding the geographical sources of such bank lending to Latin America. However, according to estimates provided by the BIS, around a third of the stock of international bank lending to Latin America in the last three years originated in flows from Europe.

An important and potentially problematic recent feature of international bank lending, to Latin America as well as more generally, is a fairly significant shortening of the average maturity of such lending. Thus, for non-OPEC Latin American countries, the share of loans of up to one-year

Table 2.14   BIS Reporting Banks' Lending to Different Categories of Countries
(outside the reporting area)

Borrowing from Reporting Banks	Changes, Excluding Exchange Rate Effects (billions of U.S.$)							Stocks at end-1992
	1986	1987	1988	1989	1990	1991	1992	
Non-OPEC								
Latin America	1.5	−3.7	−5.0	−16.7	−23.0	−0.3	12.1	200.1
Non-OPEC LDCs	3.1	2.2	−2.4	−19.6	−5.7	13.8	30.3	410.1
Total borrowing	14.4	11.6	13.5	−1.7	−11.9	8.1	63.7	813.2

Source: BIS (1993), 63rd Annual Report, Basle, June.

maturity rose from 42.5 percent of total bank loans at the end of 1991, to 45.1 percent in mid-1992, and to 47.4 percent at the end of 1992. For all LDCs this share went up in a similar proportion, from 49.4 percent at the end of 1991 to 54.1 percent at the end of 1992, although at a somewhat higher share of short-term loans. Within Latin America, particularly rapid increases in the share of loans of up to one-year maturity occurred during 1992 in Argentina, Chile, and Colombia. This trend, for Latin America and for the rest of the developing world (as well as for all bank lending) reflects banks' increased preference for short-term lending, shown by the nonrenewal of maturing long-term loans and increased emphasis on trade-related credit.

Motivations of European Securities Investors

A noteworthy point that emerged from the interviews in this study was the general impression that specific European investors (e.g., pension funds) seem to decide first whether they like a particular country or region. Once they decide to go into a particular region or country, they tend to invest in the whole range of instruments in that particular country, including equity, bonds, and short-term instruments. The extent to which they prefer one set of instruments to another depends mainly on their general preferences. Thus, U.K. investors in general prefer to invest in equities; this same preference is reflected in their general international assets and in their investments in Latin America. Similarly, German investors have a strong preference for fixed-income instruments (especially bonds), preferences that are reflected in the distribution of their international and Latin American assets.

Another important feature was that investors seem to think mainly in regional terms. Thus, they express strong views about the Latin American region in general, although they may also have some preferences for individual countries within the region. This "regionalization" of preferences works for both positive and negative trends. Thus, an anti-NAFTA speech delivered by then–U.S. presidential candidate Ross Perot reportedly caused both foreign and domestic investors to sell shares in countries as far from Mexico as Argentina, with a resulting large fall in share prices in Argentina, even though the objective connection between Argentinian economic performance and the Perot speech was very tenuous indeed.

Clearly, an important factor that encourages European investors to invest in developing-country bonds is yield. To the extent that European interest rates are consistently falling, and U.S. interest rates are relatively low, the attraction of higher yields is clearly important for European investors. To the extent that this differential in yield would be eroded (e.g., due to an increase in U.S. interest rates), the attractiveness of Latin American bonds could fall significantly. Another interesting element is that increased demand for Latin American bonds runs in parallel, and is related to, increases in the volume and prices of secondary market trading, especially of Brady bonds.

One of the most active investment banks in London in selling Latin American bonds, Morgan Grenfell, summarized the key fundamentals regarding specific country investments as: (1) relations with creditors, (2) fiscal policy, (3) consistency of policy and political stability, and (4) progress in structural reforms such as privatization. When these four criteria were applied to four countries (Mexico, Brazil, Morocco, and Poland) for two different years, Mexico emerged as the most attractive country in 1992, with a large improvement over its 1988 "performance."

The exponential growth of research on Latin American economies by large investment houses was given as an indication that there will be a likely growth in business from U.K. investors into both bonds and equities. It is important to understand the complex institutional arrangements behind the motivations of U.K.-based investors in Latin American equities. Institutional investors (such as pension funds and insurance companies) are the sources of the funds, but are only very indirectly and somewhat partially involved in the decisionmaking process. They hire pension fund consultants, who advise them on a general strategy. They also hire investment managers, to whom they tend to give fairly broad guidelines; the investment managers make suggestions within those guidelines or suggest changes in the guidelines. Finally, brokers are involved in directly purchasing the shares. Decisions are somewhat disseminated. Knowledge is also unevenly distributed—pension-fund managers would have far less specialist knowledge than investment managers on, for example, Latin American markets. It may indeed be desirable for Latin American borrowers to establish also stronger links and communication channels with pension-fund managers directly.

Some of the factors determining investment in Latin American equities are global in origin. For example, as deposit rates come down, resources are transferred on a large scale from banks into the securities markets. Furthermore, there are fears that returns on European equities could become very low or negative, and investing in emerging markets (including those in Latin America) is seen to offer possibilities of better returns and of reducing systemic risk. The latter reason is supported by research, which shows that as national trade cycles are not correlated (especially in noncrisis times) the investment of part of the portfolio in other markets can reduce systemic risk for the same return (Davies, 1991; World Bank, 1993). Furthermore, a strong reason for investing in Latin American equities is that in recent years the prices of Latin American stocks (as well as several Far East stocks) had increased far faster than that of stocks in developed countries. Indeed, in 1992 the top six best-performing markets were emerging ones.

Most fund managers seem to take a top-down approach to the selection of stocks in developing countries. Thus, they first assess the country's overall economic prospects (with some using 4–6 percent growth as a minimum threshold), and then move down to sectoral and company levels. Investment managers report a generally inadequate quality of financial information available at the company level in Latin America.

As pointed out above, U.K. institutional investors are only now beginning to invest in Latin American equities, and they are increasing their participation rather prudently. The reluctance to move faster is due to the fact that Latin America is still seen as potentially somewhat volatile, both economically and politically.

The performance of Latin America in 1993 (both in the economies and in the stock markets) is seen as good and improving; this is reflected in the significantly improved ranking of Latin American economies since 1989 in the country risk ratings published, for example, by *Institutional Investor* and *Euromoney*. However, among some U.K.-based institutional investors there were lingering (although diminishing) concerns about the sustainability of Latin America's improved economic performance.

Among the criteria attracting U.K. investors, at both the institutional and retail levels, to Latin America were: (1) a major change in economic philosophy toward more free-market economics, which is broadly seen as permanent; (2) increased growth and growth prospects; (3) prudent macroeconomic management; and (4) improved political stability. To the extent that flows (both bonds and equities) are attracted to an important degree by domestic-country factors, and these policies are maintained in Latin America, it becomes more likely that such flows will continue at a fairly significant level.

Other factors that influence the decision to invest in the Latin American market are the size of the market (with clear preference for larger markets) and domestic regulations. U.K.-based investors attach quite a lot of importance to appropriate domestic regulations in Latin American markets, which are seen to have improved significantly; however, further improvements are seen as desirable in key aspects, such as liquidity of local markets, systematic information, and clearing and settlements procedures. One aspect of Latin American countries' regulations seen as problematic by U.K.-based investors is the continuing holding period requirement imposed in Chile for the sake of macroeconomic stability.

It is important to stress that foreign fund managers tend to "hold" their investment far longer in emerging market equities than in developed-country markets. On average for the 1986–1992 period foreign fund managers turned their emerging market portfolio over 0.8 times a year, whereas foreign equity portfolios in developed-country markets are turned over 2.6 times each year. This has led Howell (1993) to conclude that while foreign fund managers are "trading" in the developed markets (increasingly with derivative instruments), searching for ever more elusive arbitrage opportunities, they are "investing" in the emerging markets, where they are steadily building up their exposure. However, average holding periods for LDC stocks are still rather short.

It would seem that holding periods are somewhat longer for U.K.-based global investors, as they are more interested in longer-term capital appreciation. There is also some evidence that for these investors the time horizon tends to be longer for investments in Asian markets, where transactions are driven more by fundamental factors, and generally shorter for investments in Latin America markets, which tend to be more trading-oriented. One reason for this is the high inflation rates in some countries (e.g., in Brazil), which complicate longer-term investment strategy.[6]

Expected and required return targets that are set before investing vary widely. Some more aggressive investment managers argue that less than a 20 percent annual return is considered "disappointing." On the other hand, some institutional investors say that fairly low returns can be tolerated, as their investment in Latin American or other emerging markets produces a valuable diversification effect.

The investment managers interviewed argued that a large outflow of funds from Latin American equity markets could occur if there were a major relevant change in the international economy (for example, if U.S. interest rates rose rapidly and significantly, or if there were a sharp increase in protectionism in the industrial world) or if there were major political unrest in one of the larger Latin American countries.

Relevant Regulations in Europe

A fairly important factor influencing European flows into Latin American investments is the issue of source country regulations. For investments by

European institutional investors, two general trends can be detected. One is that in most European countries pension funds are less restricted than life insurers regarding their ability to carry out international investments. The second is that there is quite a sharp contrast between some European countries with fairly liberal regulations (in particular the United Kingdom, but also to an important extent Holland) and countries with fairly restrictive regulations (e.g., Germany, France, and Italy). U.K. life insurance regulations stipulate that liabilities in any currency that exceeds 5 percent of the total must be matched at least 80 percent by assets in the same currency. Furthermore, firms have to prove to the supervisory authorities at regular intervals that they meet statutory solvency requirements.

In other European countries, life insurers are constrained by regulations from holding sizable proportions of foreign assets; that is, firms are not free to expand foreign asset holdings. Thus, in Germany the Law on Insurance Supervision specifies that assets held to meet contractual insurance liabilities (which represent more than 90 percent of the total) must be one of twelve specified types, and foreign assets are excluded from the list. Technically, 100 percent matching of domestic currency life insurance liabilities with domestic assets is required. Also, foreign assets may not exceed 5 percent of other assets (i.e., those reserves allocated for future bonuses). Reportedly, a European Community (EC) directive would raise this ceiling on foreign investment, but regulators would still impose other relevant restrictions.

In France, 100 percent matching of life insurance liabilities to assets is required, as in Germany; also, 34 percent must be in public bonds. Several other European countries have restrictions on life insurance assets similar to those in Germany and France. In Italy, foreign currency assets are limited to the size of foreign currency liabilities. In contrast, Netherlands has a liberal regime. There are no restrictions on asset holdings or solvency requirements, although account must be made regularly of the asset and liability positions of the firms.

The regulations passed in the context of 1992 and the single market (including the Life Insurance Directive, ensuring cross-border competition) may directly—or indirectly as a result of competition—reduce the differentials in portfolio restrictions. Competition will particularly be the case as EC firms will be able to operate under "home" country regulations, allowing foreign firms from outside Europe to compete under less stringent regulations.

In Germany, profitability is also regulated and product design is restricted. With the new EC directives, even if the products remain the same, incentives to invest overseas may increase; however, if—as is more likely—the nature of the product changes as a result of EC directives, there will be more offshore German investment.

In the United Kingdom, pension funds (as in the United States) are subject to a "prudent man rule," which requires managers to carry out sensible portfolio diversification. U.K. pension funds are not constrained by regulation in their portfolio holdings, except for limits on self-investment (5 percent) and concentration. (Trustees may, however, impose limits on portfolio distribution.) There is therefore no regulatory limit on the share of foreign assets held by U.K. pension funds.

German pension funds remain subject to the same panoply of regulations as those for life insurers (including a 4 percent limit on foreign asset holdings). In France, certain pension funds are constrained by fiscal regulations to invest in domestic assets, implying even tighter control than in Germany. Swiss limits are similar to, if slightly less restrictive than, German ones; there is a 20 percent limit on foreign assets and 10 percent on foreign shares. Finally, Dutch private funds face no restrictions, except for a 5 percent limit on self-investment. In contrast, the public service fund (ABP) faces strict limits, being able to invest only 5 percent abroad.

As regulations for institutional investors in continental Europe are likely to become more liberal—as a result of the influence of the Anglo-Saxon model and as a result of EC directives—there may be quite a large potential for increased investment by those institutions in foreign assets, including those held in Latin America. Such potentially large growth may be particularly important from those institutions whose regulations are at present particularly restrictive and from those countries where institutional assets are likely to grow.

Changes in EC regulations, not just those that regulate institutional investors but also those that regulate financial intermediaries, will influence decisionmaking on the allocation of funds globally from European sources, and therefore influence the share going to Latin America. It would be somewhat premature to assess the direction of the effects of such changes, as these have just occurred recently or will occur in the future. However, the measures described briefly below will clearly encourage cross-border activity within Europe by financial entities, and may therefore facilitate access by Latin American borrowers to a greater scale and variety of European sources of savings. On the other hand, there could be the danger that a focus on European financial integration and investment opportunities could distract attention and resources from investment abroad; this trend, which is reported to have occurred for FDI, seems less likely to occur for securities flows, however.

The creation of a single financial market in the European Community is an essential element of the 1992 Single Internal Market. It aims first to abolish capital controls within the European Community and to remove all barriers to cross-border provision of financial services. The latter aim requires two measures: (1) the recognition of a single license permitting an institution to do business anywhere in the European Community, and (2) agreement on minimum standards. For banks and other credit institutions, mutual recognition is established in the Second Banking Directive, which came into effect in January 1993. This allows a bank that is lawfully established in any member country to establish branches throughout the European Community, without needing special permission from the host country nor holding separate capital. The entire bank, including branches in other countries, is regulated by the home country, except for liquidity and risk in domestic markets. There are complementary directives and bilateral agreements on banking regulation in the EC context.[7]

Among the possible likely effects of these directives is exposing European banks, which currently display elements of monopoly, to heightened competition. Some observers also suggest that the single market may result in a shift toward the universal banking model, as the EC Second Banking Directive appears to lean toward universal banking by allowing universal banks to do business throughout the EC, while confining banks from the "Anglo-Saxon" model to the same narrow range of activities in any member country as they already do.

In the securities markets, a single passport is to be provided under the Investment Services Directive, adopted in mid-1992, and which is to come into force in 1996. This passport allows securities dealers licensed in any member country to do business anywhere in the European Community; it is supplemented by capital requirements designed to ensure the safety and soundness of dealers and brokers (specified in the Capital Adequacy Directive), which applies to securities firms and to the securities trading activities of banks.

Another important element of the single market is the sale and advertisement of products rather than the establishment of business operations. In particular, cross-border sale of shares in open-ended mutual funds was authorized in the Directive on Collective Investment, which came into force in most EC countries in 1989. It resulted in a significant increase in the volume of cross-border investment activity, although reportedly much of it apparently consists of "round-tripping." This type of round-tripping makes accurate statistical analysis of country origins practically impossible.

An EC Directive on Pension Funds establishes as a general principle freedom of investment; for example, governments cannot require pension funds to hold only domestic assets. Similar EC initiatives have been under way for life insurance companies as well as other insurors.

It is important to note that likely changes in the United Kingdom are currently being discussed regarding regulation of investments at a national European level. These changes are relevant here because some investment managers interviewed highlighted existing regulations as an important constraint for investment in Latin American shares, particularly by retail investors.

In the United Kingdom, the Securities and Investment Board (SIB) regulates securities and investment activities, mainly through a network of self-regulatory organizations. The SIB currently publishes lists of overseas exchanges, which according to its criteria provide acceptable levels of investor protection. These lists are important because investments in approved markets imply a lower capital requirement for the securities firm, and these markets are therefore more profitable for them.

The current list of markets approved for authorized unit trusts includes only Mexico among Latin American securities markets, although it includes several Asian securities markets (Korea, Malaysia, Singapore, and Thailand). Reportedly, it is relatively simple for new securities markets to be added to the list if they request to do so; however, from Latin America, only Mexico has reportedly made this request.

However, in an October 1993 review of its policy (SIB, 1993), the SIB is proposing that the concept of approved markets for authorized unit trusts be abolished. The SIB proposes replacing the list of approved securities markets by a duty, placed upon the manager of the unit trust after consultation with the trustees, to invest only in those markets that are (1) regulated, (2) operate regularly, (3) are recognized, and (4) are open to the public.

It is interesting how the SIB justifies this proposed change. It argues that, provided the manager operates within disclosed parameters, appropriate investor protection could be achieved by placing reliance on the integrity and competence of unit trust managers to make judgments about the relevant market. The SIB therefore considers that "this approach should not result in any material lessening of investor protection." It argues, then, that given accelerated globalization of investment and an increase in the number of markets in which fund managers seek to invest, it is unrealistic to expect U.K.-based regulations to make—and continually review—a judgment on each market without a significant increase in regulatory resources and costs.

If, as seems likely, this regulatory change is approved in the United Kingdom, it will imply that it will become easier for Latin American borrowers to raise funds from U.K. unit trusts. This is a potentially large source of revenues, as total U.K. unit trust assets reach around U.S.$100 billion.

Although this effect should be welcome, perhaps some concern should be raised about the apparently drastic process of liberalization of regulation that this change implies and reflects. Also of concern is the fact that apparently the issue of regulatory resources and costs, as well as the difficulties of regulating in an increasingly globalized world, very heavily influences the decision on the extent to which regulation should actually be carried out.

Terms of Inflows into Latin America:
Their Suitability for Long-Term Development
and Risks Associated with Them

As we have shown, there is at present an important supply globally of foreign capital entering Latin America, of which a fairly large share comes from Europe. Furthermore, there is evidence that at least some of the main reasons motivating such capital to flow to the region (such as the improved economic policies of many countries as well as higher interest rates and profitability in the region than in the developed countries) are likely to remain, both in the short and medium term. Therefore, there are some grounds for cautious optimism about the sustainability of these flows in the short to medium term. It is also a reason for some optimism that investors with a more long-term perspective—such as the institutional investors, which include pension funds and insurance companies—are beginning to invest in Latin America. In the case of European institutional investors, particularly those in much of continental Europe, there seems to be a great potential for increased investment in the future, as their assets are projected to grow and they are likely to increase their international diversification. In the more immediate period, institutional investors in countries such as the United Kingdom—already with very large assets and international diversification but with relatively low exposure in Latin America—could increase their exposure to the region fairly significantly. Some additional efforts may be required on the part of the borrowers to appropriately tap those new sources of funds.

Even though there are legitimate reasons for cautious optimism about sustainability of the flows in the short to medium term, it must be stressed that there are risks of volatility of such flows, particularly due to international factors. For example, if interest rates and profitability were to rise significantly in developed countries (and specifically in Europe, in the context of our analysis here), then the attraction of Latin America to foreign investors could decline. Although such a trend does not seem very likely in the short term, economic history shows that such changes do occur and that they tend to affect inflows to regions such as Latin America quite dramatically.

This is one of the main reasons it is important not to assume that flows will continue to come in at the same level as at present, and to examine what the potential for volatility of such flows is and what the negative effects of such volatility could be, as well as how policymakers should attempt to minimize both.

One additional important point needs to be made. The long-term impact on growth and development of such flows depends not just on the sustainability of these flows and on the financial terms they have (important as those factors are), but also on the use made of these flows. To what extent are these flows being channeled into investment and not consumption? In what proportion is investment in tradables, which will generate additional foreign exchange in the future to help service those flows without creating a debt crisis and/or a reduction in the capacity to import? Is there not a contradiction between very large capital inflows pushing for exchange-rate appreciation and encouraging investment in tradables? How well is that contradiction being resolved by the economic authorities of the recipient countries?

In what follows, we will emphasize more the risks and costs of these flows, with a view to minimizing them. It should be stressed, though, that if volatility is reduced and handled well, and if the foreign inflows are productively invested (with an important proportion going into tradables), there is a high likelihood that the inflows will not be beneficial just in the short term, but that these benefits will be sustained in the medium and long term. It is precisely to achieve these objectives (which are in the interests of investors, lenders, and borrowers alike) that measures may need to be taken to encourage more desirable flows and in some cases to discourage less desirable flows, particularly if these are coming in at an excessively high level.

Bonds are a very important category of Latin American borrowing. It is often stressed correctly[8] that since 1989, on the whole, yield spreads for Latin American borrowers have tended to decline and that maturities have on the whole remained constant or slightly increased. Furthermore, the total cost of bond finance was seen as low by Latin American borrowers because the interest rate level of U.S. Treasury bonds, over which spreads are usually calculated, was then fairly low. However, it should be emphasized that the average weighted spreads for Latin American bonds in the 1989–1992 period are significantly higher than they are in the 1972–1980 period.[9] Nevertheless, especially for certain borrowers, in particular the Mexican public sector and private sector (see Table 2.15), there has been an important decline in yield spread for unenhanced bonds. However, yield spreads for developing countries as a whole for the public sector have tended to increase somewhat from their 1989 levels, even though they were below their 1991 peaks.

More important, as can be clearly seen in Table 2.16, the maturity at which Latin American borrowers have been raising ever increasing amounts of bond finance are far shorter in 1989–1993 than they were in 1972–1982 (when also the amounts raised were much smaller). Furthermore, the average maturity in the 1989–1993 period (around 4.0) is extremely short.[10] This implies that much of the stock of outstanding bonds can be fairly rapidly withdrawn if bonds are not renewed; this could happen if the country/region faces domestic problems or due to changes in the

Table 2.15   Yield Spread at Launch for Unenhanced Bond Issues for Selected
Latin American Borrowers and Total LDC Borrowers
(in basis points)

	1989	1990	1991	1992	First half 1993
Sovereign borrower (total LDC)	171	181	265	220	240
Argentina	—	730	456	300	—
Other public sector (total LDC)	200	250	361	219	172
Brazil	—	—	523	416	528
Mexico	820	366	264	215	198
Venezuela	—	260	275	256	—
Private sector (total LDC)	738	530	526	379	388
Argentina	—	—	447	427	533
Brazil	—	—	655	502	578
Mexico	800	555	566	427	366
Venezuela	—	496	362	—	450
Total	216	254	347	275	274

Source: Collyns et al. (1992, 1993).

international economy. If, as a result, a serious balance-of-payments crisis were to emerge, it would be more difficult than in the case of banks in the 1980s to organize a concerted response to sustain external financing, as claims would be dispersed among numerous bond-holders. As Collyns et al. (1993) rightly point out, this would complicate the response to a renewed bout of debt-servicing difficulties. This would be further complicated by a lack of any lender-of-last-resort facilities for bond-holders, which is in contrast with such facilities (at least at an implicit level) for international bank lending.

Even though at present the cost of bonds is perceived by Latin American borrowers to be relatively inexpensive, there is excessive risk in borrowing very large amounts, particularly at such short maturities. It would seem preferable for Latin American borrowers to scale down the total level of international flows, and within it to place greater priority on sources such as more long-term loans provided by multilateral banks, as well as foreign direct investment. And perhaps Latin American borrowers should wait to borrow large amounts until they can obtain far longer bond maturities. The same line of argument can be made, but with greater strength, about excessive levels of borrowing via short-term instruments, such as Euro-certificates of deposit and Euro-commercial paper.

A final point should be made about bonds: to the extent that most bonds continue to be of fixed interest, the existing stock of bonds is not subject to the debt-servicing variations linked to changes in international interest rates. This is positive, especially in contrast to the variable interest

Table 2.16 Average Term and Total Value of Latin American International Bonds

	Average Term (in years)	Total Value (U.S.$ million)
1972	15.3	470
1973	14.6	130
1974	15.7	77
1975	14.7	408
1976	11.2	1,067
1977	7.5	3,908
1978	9.0	3,211
1979	8.7	1,473
1980	8.1	1,418
1981	8.4	2,583
1982	8.4	1,945
1983–1984	0.0	—
1985	7.0	10
1986	6.5	56
1987	7.0	50
1988	7.7	800
1989	4.3	513
1990	4.5	3,348
1991	4.3	6,420
1992	3.7	9,782
1993[a]	3.9	10,708
Total	6.6	48,378

Source: BIS estimates.
Note: [a]Data up to June. According to West Merchant Bank (1993), in the third quarter of 1993 U.S.$6.2 billion was placed in bonds by Latin America, bringing the first nine months up to U.S.$17 billion.

bank borrowing undertaken by Latin America in the 1970s. However, this should be qualified in two ways. First, because maturities are so short, there is a risk that on renewal (if renewal is possible) the cost of borrowing will increase significantly. Also, even if bonds have fixed debt-servicing costs, there is no mechanism for this servicing to vary with the borrower's ability to pay.

International equity investments have the advantage of a degree of cyclical sensitivity of the dividends paid, thus allowing a better match between debt service and ability to pay. Furthermore, there is no automatic link—as there is for variable interest rate borrowing—to variations in international interest rates. The risks of this type of investment for Latin American borrowers seem at present smaller mainly because the scale of the flows involved are somewhat more modest.

However, international equity flows also carry important risk for the recipients and recipient countries. If there were a critical situation, either real or perceived, large parts of the stock of equities could leave Latin American countries in a very short period. Furthermore, new foreign investments in equities would also cease at that time. To the extent that the shares were sold by foreigners to national residents, this would imply pressure on the balance of payments and on the exchange rate, possibly contributing to a balance-of-payments crisis and/or to a large devaluation. Conversely, if sales were made by foreign residents to other foreign residents, as with an equity instrument such as the ADR, then the effect would seem to be more on the prices in the domestic stock exchange. Indeed, even if shares were sold by foreign to national residents, the scale of the foreign exchange outflow could be stemmed somewhat by sharp falls in the prices of shares, as this could reduce the willingness of foreign equity holders to sell, so as to avoid excessive losses. Therefore, the fact that equities have a price-correcting mechanism may moderate somewhat the risk of a very large foreign exchange outflow.

Nevertheless, a sharp decline in prices of Latin American shares, caused or accelerated by sales by international investors, would also imply negative effects. Via a wealth effect, it could contribute to a decline in aggregate demand. Equally as serious, or more so, it could imply risks for the domestic financial system, and particularly for the banks; this would be particularly the case if there is strong integration between banking and securities activities, and/or if borrowers from banks have large investments in domestic shares and their ability to pay back their loans could be impaired (see Griffith-Jones, 1993). In this context, regulations that limit direct exposure of banks to volatility in equity markets (and have appropriate risk-based capital requirements for such risks) could help limit the negative effects of volatility. To the extent that an increasing amount of the foreign inflows going into Latin American shares originate in institutional investors, and these allocate their assets using more long-term criteria based on specific asset allocation and diversification targets, the risk of massive outflows from Latin American shares in the event of a crisis is somewhat decreased. However, in a very critical situation (or one that is perceived as such), even institutional investors would be likely to sharply revise their aim of greater diversification into foreign, and particularly emerging, markets.

More generally, as the debt crisis of the 1980s so clearly showed, there are always risks that in critical situations the problems in foreign flows and in domestic financial markets will perversely magnify each other. A source of concern here is that to the extent that capital flows are intermediated through the domestic banking system, a sudden burst of capital outflow can lead to a domestic financial crisis (Calvo, Leiderman, and Reinhart, 1993).

Finally, FDI flows seem on the whole far more stable and long term, and therefore would have less problematic effects in the case of a critical situation. It is therefore very positive that in recent years a far higher proportion of capital inflows to Latin America have come in the form of FDI, as compared, for example, to the 1970s (see Table 2.5). However, international companies reportedly do play speculative games with some of their funds—for example, in anticipation of a devaluation. This "speculative" behavior can be an additional, although probably a more limited, source of exchange rate instability.

More generally, Claessens, Dooley, and Warner (1993) have argued that labels on flows (short- versus long-term ones) may be less relevant in practice than has traditionally been believed; this was partly confirmed by some of the interviews from the present study. Although this argument should not be taken too far, as such distinctions do have validity and important policy implications, it does point to the need for an overall, careful aggregate analysis of individuals' and countries' exposure to foreign debt and equity.

Finally, it should be stressed that, globally, regulations of international capital flows have evolved well behind the flows themselves. This is partly due to technical difficulties, the great complexity of the task,[11] and lack of political will in the major industrial countries. Although the tide is turning, the regulatory response seems always "too little, too late." This is combined with a situation of large pressures from global liquidity to find profitable investment via mechanisms that have often only recently been deregulated. Therefore, it may primarily fall to the Latin American governments themselves to carry out any necessary regulation of capital inflows such that their benefits can be maximized and their potential costs minimized. However, it should be emphasized that any such regulation should be limited to that which is essential for such purposes, so as to avoid overregulation that could discourage desirable foreign capital flows.

Notes

Valuable insights and information were gathered during interviews at the BIS, in Basle, the Bank of England, the SIB, and in several London-based private financial institutions. Valuable comments by Peter West and Rodrigo Vergara are acknowledged, as are comments by other participants in the workshop, and in particular those of Ricardo Ffrench-Davis. Research assistance by Joel Climaco is gratefully acknowledged. Angela Cozzini's estimates in Table 2.10, given the lack of available information, are thankfully recognized here.

1. Interview material and Collyns et al. (1992).
2. Interview material; see also Howell (1993).
3. See Baring Securities (1993); also interview material.
4. Interview material; see also Baring Securities (1993).
5. Based on estimates by Intersec Research.
6. The author thanks Kwang Jun for providing this information, based on interview material.

7. For more details, see, for example, Griffith-Jones (1993).

8. See, for example, Collyns et al. (1992); see also, for recent data, West Merchant Bank (1993).

9. Data provided by Von Kleist of the BIS. The comparability is somewhat limited by the fact that in the later period there is a higher proportion of private sector borrowers, whose spreads tend to be higher than those of public sector borrowers.

10. It should be stressed that some borrowers have recently been able to raise bonds with very long maturities; for example, PEMEX raised a 30-year bond in late 1993. But at present these seem only the exception.

11. For a more detailed discussion, see, for example, Griffith-Jones (1993).

References

Bank for International Settlements (BIS) (1994), "International banking and financial market developments," Basle, February.

Baring Securities (1993), *Cross border capital flows. A study of foreign equity investment, 1991/1992 review*, London.

Beetz, C., and W. van Ryckeghem (1993), "Trade and investment flows between Europe and Latin America and the Caribbean," IDB, Washington, D.C.

Calvo, G., L. Leiderman, and C. Reinhart (1993), "The capital inflows problem," *Paper on Policy Analysis and Assessment*, IMF, Washington D.C., July.

Claessens, S., M. Dooley, and A. Warner (1993), "Portfolio capital flows: Hot or cold?" paper presented to the World Bank Symposium on Portfolio Investment in LDCs, September 9–10.

Collyns et al. (1992), "Private market financing for developing countries," *World Economic and Financial Survey*, IMF, Washington, D.C., December.

Collyns et al. (1993), "Private market financing for developing countries," *World Economic and Financial Survey,* IMF, Washington, D.C., December.

Davies, E. P. (1991), "International diversification of institutional investors," *Discussion Paper No. 44*, Bank of England, London, September.

———— (1993), "The structure, regulation and performance of pension funds in nine industrial countries," *Policy Research Working Paper*, no. 1229, World Bank, Washington, D.C.

Griffith-Jones, S. (1993), "Globalization of financial markets and impact on flows to LDCs: New challenges for regulation," in R. Cooper et al. (eds.), *In search of monetary reform*, FONDAD, Holland.

Howell, M. (1993), "Institutional investors as a source of portfolio investment in developing countries," paper presented to World Bank Symposium on Portfolio Investment in LDCs, September 9–10.

Instituto de Relaciones Latinoamericanas (IRELA) (1993), *El mercado único europeo y su impacto en América Latina*, Madrid.

Inter-American Development Bank/Instituto de Relaciones Latinoamericanas (IDB/IRELA) (1992), *Foreign investment flows to Latin America*, Madrid.

International Monetary Fund (IMF) (1993), *World Economic Outlook*, Washington, D.C., October.

Ministerio de Industria, Comercio y Turismo, (1990), *Sector exterior*, Secretaría de Estado de Comercio, Madrid.

Organization for Economic Cooperation and Development (OECD) (1993), *Financial Market Trends*, June.

Securities and Investment Board (SIB) (1993), *Discussion paper on regulated collective investment schemes*, London, October.

West Merchant Bank (1993), *Investment Review*, London, October.

World Bank (1993), *Global economic prospects and developing countries 1993*, Washington, D.C.

3

Latin American Financing in Japan's Capital Markets

PUNAM CHUHAN & KWANG W. JUN

Latin American countries have seen a remarkable turnaround in private capital flows in recent years. Long-term private capital flows have surged from less than U.S.$9 billion in 1989 to more than U.S.$27 billion in 1992, and account for much of total capital flows to the region (Table 3.1). Most of this new capital inflow has been in the form of portfolio investment, both bond and equity. These flows have been fueled by a record amount of new bond issues in international markets. Following Mexico's successful return to the international markets in 1989, Latin American borrowers from Argentina to Venezuela have tapped the international bond markets, raising U.S.$10.6 billion in 1992 and a record U.S.$27 billion in 1993. In addition, successful implementation of privatization programs in several countries, including Mexico and Argentina, have spurred foreign investment in the regions's stock markets and companies.

Although much of the increase in flows to Latin America has represented repatriated flight capital, investment by industrial countries, notably the United States, has also risen. Chuhan (1994) has found that net portfolio investment in developing countries by four major industrial countries—Canada, Germany, Japan, and the United States—accounted for nearly 30 percent of the international bond and equity issuance (gross) by developing countries in 1992. Likewise, the share of U.S. portfolio flows in Mexico's total foreign portfolio flows was large, at 43 percent in 1992. Spurred by low interest rates in the United States and other major OECD countries, high potential returns on developing-country bonds and equities, and an increasing trend in favor of diversification, industrial-country

75

Table 3.1   Portfolio and Other Long-Term Flows to Latin America
(billions of U.S.$)

Type of Flow	1989	1990	1991	1992	1993	1989–1992
Bonds	0.8	2.7	6.8	10.6	27.0	20.9
Equity[a]	0.4	0.7	5.4	4.3	6.6	10.8
Country funds	0.4	0.6	0.7	0.3	0.1	2.0
International issue	0.0	0.1	4.7	4.0	6.5	8.8
Net FDI	7.1	7.7	12.4	14.5	17.5[c]	41.7
Official (excluding grants)	3.4	6.5	2.4	0.3	3.4[c]	12.6
Commercial banks	−3.5	−0.7	0.5	0.0	n.a.	−3.7
Other private long-term flows	0.1	−0.1	−1.7	−2.3	n.a.	−4.0
Total	8.3	16.8	25.8	27.4	54.5	78.3
All portfolio flows[a,b]	1.4	3.4	14.2	16.9	35.6[c]	35.9

Source: World Bank, World Debt Tables; International Financing Review.
Notes: [a]Does not include direct equity investment.
[b]Included for comparison.
[c]Estimates.
n.a. = not available.

investors have raised their investment in these countries' securities. At the same time, privatization programs and the opening up of sectors previously closed to foreign investors have attracted FDI flows.

Notwithstanding Japan's position as a major capital exporter, Japanese private investment in Latin America has been low, contrasting sharply with the global trend and particularly with the trend observed among U.S. investors.[1] This chapter focuses on the source-side factors that constrain Japanese private investment in Latin America. The factors viewed as limiting Japanese private investment in the region can be categorized under three broad groups: transitory or special factors, institutional factors, and long-term factors.

Transitory or special factors are those that are assumed to reverse in the near to medium term. They consist of economic and financial conditions, such as the broad-based decline in Japan's financial markets, appreciation of the yen vis-à-vis the U.S. dollar, and protracted downturn in industrial production. Primarily working through the wealth effect, these factors are believed to have played a large role in depressing Japanese outward investment flows. A reversal of these transitory factors could boost Japanese overseas investment as well as lift flows to Latin America, but a boom in capital flows to the region is unlikely because of factors that will be explained below.

Institutional factors inhibiting foreign borrowing in Japan's capital markets include regulations restricting access to Japan's bond market, investor perceptions influencing investment decisions, and common practices by major groups of investors. The continuing effort by the Ministry of Finance

(MoF) to liberalize Japan's capital markets, coupled with a worldwide trend of increased globalization of financial markets, are likely to favorably impact foreign borrowing in Japan's capital markets as well as Japanese overseas investment. As Latin American entities diversify sources of funds, they are increasingly expected to tap Japanese investors. But because of a desire for high credit quality and a continuing wariness over Latin American exposure, Japanese investment in the region is likely to be modest.

Long-term factors are assumed to include trade relations, locational characteristics, and historical ties—features that have dominated Japan's investment patterns. Recent patterns of trade and direct investment reflect the growing importance of East Asia to Japan and the increasing economic integration of Japan with this region. Although Japanese investors are likely to continue to heavily favor Asian economies, the importance of Latin America to Japanese investors could be increased by the recent shift toward outward-oriented policies in Latin America. Combined with better growth prospects based on appropriate policies and the adoption of NAFTA, the attractiveness of this region to Japanese investors could be enhanced. However, Japanese investors are unlikely to shift their investment focus from the dynamic Asian economies to Latin American ones.

Japanese Investment in Latin America

Broad Trends in Japanese Private Capital Flows

Foreign private capital flows from Japan remain depressed from their peaks of the late 1980s, when Japanese overseas investment soared in the midst of the so-called bubble economy. Total private capital outflows shrank from U.S.$209 billion in 1989 to U.S.$63 billion in 1992 (Table 3.2).[2] Although this declining trend is mirrored in all the major investment flows, the largest contraction (in size) is observed in net purchases of foreign securities, which fell by more than U.S.$81 billion in this period.

The 1980s saw a rapid growth of portfolio flows. The deregulation of the Japanese financial sector in the 1980s created strong competition for domestic savings between commercial banks and other financial institutions such as life insurance companies, trust banks (mutual funds and investment trusts), securities firms, and the postal saving system (Tatewaki, 1991). Japan's high savings ratios coupled with individual investors' heavy use of financial intermediaries (especially in the fixed-income market),[3] caused total assets of all financial institutions to increase more than sixfold between 1980 and 1991, and the assets of insurance companies and pension funds grew even more rapidly (a sevenfold increase). This period of robust asset growth was accompanied by portfolio diversification as

Table 3.2   Japanese Private Sector Foreign Investment and Loans
(in U.S.$ millions)

| | Long-term Assets (excluding export credit) | | | Short-term Assets | | |
	FDI	Loans Extended	Securities	Loans Extended	Securities	Total
1982	4,540	7,902	9,743	162	1,427	23,774
1985	6,452	10,427	59,773	116	530	77,298
1986	14,480	9,281	101,977	3,869	3,700	133,307
1987	19,519	16,190	87,757	27,373	3,242	154,081
1988	34,210	15,211	86,949	16,903	1,902	155,175
1989	44,130	22,495	113,178	26,002	3,304	209,109
1990	48,024	22,182	39,681	29,588	6,291	145,766
1991	30,726	13,097	74,306	14,224	9,428	141,781
1992	17,222	7,623	34,362	3,065	628	62,900
1993[a]	9,061	6,950	14,138	−6,737	−5,096	18,316

Source: Bank of Japan, *Balance of Payments Monthly,* various issues.
Notes: Figures calculated on a balance-of-payments basis.
[a]Preliminary values for January through September.

financial institutions invested large sums overseas. For example, foreign securities of insurance companies and pension funds climbed from less than U.S.$5 billion (less than 3 percent of total assets) in 1980 to U.S.$183 billion (11 percent of total assets) in 1992. Apart from the deregulation of the financial system, Japanese overseas investment was propelled by high interest rates abroad through most of the 1980s, an easing of domestic demand for funds, and accounting restrictions on some investors (for example, insurance companies were required to pay policyholders dividends out of income but not capital gains) that increased the attractiveness of high-interest securities, namely U.S. Treasury bonds.

After rising through most of the 1980s, foreign bank lending by Japanese banks collapsed in 1991. Long-term bank lending flows (net) soared from less than U.S.$8 billion in 1982 to U.S.$22.5 billion in 1989. By 1992, this figure had again fallen to less than U.S.$8 billion. Net short-term lending also fell sharply, from U.S.$30 billion in 1990 to U.S.$3 billion in 1992. And Japanese banks' foreign claims have fallen in tandem with the shrinking lending activities.

Also in the 1980s, Japan emerged as the largest source of foreign direct investment. Japanese outward FDI in this period was spurred by several factors.[4] The sharp appreciation of the yen between 1985 and 1988 and rising labor costs at home prompted companies to seek overseas production bases. Frictions with major trading partners, namely the United States and Europe, and fear of trade restrictions also pressured firms to locate production in major export markets. At the same time, the rapidly rising stock market and a robust economy allowed firms, awash with funds, to finance foreign investment relatively cheaply.

But after peaking at U.S.$67.5 billion (on a notification basis) in 1989, Japanese FDI has trended downward. During 1992, FDI flows originating from Japanese corporations amounted to U.S.$34 billion, compared with U.S.$42 billion in 1991 and U.S.$57 billion in 1990.[5] The size of FDI flows to developing countries is substantial, and despite a general decline in Japan's direct investment overseas, FDI flows to developing countries have been maintained (thus the share going to developing countries has grown). There are divergent patterns across the various regions, however.

Borrowing by Latin American Countries in Japan's Bond Market

The return of Latin American borrowers to the international bond markets partially coincided with the downturn in Japanese outward investment. Anecdotal evidence suggests that Japanese investors have not been a major source of the funds raised by Latin American entities in international markets. Portfolio flow data (bond and equity flows are not available separately) also reveal that Japanese investment in Latin America has been low and uneven, in sharp contrast with U.S. investment in this region.[6] Another indicator of the extent to which Latin American borrowers have tapped Japanese investors is the level of issuance activity in the yen-denominated fixed-income market.[7] Issuance by Latin American borrowers in Japan's bond market—one of the largest in the world (second only to that of the United States)—has until recently been virtually negligible.

Latin American borrowers raised about U.S.$48 billion in international bond markets during 1989–1993, hardly any of it in the Japanese market. The near absence of Latin American borrowers from the Japanese bond market is in contrast to some other emerging market countries, which have successfully tapped the Japanese bond market. Total yen issues by emerging market country borrowers in the Samurai, private placement, and Euroyen markets were U.S.$5.6 billion in 1992, and doubled to U.S.$11.4 billion in 1993 (Tables 3.3 and 3.4). Emerging market issuers have favored the Samurai sector over issuance in the private placement and Euroyen markets, although these borrowers' issuing activity in both the Euroyen and private placement markets rose dramatically last year. The recent easing of the lock-up period (applicable to Japanese investors) on new Euroyen issues as well as the easing of purchase and resale restrictions in the private placement market are expected to further boost activity in these two sectors.

Some emerging market issuers have been attracted to the Japanese bond market by a cost differential in this market vis-à-vis the Eurodollar

Table 3.3   Total Yen-Denominated Bond Issues by Emerging Market Issuers
(millions of U.S.$)

	1989	1990	1991	1992	1993
Total	2,142	1,413	3,173	5,561	11,360
Samurai	1,769	1,237	2,545	5,079	6,617
Euroyen	0	110	224	150	2,290
Private placement	373	66	404	332	2,453

Source: Euromoney Bondware.

Table 3.4   Total Yen-Denominated Bond Issues by Emerging Market Issuers by Region
(as a percentage of total bond issues)

	1989	1992	1993
Asia	10.87	4.29	5.95
China	1.86	2.96	1.84
Korea	2.56	1.33	2.29
Europe and Central Asia	15.47	18.84	12.20
Greece	5.47	8.80	4.10
Turkey	1.80	8.05	3.62
Hungary	5.41	2.00	2.88
Latin America	0.00	0.00	1.54
Brazil	0.00	0.00	0.66
Mexico	0.00	0.00	0.56
Total bond issues by emerging markets (in billions of U.S.$)	8.13	24.05	57.69

Source: Euromoney Bondware.

market. This is evidenced by the fact that several emerging market borrowers have swapped funds raised in the yen market into dollars. One reason for the lower overall funding costs for some borrowers in the Japanese bond market is that this market does not appear to translate differences in ratings into differentiation in pricing to the same degree as in the Euromarkets or the U.S. market.[8] Among emerging market issuers, the largest amount of borrowing (54 percent in 1993) in the yen-denominated market was accounted for by Greece, Hungary, and Turkey. At U.S.$4 billion, the Bank of Greece (with an "A" rating from the Japan Bond Research Institute) is the largest borrower since 1989. The National Bank of Hungary (with a "BBB+" rating from Nippon Investors Service) has borrowed U.S.$1.6 billion in the yen-denominated market, and the Republic of Turkey (with a "BBB–" rating from Standard and Poor's) has borrowed U.S.$1.8 billion during this period.

As Latin American borrowers diversify funding sources to lower borrowing costs and obtain larger amounts of funds, they turn to the Japanese markets. Last July, the United Mexican States (UMS) launched a benchmark offering in the Japanese bond market with a three-year 10-billion-yen issue. This marked the first time that the UMS tapped the Samurai sector since 1977. Demand for the issue was reported to be strong, although the paper was placed with retail investors and regional institutions. Participation by commercial banks and life insurance companies, the largest holders of foreign securities, was reportedly low (World Bank, *Financial flows,* November 1993). Despite an improvement in Mexico's economic performance, major institutional investors and commercial banks still appear to be cautious about Latin American risk.

So far, the demand for high-yield yen-denominated Latin American paper has been limited to a small investor base, composed mostly of Japanese regional banks and credit unions. These institutions' demand is a result of low borrowing by domestic corporations (due to weak Japanese economic activity) and a strong yen, which has depressed returns on foreign currency–denominated securities. Latin American borrowers have sought to tap this investor base, and in the fourth quarter of 1993 there was a flurry of issues by top Latin American credits. In October, the Mexican development bank, Nacional Financiera (Nafinsa), entered the Samurai sector with a debut three-year 10-billion-yen issue, and in December, the Republic of Colombia made its debut in the Samuari market with a 10-billion-yen offering. Also in that quarter, Brazil's Telebras and Petrobas raised more than 40 billion yen in the Euroyen market.[9]

Equity Issuance by Latin American Corporations in Japan's Stock Market

In step with bond flows, foreign equity flows to Latin America have also grown explosively. Gross equity issuance by Latin American countries was U.S.$6.6 billion in 1993, with initial public offerings (IPOs) offered in the context of privatization accounting for a large share. For example, the recent (June 1993) sale of Argentina's oil company, Yacimientos Petrolíferos Fiscales, raised U.S.$3 billion, or more than 70 percent in international markets. Likewise, the 1991 sale of Mexico's national telephone company, Teléfonos de México (Telmex), fetched U.S.$2 billion through an international IPO.

Japanese investors, however, have invested very little in emerging stock markets, typically lagging U.S. and U.K. investors. Employing data on the geographic composition of foreign stocks registered on the Japanese Securities Dealers Association, Chuhan (1994) has estimated that emerging market equities comprise less than 2 percent of the foreign equities of Japanese investors and about 0.2 percent of total assets. Japanese investors, although they recognize the improved creditworthiness of several

Latin American countries, have directed little of their equity investments to this region. The investment in Latin American shares has mostly been through country funds and, more recently, ADRs. Direct investment in equity markets has been a less important means for investing in these countries.

The continuing slump in the Japanese stock market has tended to discourage Latin American corporations, as well as all issuers, from using this market to raise funds or to list shares. By contrast, the U.S. market has seen a burst of issuing activity by Latin American corporations. The U.S. private placement market under Rule 144-A (see Chapter 1) has been popular with the smaller and less well-known (blue-chip) emerging market companies looking to raise equity capital. Companies that are already traded in the United States or that have large issues have tended to favor the U.S. public market. Mexico has accounted for the bulk of the equity capital raised by Latin American companies as well as by all emerging markets. The Rule 144-A market is somewhat limiting in terms of access to a wide range of investors, however, and several companies that used the Rule 144-A private market to test the demand for their shares are now moving into the public market.[10]

Japanese Bank Lending to Latin America

In sharp contrast to borrowing in overseas bond markets, Latin America's access to syndicated bank credits remains rather limited. Following the trend in most major industrial-country banks, Japanese banks have been very cautious and do not appear to be ready to resume lending to developing countries in a major way. Japanese banks' claims on developing countries have been scaled back sharply, with claims contracting from U.S.$78.5 billion at the end of 1988 to U.S.$51 billion at the end of 1992 (Table 3.5).[11] The country's banks have been selective in their lending to developing countries, focusing primarily on creditworthy borrowers in the Asia region and, even then, typically restricting lending to project finance and short-term credits. Japanese banks' exposure to Latin America has shrunk to U.S.$16.9 billion in 1992, less than half of what it had been in 1989. Although U.S. commercial bank lending to the region is also subdued, with claims to the region shrinking from U.S.$53 billion at the end of 1989 to U.S.$46 billion at the end of 1992, the decline in U.S. banks' claims has been less severe. Japanese financial institutions have been quite unresponsive to the incentives provided by the Japanese government to increase private lending to Latin America. The government's U.S.$65 billion "surplus recycling plan" (announced in 1987) anticipated major participation of Japanese banks as cofinanciers. However, banks were reluctant to participate in lending, especially to Latin America.

Table 3.5   Outstanding Japanese Commercial Bank Lending to Foreign Sovereign Borrowers

Region	1988 Millions of U.S.$	Percent of Total	1989 Millions of U.S.$	Percent of Total	1990 Millions of U.S.$	Percent of Total	1991 Millions of U.S.$	Percent of Total	1992 Millions of U.S.$	Percent of Total
Asia	23,815	15.7	24,070	16.0	21,732	17.4	24,196	19.3	20,903	17.9
Middle East	596	0.4	799	0.5	734	0.6	1,776	1.4	2,440	2.1
Eastern Europe	15,220	10.0	15,483	10.3	11,357	9.1	9,273	7.4	8,488	7.3
Africa	3,876	2.6	3,504	2.3	2,885	2.3	2,606	2.1	2,276	2.0
Latin America (including Caribbean)	35,020	23.1	33,198	22.1	18,779	15.1	17,791	14.2	16,929	14.5
Total for above	78,527	51.8	77,054	51.2	55,487	44.5	55,642	44.4	51,036	43.8
Total outstanding commercial bank lending to foreign sovereign borrowers	151,472		150,268		124,574		125,251		116,709	

Source: Japanese Ministry of Finance.

Emphasis on improving profitability and reducing international risk could prompt Japanese banks to seek credit enhancements, including offshore escrow accounts and government guarantees in new lending. In this context, the Export-Import Bank (EXIM) of Japan's extension of its guarantee (of principal and interest payments) to loans involving solely cofinancing arrangements by the private sector could be viewed favorably by banks. Although these guarantees were authorized by a 1985 amendment, they are being used now in accordance with the country's new U.S.$120 billion (over five years, 1993 to 1997) Funds for Development Initiative. Under its expanded guarantee facility, Japan's EXIM recently guaranteed a U.S.$300 million syndicated loan to Venezuela's Corpoven.

Japanese Foreign Direct Investment in Latin America

Better economic policies, improved growth prospects, and adoption of privatization programs have spurred FDI in Latin America. The amount of FDI to the region jumped from U.S.$7.1 billion in 1989 to an estimated U.S.$17.5 billion in 1993 (Table 3.6). The increase in FDI has been concentrated in a few countries, however. With flows of U.S.$5.4 billion and U.S.$4.2 billion in 1992, Mexico and Argentina have received the largest share of this increase.

Although FDI to Latin America has grown from 1989 to 1993, Japanese direct investment flows to Latin America and the Caribbean have exhibited an opposite trend. (There is some gain in the regional share in total Japanese FDI, however.) At U.S.$1.6 billion (on a notification basis) in 1992, FDI flows are well below the yearly average of U.S.$2.5 billion over 1989–1991.

The dominant share of Japanese investment in the region continues to be in tax havens or "flag of convenience" countries.[12] For example, combined flows to Argentina, Brazil, Chile, Mexico, and Venezuela were about one-third of FDI flows to Panama alone in 1991. Tax havens such as the Cayman Islands, the Bahamas, Bermuda, the Virgin Islands, and the Netherlands Antilles, as well as Panama, received nearly three-quarters of Japanese FDI to Latin America and the Caribbean in 1991. Although investment in these tax haven countries declined, mirroring the overall decline in Japanese FDI, Panama is still the largest regional recipient of FDI, with more than U.S.$900 million in 1992.

Investment in the manufacturing and tertiary sectors of major Latin American countries is small, reflecting that the region is not an important production base for Japanese manufacturers nor is it a significant market for Japan's trade.[13] The share of manufacturing investment in total Japanese FDI to Latin America was less than 13 percent (Jun et al., 1993). The recent implementation of a North American free trade zone (under NAFTA) could help pull Japanese FDI to the region.

Table 3.6   FDI Outflows to Developing Regions
(millions of U.S.$)

	1989	1990	1991	1992
Total				
All Developing Regions	23,320	24,008	33,916	47,156
Sub-Saharan Africa	2,476	669	1,746	1,618
East Asia and Pacific	9,071	10,885	13,021	20,491
Europe and Central Asia	2,790	3,282	5,306	8,312
Latin America and the Caribbean	7,135	7,725	12,776	14,506
Middle East and North Africa	1,619	1,156	711	1,665
South Asia	229	291	356	564
From Japan				
All Developing Regions	7,576	7,487	7,668	7,330
Sub-Saharan Africa	644	532	707	234
East Asia and Pacific	4,055	4,140	4,399	4,679
Europe and Central Asia	133	184	273	69
Latin America and the Caribbean	2,614	2,545	2,231	1,566
Middle East and North Africa	28	2	18	563
South Asia	102	84	40	219
From United States				
All Developing Regions	6,377	6,391	7,380	7,196
Sub-Saharan Africa	−239	−300	34	−855
East Asia and Pacific	1,014	1,712	1,215	994
Europe and Central Asia	22	337	492	784
Latin America and the Caribbean	5,843	4,388	5,062	5,975
Middle East and North Africa	−288	259	468	209
South Asia	25	−5	109	89

Sources: Japanese Ministry of Finance, U.S. Department of Commerce, and World Bank, *World Debt Tables,* various issues.

Notes: The numbers for total FDI are based on host-country reporting. The numbers for Japan are on a notification basis (Ministry of Finance).

Factors Contributing to the Low Level
of Japanese Investment Flows to Latin America

The recent increase in capital flows to many developing countries has raised questions regarding the importance of "push" and "pull" factors. On the one hand, global factors such as the sharp decline in U.S. and global interest rates and the slowdown in U.S. and other major OECD countries' economic activity are believed to have played an important role in increasing the attractiveness of emerging market securities and assets, pushing foreign investment in developing countries. On the other hand, improved economic prospects in many developing countries are believed to have been instrumental in attracting (pulling) capital to these countries. A study by Calvo, Leiderman, and Reinhart (1993) argues for the importance of global factors in explaining these flows. It concludes that a reversal of these global factors could induce a capital outflow from these countries.

Using flow data, Chuhan, Claessens, and Mamingi (1993) have been able to demonstrate the importance of both global and country-specific factors in attracting capital flows. They have found that these domestic factors are also important in explaining capital flows as global factors. From the literature on the determinants of international capital flows, we can attempt to identify factors that are likely to play a key role in motivating capital flows. Country-specific factors, including stock market returns, credit ratings, and secondary market prices of sovereign debt are indicative of the risk and returns of investing in the country. Over the past few years most of these country-specific indicators posted substantial gains, as several developing countries liberalized their economies and adopted comprehensive economic reform programs. For example, the rates of returns on emerging stock markets rose sharply: the IFC's dollar-based composite price index for Latin America rose 351 percent over 1989–1993, whereas the Standard and Poor's 500 index rose 69 percent and the Nikkei Index was down 44 percent (January 1989–December 1993) (Table 3.7). Credit ratings (as measured by *Institutional Investor*) also improved during this period. *Institutional Investor*'s market survey of country risk shows the region's rating at a 10-year high. Latin America's credit rating, on a scale of 0 to 100, has climbed steadily to 24.4 last September from 20.2 in September 1989. The improvement is broad-based, reflecting both better economic policies and stronger medium-term growth prospects in the region. Recently, several Latin American credits have been rated investment grade (for example, Chile and Colombia by Standard and Poor's and Mexico by Duff and Phelps). Latin American countries have also seen a sharp rise in the secondary market prices of sovereign debt. These prices have risen from less than 30 cents to the dollar at the end of 1989, to about 65 cents to the dollar in December 1993.

The low level of Japanese investment in Latin America, despite the improvement in country-specific factors in the region, suggests that factors particular to Japan were instrumental in constraining these investment flows to Latin America. The source-side factors can be viewed as falling into the three categories: transitory, institutional, and long-term.

Transitory Factors

The return of Latin American borrowers to the international bond and equity markets partially coincided with the downturn in Japanese outward investment. Foreign flows from Japan remain depressed from their peaks of the late 1980s. The protracted collapse of the Japanese stock market, the steep decline in the property market, the appreciation of the yen vis-à-vis the U.S. dollar, and weak economic growth have all combined to depress outward investment flows from the country.

Table 3.7   Selected Latin American Stock Market Performances

	Market Capitalization (millions of U.S.$)		Monthly Value Traded (millions of U.S.$)		Annualized Mean Return (U.S.$: 5 years ending Dec. 1993)	Annualized Std. Deviation (U.S.$: 5 years ending Dec. 1993)	IFC Price Indexes 12-month % change Dec. 1993
	end-1989	end-1993	1989[a]	Dec. 1993			
Argentina	4,225	43,967	160	1,158	94.44	116.12	80.48
Brazil	44,368	99,430	1,397	6,217	43.68	75.59	153.44
Chile	9,587	44,622	72	343	35.52	25.98	39.54
Colombia	1,136	8,755	9	94	43.92	37.34	69.11
Mexico	22,550	200,671	519	12,314	44.15	26.43	67.42
Venezuela	1,472	6,587	8	182	36.12	50.78	3.16
Latin America					35.04	30.62	78.66
Nikkei Index					−3.84	31.73	36.49
Standard and Poor's 500 Index					11.28	12.89	9.76

Source: International Finance Corporation Emerging Market database.
Note: [a]Numbers for 1989 are monthly averages.

The current weakness in portfolio flows stems from several factors, the most important being the huge loss in wealth associated with the unprecedented decline of the stock market and the collapse of property prices in the early 1990s (Figures 3.1 and 3.2). A deep overall decline in Japanese stock market prices for the fourth year in a row has depressed the value of investors' portfolios. Despite efforts by the MoF to support share prices, such as a near halt on new listings on the Tokyo exchange for about three years, the market has performed poorly. Domestic investors are also cautious of investing in this stock market because of lack of confidence and policies such as the minimum amount of shares that an investor must purchase, low dividend policies of firms, and weak disclosure requirement for

Figure 3.1   Nikkei Stock Index Monthly Averages (yen, January 1989–December 1993)

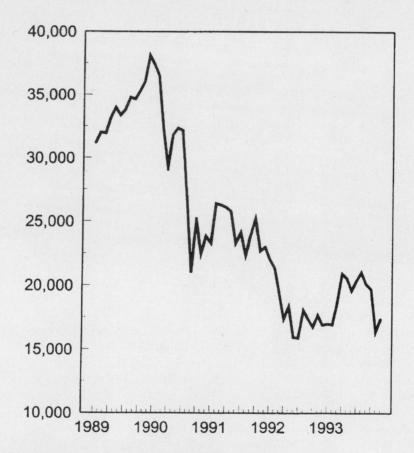

Source: Bank of Japan, *Economic Statistic Monthly.*

**Figure 3.2 Nominal Commercial Property Prices: Tokyo
(annual percentage changes)**

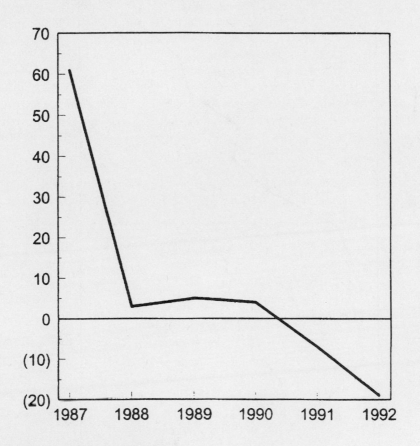

Source: Various private communications.

companies. Foreign investors have also curtailed investment in this market. A report in the *New York Times* (November 8, 1993) stated that U.S. investors, who are investing vast sums in overseas shares, have invested little in the Japanese stock market in recent periods.

Japanese investors' portfolios have been adversely affected by the sharp drop in property prices. Apart from this, currency movements—the fall of the dollar vis-à-vis the yen—have also eroded the value of overseas assets (the bulk of which are dollar-denominated), exacerbating the wealth effect and making investors wary of overseas investment.

In addition, weak economic growth witnessed since 1991 has worsened business conditions and caused corporate bankruptcies (Figure 3.3).

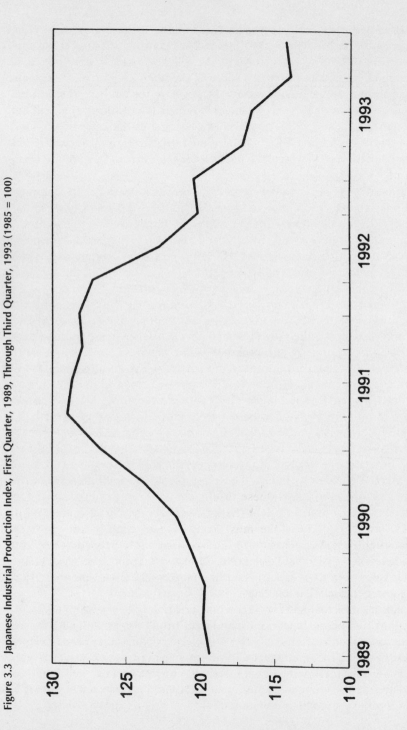

Figure 3.3   Japanese Industrial Production Index, First Quarter, 1989, Through Third Quarter, 1993 (1985 = 100)

Source: IMF, *International Financial Statistics,* various issues.

The drop in profits arising from the deteriorating economic conditions and the sharp appreciation of the yen means that companies no longer have the substantial investible cash flows of the 1980s. Business confidence, as measured by the Bank of Japan's surveys, shows continuing weakness, and some forecasts put annual growth to be negative for the first time in nineteen years. At the same time, business is reluctant to retrench (i.e., cut employment and costs) and invest overseas because of the low rate of return on previous Japanese FDI, especially the rate of return on Japanese FDI in the United States (which has been lower than that in developing countries of Asia).[14]

Moreover, retrenchment (a cutback on new lending) by Japanese banks and an increased issue of subordinated debt (raising of new capital) in the domestic market by Japanese banks to meet BIS capital adequacy requirements (by the end of March 1993) have been behind the shrinking of institutional funds available for foreign portfolio investment.[15] Weak banking sector performance—Japanese banks have seen a contraction in profits for four consecutive years—has in turn curtailed the lending activity of banks as well as their purchases of foreign securities. Bank performance has been hurt by the underlying trends of steep decline in real estate and weak economic growth, which have worsened business conditions and caused corporate bankruptcies.[16] Major Japanese banks still carry a high level of nonperforming loans in their portfolio, and loan-loss provisioning remains high. In the twelve months ending in March 1993, nonperforming loans at the eleven city banks amounted to 8.4 trillion yen (U.S.$78 billion), and in September 1993 these loans had climbed to 9.2 trillion yen (U.S.$87 billion). Details on nonperforming loans, published by the banks for the first time in March 1993, show that the share of these loans in total loans outstanding were in the range of 1.6 percent to 4.8 percent for the eleven city banks. These figures do not include restructured loans as problem loans, so these results are believed to substantially underreport exposure to bad debt (Salomon Brothers, 1993). Japanese city banks, which have been the most aggressive in dealing with problem loans, could be under pressure to increase lending to boost earnings, but they are likely to remain selective. Long-term credit and trust banks, which have been slow to dispose of nonperforming loans, are unlikely to see an early recovery in lending.

All these factors have weakened the position of Japanese financial institutions, including Japanese institutional investors, as well as other investors as a source of funds, both portfolio flows and other private capital flows, for developing countries. Without an improvement in underlying factors—namely, recovery in the share and property markets and faster domestic economic growth—institutional and other investors are not likely to favor foreign securities in the near term.

Another factor that could explain part of the drop in overall foreign portfolio investment, even though Japanese interest rates are at record low levels, is the narrowing of the spread between U.S. and Japanese interest rates. According to Nikko Research Center in Tokyo, a 3 percent to 5 percent interest rate spread between U.S. Treasury bonds and Japanese government bonds in the 1980s prompted Japanese investors to regularly purchase as much as a third or more of U.S. Treasury bonds auctioned. In fact, U.S. Treasury bonds accounted for more than 60 percent of the total foreign bond portfolio of Japanese institutional investors at the end of 1985. The narrowing of this interest rate differential to 1 percent to 2 percent in the 1990s has led to a steep drop in the share of foreign bond holdings U.S. bonds have, to about 35 percent. Although Japanese investors have shifted into other foreign bonds, their overall purchases of foreign bonds have been much reduced. Moreover, this diversification has not tended to favor Latin American securities because Japanese investors remain cautious of holding below–investment-grade paper.

Institutional Factors

Since the late 1980s, the MoF has introduced wide-ranging reforms in the Japanese bond market in order to improve the liquidity, efficiency, and transparency of Japan's capital markets. It has eliminated collateral requirements, removed stringent balance-sheet restrictions, allowed new issue structures, and attempted to lower funding costs through increased competition. It has also moved to improve access to this market, although access continues to be primarily determined by creditworthiness. This differentiation on the basis of creditworthiness means that lower-rated (non–investment-grade) borrowers are not afforded access to this market.

The relaxation of quality guidelines for Samurai bond issues was perhaps the most important event affecting developing-country borrowing in Japan's capital markets. Effective August 1, 1992, the MoF eased issuance regulations. All borrowers now need a rating of BBB or higher, instead of the previous A rating, from an approved rating agency to be eligible to issue in the Samurai sector. The rating has to be assigned by one of the following rating agencies: Fitch Investor Services, Japan Bond Research Institute, Japan Credit Rating Agency, Moody's, Nippon Investors Services, and Standard and Poor's. Since the more liberalized rule was introduced, a number of developing-countries' deals were launched, including those by China, Hungary, and Turkey.

A recently implemented important development was the relaxation of rules in the private placement market (Yamaichi Securities, 1993). In its ongoing wide-ranging reform of Japan's financial system, the government has liberalized the rules relating to the private placement market for non-Japanese issuers, that is, the Shibosai market.[17] Effective April 1, 1993, the Securities and Exchange Law has been amended to enhance the attractiveness of this market for both investors and issuers. The new rules aim to broaden the investor range, improve tradability of issues in the secondary market, and enhance issue terms such as size, maturity, and minimum spread requirements.

Under the new rules, two new types of bonds are allowed: a Q'bond and a 49er. A foreign issuer can sell a Q'bond to any number of qualified institutional investors. A 49er bond can be sold to forty-nine or fewer domestic buyers, including corporates and individuals. Under the old rules, foreign bonds could be sold only to forty-nine or fewer qualified institutional investors. Previously, there were restrictions also on the amount that an investor could purchase. The 20 percent maximum ceiling has been abolished, although the maximum that an arranger can hold is still restricted to 10 percent. The new rules have also expanded the definition of qualified institutional investor to include fifteen investor categories compared to a previous eleven. The additional categories of investors are securities companies, Japanese branches of foreign securities firms, licensed investment advisory companies, and agricultural cooperatives and federations of fishing cooperatives that are involved in deposit taking. Resale rules have also been eased, allowing both partial resale as well as sale to more than one investor after two years from the date of issue of the security. Previously, resale was limited to a lump sum sale to only one buyer, following a two-year period from the date of purchase of the bond.

The new rules have also eased restrictions on issue size. AAA-rated issuers are allowed to raise a maximum of 30 billion yen, and borrowers rated AA and lower (including unrated issuers) are allowed to issue up to 20 billion yen. This compares with ceilings of 30 billion, 20 billion, and 10 billion yen for issuers with AAA, AA, and A or lower ratings (including unrated), respectively, under the old rules. Restrictions on the maximum and minimum maturity terms of bonds has been eased, and the range now is from two years to twenty years. Minimum spread requirements have been removed, and spreads are determined by market conditions. Previously, minimum spreads had been established based on the rating of the borrower.

Although they recognize the improved creditworthiness of Latin American issuers, Japanese institutions are still wary of purchasing Latin American paper because of the large amount of loans they had outstanding to the region that were affected by the 1980s debt crisis. Moreover, Japanese investors have traditionally tended to be cautious in their investments, commonly purchasing only high-investment-grade securities. Since most Latin American issuers do not meet this investment criteria, they have not been favored by Japanese investors, particularly institutional investors.

Chuhan (1994) has found that even though institutional investors, such as insurance companies and pension funds, have regulatory ceilings on the percent of assets they can hold in foreign securities (30 percent), a more binding constraint to investing in emerging market securities has been the industry practice of favoring high credit investments.

Japanese investors are cautious of investing in Latin America because they are concerned about their limited knowledge of and experience in Latin America, which has hindered Japanese investors from better differentiating between the different countries in the region. Brazil is by far the most important country in Latin America for Japan, but difficulties in Brazil have cast a shadow over the whole region. Stallings (1990) has pointed out that even in the 1970–1982 period, when foreign bank lending to Latin America was large, Japanese banks were not the leading banks in Latin America. On the contrary, they followed U.S. banks (which had banking relationships with the region since the 1920s, as well as greater experience with the region), attracted by potentially high profit margins and in response to rapid growth of the Japanese economy. Initially Japanese banks participated in lending as syndicate members rather than as lead managers.[18] And although Japanese banks helped finance large national projects, these typically involved Japanese government participation.[19]

With banks reluctant to lend to Latin America, the linkage between bank lending and FDI is another factor negatively influencing Japanese business investment in the region. Each of Japan's Keiretsu, industry groups, has a special relationship with a variety of industries and one major bank. This industrial arrangement influences the behavior of the companies in the group. Japanese companies rely on banks to finance a large part of their foreign investment. Data from the late 1980s show that a third of Japanese companies' direct investment in Latin America was financed by Japanese banks. If a major bank is reluctant to lend to a country, the manufacturing companies of the group with which it is closely associated would be restricted from investing in the country because of the lack of financial backing from this source.

Long-term Factors

Historical ties, locational characteristics, and trade relations and patterns have in the past been instrumental in shaping Japanese investment flows. The focus here is on assessing the role of trade relations and patterns.

Since the mid-1980s, Japan's pattern of trade reflects the growing importance of East Asia to Japan. Although there is no formal trading bloc covering Japan and other East Asian economies, economic integration and regionalism have evolved driven by market forces. Bannister and Braga (1993) have found that since 1985 there is an increasing intraregional trade bias for Japan with this region as measured by a trade intensity index.[20]

Japan's pattern of FDI, with an increasing share going to East Asia, also strengthens the case for a growing integration with this region. Japanese FDI in Asia has had particularly strong "trade creating" characteristics, with Japanese manufacturing companies investing in Asian economies, attracted by cheap labor, favorable or lax regulations, and other financial incentives. A significant part of Japanese transnational corporations' output is targeted for the Japanese or U.S. market. Whereas Japanese FDI in Asia has trade links, that in Latin America has had less of an export orientation. This can be explained by the different policies in these two regions in the 1980s. East Asian countries generally had more export-oriented policies and those in Latin America were more inward-oriented. With a move toward trade liberalization in Latin America, as well as the integration of the Mexican market with that of the United States and Canada under NAFTA, the pattern of FDI to this region is likely to be affected. Nevertheless, the growing trade-investment (and aid) links with Asia suggest that Japanese businesses and investors are unlikely to leave that area in favor of Latin America.

Prospects of Japanese Investment Flows to Latin America

Although Japanese portfolio flows and other private capital flows to Latin American countries have been low in recent years, several factors point toward an increase, although no large surge, in these flows in the medium term. As noted earlier, the return of Latin America to international capital markets occurred at a time when Japanese overseas investment contracted sharply. The downturn was the result of transitory factors working through the wealth effect. A reversal of these factors is likely to fuel total private capital outflows, especially portfolio flows. Although some institutional and long-term factors are expected to constrain flows to Latin America, several developments support a modest increase in these flows.

Factors favoring increased bond and equity financing of Latin American entities are the efforts by the MoF to liberalize Japan's capital markets. The increasing accessibility of Japanese markets will prove attractive to emerging market borrowers, including those from Latin America. Moreover, the increasing financial integration of emerging markets with the global market will promote cross-border securities flows between Japan and Latin America. The attempt to diversify funding sources and lower borrowing costs will further attract Latin American borrowers to the Japanese markets.

Developments in host countries are likely to provide a positive impetus to Japanese investment, especially FDI, despite the trend of growing economic integration of Japan with East Asian economies. Positive developments include the improved growth prospects in Latin America resulting from better economic management.[21] Another positive development is the recent implementation of a North American free trade zone under NAFTA. Improved growth prospects for Mexico under NAFTA, as well as guaranteed access to the U.S. market, are likely to attract Japanese FDI to that country.

Notes

The authors are members of the Debt and International Finance Division of the World Bank. The opinions expressed in this chapter are those of the authors and do not necessarily represent those of the World Bank or its board of directors. The participants of ECLAC-IDRC Workshop II, especially Ricardo Ffrench-Davis, Hernan Somerville, and Barbara Stallings, as well as Umran Demirors, Persephone Economou, Leonardo Hernandez, Mika Iwasaki, Saori Katada, Nlandu Mamingi, and Setsuya Sato, are acknowledged for their useful comments. Himmat Kalsi is thanked for data support.

1. Although Japan's private sector provided little financing to Latin America in the late 1980s and 1990s, the Japanese government has increased its overseas development aid (ODA) and other official flows (OOF) to the region.

2. Claessens, Dooley, and Werner (1993) argue that because of substitution among the different types of flows, it might be more meaningful to look at aggregate private capital flows rather than one or a few components of these flows. Using time series data on four categories of flows—FDI, portfolio equity, long-term flow, and short-term flow—for five industrial and five developing countries, they have found that short-term flows are at least as predictable as long-term flows and that long-term flows are also not systematically more predictable. The present study finds Japan to be an exception, however, with FDI and equity flows showing high positive autocorrelations, whereas the short-term flows exhibit negative autocorrelations. Nevertheless, we study both aggregate private capital flows and the various components of these flows.

3. In Japan, more so than in many other major industrial countries, individual investors tend to make heavy use of financial intermediaries—a trend that is likely to continue.

4. See Jun et al. (1993) for a comprehensive study of the trends and determinants of Japanese FDI.

5. These flows are on a notification basis and are larger than FDI flows reported on a balance-of-payments basis, as shown in Table 3.2.

6. Because a large part of Japanese financial institutions' purchases of Latin American securities are made through these institutions' branch offices in New York or London, Japanese portfolio flows to Latin America could be understated in the country's balance-of-payments accounts.

7. Total foreign issues in the Samurai sector account for about 2 percent of the Japanese public bond market. Foreigners can also issue yen debt in the Shibosai sector of the private placement market and in the Euroyen sector. Euroyen bonds are denominated in yen, but issued outside Japan. Close to 95 percent of these bonds end up with Japanese investors.

8. *Euroweek* (1993) reports that investors in the Japanese market have enjoyed a high level of "credit protection" in the past. Thus when a (Japanese) corporation was unable to meet its bond debt obligations (i.e., was in default), related companies

or the corporation's bank would intervene to protect investors from loss. Stringent regulations, such as collateralized bonds and balance-sheet restrictions applying to borrowers, further added to the high level of credit protection for investors. Since 1987, the requirements for collateral have been progressively reduced, bringing the market more in line with international standards. With the removal of the collateral requirement, investors have slowly begun to evaluate credit risk.

9. Several other emerging market borrowers are also interested in the Samurai market. For example, the Czech National Bank issued a seven-year 35-billion-yen issue last July, marking the first time that the new Czech Republic has come to this sector. Japanese institutional investors were reportedly attracted to the issue because the Czech Republic has been able to avoid serious debt problems.

10. For example, a Venezuelan company, Corimon, converted its Rule 144-A depositary receipts to American Depositary Shares (ADSs) listed on the New York Stock Exchange (NYSE) in April. Another Latin American company, Argentina's Baesa, also listed new ADSs on the NYSE. However, investors are finding the lack of liquidity of the Rule 144-A market to be costly in terms of unloading positions in this market.

11. Following a change in policy by the Japanese government in 1990, Japanese banks began to unload their Latin American debt through secondary market sales and exit bonds under Brady-type debt operations.

12. Tax haven and "flag of convenience" countries often show up as receiving large investments. The investment inflows usually do not reflect normal FDI activity, and are often the result of transnational corporations channeling funds through affiliates established in these tax havens for lending/investing elsewhere.

13. As is the case in several other countries, Japanese FDI and trade exhibit strong links, especially in the East Asian region.

14. The pattern of Japanese FDI reflects the shrinking of industrial-country shares in these flows, but an increase in the share going to developing countries, particularly in Asia.

15. The steep decline in stock prices has eroded the value of banks' capital reserves, also exacerbating the problems facing banks.

16. About 20 to 25 percent of the leading commercial banks' outstanding loans are for real-estate activity, and close to 40 percent of total loans are collateralized by land. The sharp downturn in the property market has made the mortgage market highly illiquid, and banks have found it exceedingly difficult to unload property held as collateral, even at a substantial discount. A bank-funded initiative to purchase these assets through the newly created Credit Cooperative Purchasing Company (CCPC) has so far had limited success. The CCPC has purchased only a fraction of property from leading banks (less than 1 percent of these banks' loan portfolio) at an average discount of 40 percent of the face value.

17. The Shibosai market, like the U.S. private placement market, has a lower level of disclosure requirement than the public market and does not have stipulated minimum rating requirements, as the Samurai sector does. However, common practice may dictate that only high credits are successful in raising funds in this market.

18. For example, Japanese banks managed only about 10 percent of Latin American loans, compared with 42 percent by U.S. banks.

19. Such projects included a pipeline project in Peru and development of the steel sector in Mexico.

20. This is not the case for other East Asian economies, which do not show an increase in trade intensity with the region although they do show a regional trade bias, that is, trading more intensively with this region than with the world.

21. There is some evidence, however, that in the short term trade liberalization in Latin America has had the unexpected effect of cutting some Japanese investment, especially in manufacturing, because it is now cheaper to export from Japan rather than assemble in Latin America.

References

Bank of Japan, *Balance of Payments Monthly,* various issues.
————, *Economic Statistics Monthly,* various issues.
Bannister, G., and C.A. Primo Braga (1993), "Intra-Asian investment and trade: Prospects for growing regionalization in the 1990s," mimeo, World Bank, International Trade Division, Washington, D.C.
Calvo, G., L. Leiderman, and C. Reinhart (1993), "Capital inflows and the real exchange rate appreciation in Latin America: The role of external factors," *IMF Staff Papers,* vol. 40, no. 1, March.
Chuhan, P. (1994), "Are institutional investors an important source of portfolio investment in emerging markets?" *World Bank Policy Research Working Paper,* no. 1243, Washington, D.C.
Chuhan, P., S. Claessens, and N. Mamingi (1993), "Equity and bond flows to Asia and Latin America: The role of global and country factors," *World Bank Policy Research Working Paper,* no. 1160, Washington, D.C.
Claessens, S., M. Dooley, and A. Werner (1993), "Portfolio capital flows: Hot or cold?" paper presented to the World Bank Symposium on Portfolio Investment in LDCs, September 9–10.
Euromoney Bondware, various issues.
Euroweek (1993), "Financing Japan's top credits," September.
Jun, K., F. Sader, H. Horaguchi, and H. Kwak (1993), "Japanese foreign direct investment: Recent trends, determinants, and prospects," *World Bank Policy Research Working Paper,* no. 1213, Washington, D.C.
International Financing Review, various issues.
International Monetary Fund (IMF), *International Financial Statistics,* various issues.
New York Times, November 8, 1993.
OECD, *Financial Market Trends,* various issues.
Salomon Brothers (1993), *International Financial Market Trends,* New York.
Stallings, B. (1990), "Reluctant giant: Japan and the Latin American debt crisis," *Journal of Latin American Studies,* vol. 22, part 1.
Tatewaki, K. (1991), *Banking and finance in Japan,* Routledge, London.
World Bank, *World Debt Tables 1992–1993,* various issues.
———— (1993), *Financial flows and the developing countries,* various issues.
Yamaichi Securities (1993), *New Shibosai Rules,* Tokyo.

4

Capital Movements, Export Strategy, and Macroeconomic Stability in Chile

RICARDO FFRENCH-DAVIS, MANUEL AGOSIN
& ANDRAS UTHOFF

This chapter analyzes the determinants and macroeconomic management of foreign capital flows, and their effects on the Chilean economy. In the period 1982–1987, the main constraint on the Chilean economy was the shortage of foreign exchange brought about by the debt crisis. Since then, Chile has had to face the opposite conjuncture, resulting first from a substantial rise in the price of copper and then from the abundance of foreign capital. The main effects of the renewed capital inflows have been the positive impact on investment and the pressure on the level of economic activity, such as on money supply and toward exchange rate appreciation. To counter the effect on the exchange rate, the authorities have adopted a number of measures that have driven a wedge between the domestic and external short-term financial markets. The main aim has been to prevent an exchange rate appreciation like the one experienced in the previous period of abundant capital inflows (1978–1981), and to make space for domestic monetary policy. In so doing, the Central Bank of Chile can avert its negative effects on the sustainability of macroeconomic balances and on the growth of exports, which have led Chile's recent economic growth. The monetary effect of Central Bank intervention in the foreign-exchange market has been offset by sterilizing the corresponding increase in liquidity.

Four basic instruments have been used to neutralize any effects that, as a result of the influx of short-term capital, may be inconsistent with the objectives of the export development strategy. These instruments are the application of taxes and reserve requirements to capital inflows, an exchange-rate policy based on "dirty" floating of the exchange rate in relation to a reference value pegged to a basket of currencies, open-market operations to sterilize the monetary effects of exchange rate dealings, and the prudent supervision of financial markets.

These measures have succeeded in moderating the inevitable exchange-rate appreciation that the new capital inflows entail. Even so, between the first quarters of 1991 and 1993, there was a 15 percent revaluation in real terms;[1] then, in 1993, the real exchange rate recovered slightly. It is difficult to determine with any certainty what impact the appreciation has had on investment in exportables. It is likely that the growth of nontraditional exports, as well as investment in them, involves a large measure of inertia.

Although this analysis concentrates on the period 1987–1993, it also refers to the period 1978–1981, when most of the liberalization of external financing took place in Chile. These two periods were marked by massive capital inflows, which the economic authorities managed in very different ways.

One finding of this study is that, partly as a result of the policies pursued, capital flows have tended to take the form primarily of FDI rather than formal portfolio investment or other speculative flows. Although not all FDI involves new investment (it sometimes is simply the purchase of existing assets), an attempt is made to determine roughly the effective contribution of FDI to overall investment.

The regulation of capital movements in Chile has achieved important, closely interrelated objectives: first, the development of policy instruments that serve as incentives/barriers to capital inflows and outflows; second, the regulation of foreign exchange and money markets to influence basic macroeconomic relative prices, trying to ensure that the latter do not deviate significantly from the target of long-term equilibrium and thereby affecting the allocation of resources and sustainable growth; and third, a degree of control over monetary aggregates and the determinants of aggregate demand, so as to have a positive influence on capital formation and its productivity. However, a gradual liberalization of diverse capital flows, together with a sharp improvement of the terms of trade, made regulation of the exchange rate by the Central Bank more difficult in 1994.

Characteristics of the New Capital Flows

In the last two decades, the drastic liberalization of the Chilean economy has been reflected in all spheres of economic policy. In the trade sphere, all nontariff measures were eliminated between 1974 and 1979, and tariffs were reduced to a uniform rate of 10 percent (now 11 percent). With respect to the balance-of-payments capital account, most of the liberalization of capital inflows and of the domestic financial market took place in the 1970s and early 1980s, although inflows and outflows are still subject to certain controls that were partially liberalized in 1991. However, a strict system of prudential supervision of banking institutions was introduced in 1986 and various regulations were reimposed in 1991 to deal with the abundance of foreign exchange.

Economic growth, which has fluctuated widely in the last quarter of a century, has been led by exports, whose share of the gross domestic product (GDP) has risen substantially (from less than 15 percent in 1974 to over a third at present, at 1977 prices). The greatest growth has been in a group of new exports, including horticultural products and fruit, forestry, seafood (particularly fishmeal and salmon), and a growing group of manufactures, especially paper and pulp plus miscellaneous products. Investment in fixed capital has been low for virtually the entire period. However, such investment began to pick up toward the end of the 1980s and has since grown, reaching well over 20 percent of GDP (at 1977 pesos) in 1993.[2]

Since the 1982–1983 depression, during which GDP fell by 15 percent, Chile's economy has been enjoying a period of sustained recovery, interrupted briefly in 1985 as a result of deliberate policies to rebalance the external and fiscal accounts, and again in 1990 to reduce the inflation and excess of aggregate demand over production capacity, generated by a massive spending increase in the last biennium of the military government. This growth of GDP has been accompanied by a boom in nontraditional exports, a recovery of investment, a very high copper price, and, subsequently, a major private capital inflow.

Private voluntary capital flows began to recover in 1987 (Table 4.1). From then until 1989, capital inflows increased steadily, but to amounts below the average level for 1983–1986. Debt-for-equity swaps grew spectacularly. Cash inflows began to take off in 1990, rising sharply in 1993. The most important item has been effective foreign direct investment.[3] Other significant components between 1989 and 1993 were private short-term loans and the return in 1991 of medium- and long-term voluntary private loans.

Portfolio investments, which made their appearance in 1989, are a relatively new phenomenon. The bulk of these investments go through two channels: foreign mutual funds, organized specifically for investing in the shares of Chilean and other Latin American corporations, and offerings of shares of a number of Chilean companies on the New York Stock Exchange through American Depositary Receipts (ADRs).

Another somewhat recent development, albeit in the opposite direction, was the beginning, in 1991, of a significant outflow of capital by

Table 4.1   Chile: Capital Account, 1980–1993 (millions of U.S.$)

	1980–1982	1983–1985	1986	1987	1988	1989	1990	1991	1992	1993
Total Capital Account	3,026	1,278	741	945	1,009	1,264	3,049	829	2,883	2,763
Foreign Investment	421	113	380	1,068	1,305	1,677	1,690	761	703	1,768
Investment from abroad	448	118	383	1,075	1,321	1,687	1,698	883	1,082	2,289
Effective FDI[a]	332	92	60	104	124	182	235	562	730	896
Net loans associated with DL 600[b]	115	–1	67	185	388	311	749	336	51	615
Disbursement	134	53	108	226	524	437	888	458	328	847
Debt/equity conversion	0	27	255	786	809	1,107	355	–40	–32	–55
Portfolio investment	0	0	0	0	0	87	359	25	332	833
Investment funds[c]	0	0	0	0	0	87	254	56	50	40
American Depositary Receipts	0	0	0	0	0	0	105	–31	282	793
Investment abroad	–27	–5	–3	–7	–16	–10	–8	–122	–378	–521
Other Capital	2,605	1,164	361	–123	–296	–413	1,358	68	2,179	996
Medium- and long-term capital	2,080	1,438	–41	–968	–986	–1,616	–57	–419	239	–96
Medium- and long-term disbursements	3,613	1,623	1,144	829	998	1,009	1,328	1,152	1,376	1,438
Loans	3,572	1,623	1,144	829	998	1,009	1,328	952	1,256	1,114
Disbursements through Article 15	65	23	16	27	42	232	395	210	104	187
Suppliers credits	237	124	159	197	124	134	86	85	77	129
Official loans	80	445	510	535	765	558	652	508	656	290
Banks	3,176	1,021	459	69	68	67	164	87	386	448
Companies and persons	15	10	0	0	0	18	32	61	32	60
Bonds	41	0	0	0	0	0	0	200	120	324
Amortization of foreign loans	–1,487	–638	–1,192	–1,804	–2,381	–2,636	–1,432	–1,546	–1,174	–1,506
Effective amortization[d]	–1,487	–552	–432	–269	–513	–690	–604	–863	–838	–1,230
Foreign debt conversions	0	–85	–760	–1,535	–1,868	–1,946	–828	–684	–336	–276

(continues)

Table 4.1 continued

	1980–1982	1983–1985	1986	1987	1988	1989	1990	1991	1992	1993
Other medium- and long-term capital (net)[e]	−46	452	7	8	397	11	48	−24	38	−28
Short-term capital	525	−273	402	845	690	1,203	1,415	487	1,940	1,091
Short-term lines	729	−165	242	141	371	819	549	−998	1,879	154
Nonfinancial public sector	249	−26	22	5	44	161	−101	−600	61	−12
Private and banking sector	480	−139	220	136	328	658	650	−398	1,818	165
Short-term direct commercial	58	−19	−47	−99	−3	105	251	400	−217	207
Short-term assets	−346	248	563	577	546	273	610	1,094	280	732
Foreign debt conversion counterpart[f]	0	44	478	750	991	606	473	665	263	135
Others	−346	204	85	−172	−445	−332	137	429	17	597
Other short-term capital (net)	85	−338	−357	225	−225	5	5	−9	−1	−1

Source: ECLAC on the basis of data from the Central Bank of Chile.

Notes: [a]Corresponds to net income via Decree Law No. 600 and Chapter XIV of CNCI.

[b]Although not risk capital, strictly speaking, it is a loan directly related to the investment process.

[c]Includes only funds established according to Law No. 18657.

[d]Not counting amortization of loans associated with DL 600.

[e]Includes amortization refinancing, interest retiring, deferred amortization to the Club of Paris, and other medium- and long-term assets and liabilities. In 1983, corresponds to refinancing within the debt-restructuring agreement of that year. In 1988, corresponds to the interest retiring established within the debt-restructuring agreement of that year.

[f]Reflects the decrease in private sector assets to finance debt conversions made with informal market resources, which have no counterpart in other items of the balance of payments.

Chilean companies in the form of direct investments and the purchase of assets abroad, especially in Argentina.

It is interesting to place the 1987–1993 capital flows in the context of trends in those flows since 1978.[4] Net capital inflows during the period 1979–1981 accounted for between 11 and 14 percent of GDP at current prices (Table 4.2). If this proportion is measured at 1977 prices, the range is 11 to 18 percent. Although there was a considerable accumulation of reserves, between 54 and 100 percent of capital inflows financed massive current account deficits (caused by the increasing real overvaluation of the peso and the rapid rise in aggregate demand). During the current period, capital inflows have been smaller, both in nominal terms and as a percentage of GDP. The only year in which capital inflows reached levels similar to those between 1978 and 1981 was 1990, when they climbed to 11 percent of GDP at current prices. However, the current account deficit that year was small and shrinking, whereas the accumulation of reserves reached 77 percent of capital inflows.

A subsequent, marked change in the trade balance has also been reflected in the current account. After showing a surplus in 1991, the current account deteriorated rapidly, reaching nearly 5 percent of GDP in 1993. The sharp switch was associated with: (1) a change in the domestic economic conjuncture—the economy grew very slowly in 1990 and rebounded strongly in 1992–1993; (2) the terms of trade, which changed from favorable (clearly above "normal") to unfavorable;[5] and (3) the lagged effects of the 1991–1992 currency appreciation and of a tariff reduction in 1991.

Obviously, the external sector balance may fluctuate dramatically because of external shocks and changes in the short-term domestic macroeconomic situation. Consequently, a shortsighted horizon can lead to costly mistakes, as happened in 1978–1981. The present economic authorities seem to have had this lesson well in mind when they tried to curb the pressures toward exchange rate appreciation in 1991, even though there were trade and current account surpluses that year.

The composition of capital inflows has varied more markedly than their overall volume (see Table 4.1). In 1978–1981, capital inflows took the form primarily of medium- and long-term loans from international banks to the domestic private sector. Given the abundant supply of foreign bank loans, this situation was partly attributable to the steady relaxation of the limits imposed on banks' external indebtedness in order to provide loans in pesos and a relaxation of the guarantees that banks could extend to the external indebtedness of nonbanking firms.

Four main components of capital flows—foreign direct investment, portfolio investments, "hot" money, and Chilean investment abroad—warrant further analysis.

Table 4.2   Summary of Chile's Balance of Payments, 1979–1993 (millions of U.S.$)

	Trade Balance (goods)	Financial Services	Current Account	Capital Account[a]	Errors and Omissions	Accumulation of Reserves	Net Capital Inflows to GDP (%)	
							In Nominal Dollars	In 1977 Dollars[b]
1979	−355	675	−1,189	2,247	−11	1,047	10.8	11.2
1980	−764	930	−1,971	3,165	50	1,244	11.5	13.0
1981	−2,677	1,464	−4,733	4,698	102	67	14.2	17.9
1982	62	1,921	−2,304	1,215	−76	−1,165	4.8	5.5
1983	986	1,748	−1,117	508	68	−541	2.6	2.3
1984	363	2,025	−2,111	1,940	188	17	10.1	8.5
1985	884	2,043	−1,413	1,384	−70	−99	9.6	5.9
1986	1,092	1,892	−1,191	741	223	−227	4.4	2.8
1987	1,229	1,700	−808	945	−91	45	5.0	3.0
1988	2,219	1,920	−167	1,009	−110	732	4.2	2.8
1989	1,578	1,926	−705	1,264	−122	437	5.0	3.2
1990	1,273	1,811	−648	3,049	−32	2,369	11.2	7.6
1991	1,576	1,809	15	829	394	1,238	2.6	1.9
1992	749	1,860	−743	2,882	359	2,498	7.4	6.1
1993	−979	1,503	−2,092	2,764	−94	578	6.7	5.5

Source: Central Bank of Chile.
Notes: [a]Net capital inflows. This column plus errors and omissions and minus the change of reserves (in the balance of payments) is equal to the net financing of the current account.
[b]GDP (in 1977 pesos) was converted to dollars using the average exchange rate for 1977. Capital inflows were deflated by Chile's external price index.

Foreign Direct Investment

Foreign direct investment has played a leading role in the current period of capital inflows. Since 1974, FDI has been regulated by Decree Law 600, which has been slightly modified subsequently. The principles underlying this decree are national treatment for foreign investors, their free access to domestic markets, and the virtual absence of state oversight of the activities of foreign corporations and the sectoral destination of their resources. At present, capital can be repatriated one year after an investment has been made. Foreign investors are guaranteed the right to profit remittances and can choose between the tax regime applicable to national corporations or a fixed rate of taxation on their profits, which is guaranteed for a certain period of time. When investments for export projects exceed U.S.$50 million, corporations may hold escrow accounts outside Chile to pay interest, dividends, and royalties, and to purchase raw materials and capital goods. Because these benefits are not available to national investors, present legislation can be said to give preferential treatment to foreign investors.

Another intensively used channel for investing in Chile was through the debt-for-equity mechanism provided for in Chapter XIX of the Central Bank's CNCI, introduced in 1985. However, this mechanism represented not an effective net capital inflow, but rather a debt swap.[6] Chapter XIX investments were subject to approval by the Central Bank on a case-by-case basis. Moreover, there were some limitations on the use of this mechanism: in the case of major investment projects in mining, only 10 percent of investments could be made through debt conversions. When the mechanism was introduced, profits could not be remitted for a period of four years and capital could be repatriated only after ten years.

Foreign direct investment has accounted for a growing proportion of net capital inflows, reaching 32 percent in 1993. This proportion increases to 55 percent if we add to it net credits associated with DL 600. A change of composition between risk capital and associated credits in favor of the former can also be observed and may be related to the policies discouraging short-run financial inflows.

Apart from the long-term stability of the rules governing foreign investment and the stability and good prospects of the Chilean economy as a whole, debt-for-equity swaps were obviously a favorable factor in the increase in the presence of foreign investors. While they were in action (1985–1990), debt-for-equity swaps accounted for well over half of all the foreign investments entering Chile[7] (Figure 4.1). The controversy about the degree of additionality that these resources represented is difficult to resolve.[8] Investors who used this channel to enter Chile benefited from a substantial subsidy that was not available to those using DL 600. Ffrench-Davis

Figure 4.1   Chile: Net Foreign Investment

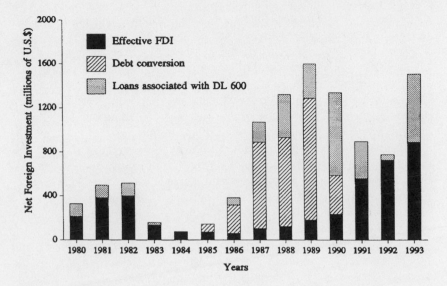

Source: Central Bank of Chile and Table 4.1, this chapter.

(1990, table 6) estimated that between 1985 and 1989 the subsidy implicit in the mechanism amounted to 46 percent of the value of investments (the greater value received in Chile by the investor of the notes divided by their purchase price in international markets). At current values, these investors brought in paper valued at U.S.$1.9 billion in international markets and at U.S.$2.8 billion in Chile.[9]

The international publicity surrounding the introduction of the mechanism probably helped create a favorable climate among foreign investors and tended to attract them to Chile. Moreover, it helped to mitigate the debt crisis and reduce the debt service at a very opportune moment, when external restrictions predominated. Partly because the debt stock was reduced as a consequence (and partly because the quantum and price of exports rose sharply), the debt-export ratio fell from 5 in 1984 to less than 2 in 1989. When the price of Chilean debt notes rose in international markets, conversion ceased to be a good deal for investors. In fact, no new operations have been conducted since 1991.

A large share of FDI has gone to export sectors. Between 1985 and 1992, mining projects absorbed more than half the capital flows brought in by DL 600. Two major copper-mining projects (La Escondida and La Disputada de Las Condes) accounted for a substantial proportion of such investments in 1987–1990. The only other sectors of any significance were manufactures and services. On the basis of information available for investments worth more than U.S.$100 million, most projects in manufacturing relate to the forestry, paper, and pulp industries, geared basically to external markets. Therefore, approximately two-thirds of FDI brought in through DL 600 has gone to export sectors. With regard to services, investment has been concentrated in the financial sector. In some cases, whose share of the total is difficult to determine, these investments may not represent the creation of new assets but the purchase of existing ones, meaning that not all FDI contributes directly to increase gross capital formation.

Chapter XIX has treated sectors somewhat selectively. The limits imposed on mining explain the sector's low share of these sources. On the other hand, some export-manufacturing sectors (processed foods, paper and pulp), forestry, fisheries, and agriculture for export have received a large share. Investments in services have been concentrated in telecommunications (privatized in the late 1980s), private pension funds (AFPs), banks, electricity-generating corporations (also recently privatized), and hotels. To sum up, from one-half to two-thirds of debt-equity swaps has gone to export sectors, but largely through the purchase of existing assets. By contrast with DL 600, such investment has been concentrated in mining or in the processing of nonmineral raw materials. Investment in manufactures unrelated to the commodities in which Chile enjoys natural comparative advantages do not figure significantly in either DL 600 or Chapter XIX flows.

The purchase of existing assets has undoubtedly been more important among Chapter XIX investments than among DL 600 operations. A large proportion of Chapter XIX dealings in the services sector involved purchases of existing firms. Even in some export sectors, some joint ventures with national entrepreneurs included purchases of stock in local corporations. An estimate based on data from the Central Bank shows that purchases of existing firms accounted for somewhat over one-half of all debt-equity swaps. This high percentage prompted the Central Bank in 1990 to give new investment in tradables priority over the purchase of existing assets.

Portfolio Investment

The newest kinds of flows that have been taking place recently, portfolio investment, enter the country through foreign capital investment funds (FICEs) and through the sale of shares on U.S. stock markets in the form of ADRs. As can be seen from Table 4.1, FICEs were quantitatively more significant in 1989 and 1990. ADRs, on the other hand, after a first operation in 1990, gained importance only since 1992. They have aroused increasing interest among local firms and foreign investors but also have generated significant, unwarranted, macroeconomic effects in the Chilean economy.

There are two radically different forms of ADRs. The original one ("initial offering") is subject to stringent requirements; for instance, the issuer must fulfill given capital and gross income minimums, exceed solvency classification, and—most significant of all—ADRs must correspond to an increase of the capital of the firm and must be placed on the U.S. stock markets. The second form ("inflows," or secondary ADRs) corresponds to purchases made in the local stock exchanges of any existing shares of the firms that have fulfilled the first stage mentioned above. Subsequently, they are converted into ADRs tradable in the United States, with the benefits in Chile of tax exemptions on capital gains and of access to the formal foreign exchange market. There are also flowbacks, which are opposite operations that involve converting ADRs to shares and reselling the latter on the local market. All such operations rely on access to the formal foreign exchange market for converting U.S. dollars to Chilean pesos and vice versa. A large majority of all outstanding ADRs corresponds to the second category (Table 4.3).

Interest in Chilean securities grows when major price differentials arise between the local and the foreign stock exchange markets as well as in the price/profit ratios. When foreign investors take advantage of these differentials, this gives rise to inflow operations. In any event, the inflow is more prevalent at present; the amount brought in in the form of inflows totals U.S.$640 million, compared to only U.S.$466 million in initial offerings by the end of 1993 (see Table 4.3). Most of this flow of funds was associated with old stock. This phenomenon intensified significantly in 1994. As a matter of fact, U.S.$1 billion in secondary ADRs were operated in 1994, representing an additional net capital inflow of 2 percent of the GDP. This may become a significant source of instability.

There are two kinds of foreign capital investment funds in Chile: those financed with debt swaps (regulated by annex 2 to Chapter XIX of the CNCI), now reduced to already existing funds, and those regulated by Act No. 18.657 of DL 600.[10] Most resources for establishing these funds have been channeled through the latter mechanism (Table 4.4). By May 1994, the Superintendency of Securities and Insurance had authorized the functioning of eighteen funds, which by that time had brought in U.S.$505 million. With respect to the composition of the funds' portfolios, 97 percent corresponded to shares in 120 corporations. However, just five domestic firms accounted for 45 percent of the funds' total portfolio.[11]

On the other hand, the three funds set up under the debt conversion mechanism had brought in U.S.$130 million. In early 1990, the Central Bank announced more selective rules for the application of Chapter XIX and excluded new investment fund inflows from it.[12]

Table 4.3   ADRs Registered on the U.S. Stock Markets
(millions of U.S.$ as of November 1993)

Company	Date	Initial Offering	Inflows[a]	Total[b]	Flowback[c]	Percent of Company in ADRs	Nominal Variation (%)[d]
CTC	July 20, 1990	89.0	416.6	505.6	46.1	24.2	416.9
CHILECTRA	February 19, 1992	72.7	36.7	109.4	14.0	10.6	25.0
CCU	September 24, 1992	57.0	19.8	76.8	6.7	9.7	116.0
MADECO	June 7, 1993	55.0	34.6	89.6	2.4	15.8	103.6
MASISA	June 16, 1993	54.0	45.7	99.7	0.0	27.0	26.2
SOQUIMICH	September 28, 1993	75.2	47.1	122.3	0.0	22.7	−8.4
ENERSIS	October 26, 1993	63.5	39.2	102.7	0.0	9.5	9.0
Total		466.4	639.7	1,106.1	69.2	—	—

Source: Latin Finance Review, various issues; Chile Market, stockbrokers.
Notes: [a]Purchases made by foreigners in Chile and subsequently converted to ADRs.
[b]Chilean ADRs registered on the U.S. stock markets (initial offering plus inflows).
[c]Flowback operations correspond to ADRs converted to shares and traded on the national stock market.
[d]Nominal change in the value of ADRs on NYSE from the time of their first offering to November 1993.

Chile's favorable macroeconomic prospects since the end of the 1980s and the anticipated rise in stock exchange quotations have undoubtedly been important for attracting this kind of capital.

Table 4.4   Assets of Foreign Investment Funds
(billions of pesos as of December 1993)

	Stock	Government Securities	Other[a]	Total Assets
Funds related to DL 600[b]	649.2	6.6	13.8	669.6
Funds related to Chapter XIX[c]	25.3	0.1	0.8	26.2
Total	674.5	6.7	14.6	695.8

Source: Superintendency of Securities and Insurance, and Central Bank of Chile.
Notes: [a]Includes time deposits, mortgages, bonds, bills of exchange, and other assets.
[b]Includes seventeen investment funds.
[c]Includes only one investment fund.

It is interesting to contrast the return for the investor—and hence the payments by Chile to foreign factors—obtained by ADRs and FICEs. Both have been notably profitable for foreign investors. But primary ADRs have contributed directly to increases in the volume of stocks, whereas FICEs have contributed mostly to increases of prices of existing stocks. The primary ADRs offered between 1990 and 1993 allowed local firms to place shares at better prices than they would have been able to if limited to the domestic stock exchange. In fact, ADRs were offered at NYSE price/earnings ratios that were higher than the ratios prevailing in the Chilean market; arbitrage before and/or after the offerings of the ADRs raised the domestic ratios toward the U.S. levels.[13] Thus, in the process, local firms obtained financing at a lower cost.[14]

Notwithstanding the rather high prices achieved by issuers of ADRs, prices kept on rising. By December 1993 the market value of ADRs bought at U.S.$1.0 billion (including both categories) had climbed to U.S.$2.2 billion (plus U.S.$60 million in dividends).

FICEs, on the other hand, entered the local stock market at lower domestic prices, and this resulted later in a sharper increase in the price of their assets. FICE capital inflows originally totaling U.S.$490 million were worth the equivalent of U.S.$1.6 billion (plus U.S.$130 million in dividends) by December 1993. Both kinds of external liabilities have come to be relatively liquid and can be rapidly withdrawn from Chile through the formal foreign exchange market if investors see fit to sell their assets in the domestic market. In this sense, those funds relate more to the speculative flows discussed below rather than to FDI.

Speculative Flows

In 1975, existing regulations on the domestic financial market and controls on capital flows from abroad hindered the entry of speculative flows into the country. Only since 1978, with the liberalization of restrictions on banks' external indebtedness, has the possibility of speculative capital movements through the official exchange market been opened. Subsequently, during 1982, with the abrupt curtailment of bank loans to Latin America, the perception that Chile was a risk country and the growing expectation that the peso would be devalued led to a significant reduction of private capital flows; between then and 1986, such flows were nonvoluntary and went mostly to the public sector.[15] Only since 1987 did large private capital flows resume, an appreciable amount of which was speculative or short-term private capital.

The measurement of speculative capital flows is problematic from a statistical viewpoint, since they tend to be hidden in both the current and the capital account. Short-term (less than one year) capital, with the exception of loans to finance foreign trade, is usually considered to be speculative or "hot" money. But not all flows of less than one year are speculative; most evidently, "normal" trade credit is not. In any case, private short-term flows provide a tentative measurement of speculative capital.

When controls are placed on capital movements or measures introduced to discourage short-term flows (as in the case of Chile since mid-1991), the most common ways to enter speculative capital are overinvoicing exports of goods and principally services (such as tourism), underinvoicing imports, and leads and lags in foreign trade payments.

Another channel by which speculative capital enters is through the informal foreign exchange market (the exparallel market). Such flows are undoubtedly influenced by interest rate differentials between Chile and international financial markets (especially rates on the U.S. dollar) and expectations of depreciation or appreciation of the peso. The Central Bank makes estimates of some of these flows associated with the current account and certain capital account operations. The balance is included in the capital account under "other assets." This has made it possible to reduce the errors and omissions entry.

Recorded speculative flows are found within short-term movements carried out by the private and banking sectors and direct trade credit operations. These latter, although not speculative, clearly are responsive to interest-rate differentials. Speculative flows, therefore, can be estimated by adding the sum of short-term private flows recorded in the balance of payments and the "other assets" entries. In the period since the fourth quarter of 1991, the rise in the value of reserve requirements (a total of roughly U.S.$1 billion) associated to those credits should be subtracted from the balance-of-payment figures because banks borrowed abroad in order to comply with the reserve requirements of the Central Bank.[16]

As Figure 4.2 shows, private short-term flows behave as expected: they have been strongly positive in 1989–1992. This period was characterized by a growing gross gap between domestic and international interest rates (shown in Figure 4.4), an expectation on the part of economic agents that the Chilean peso would appreciate in real terms (due to the huge inflow of foreign exchange plus a rise in the terms of trade), and a perception that Chile's risk-country rating had improved significantly. The gross gap has been reduced significantly by a series of policy measures adopted by the Central Bank.

Investment Abroad

At the end of 1990, investment abroad was of little significance, with an accumulated total of U.S.$178 million. However, the presence of Chilean investment abroad was radically changed by the liberalization of some capital outflows in 1991; by the end of 1994 Chileans had invested an accumulated total of U.S.$1,800 million abroad.[17] A good part of these new investments were in Argentina, where Chileans own or are partners in more than fifty enterprises. Only since 1992 did the Chilean presence in

Figure 4.2   Inflows of Short-Term Capital
(quarterly data)

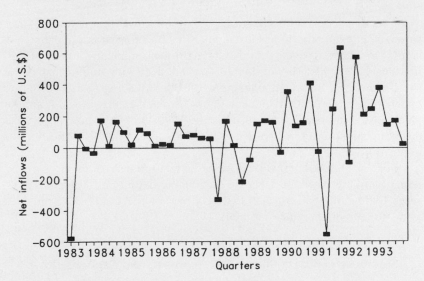

Source: Central Bank of Chile and calculations by the authors.

Argentina begin to be significant, especially through privatization programs. By the end of 1994, the Central Bank had recorded investment in Argentina amounting to U.S.$710 million. Reportedly, a significantly larger figure includes nonregistered informal portfolio investment in several Latin American stock exchanges, and associated capital gains accrued.

From the viewpoint of Chilean investors, Argentina's privatization program has been a success, as evidenced by the fact that three of the four enterprises into which the Greater Buenos Aires electric company (SEGBA) was divided wound up in the hands of consortia controlled by Chilean electric companies.[18] Chileans also participated in the privatization of Gas del Estado, and since 1992 in the purchase of a steel mill.

Another area where the Chilean presence is beginning to grow is the service sector, especially supermarkets and insurance. In manufacturing, besides the share in steel, Chilean firms have diversified by buying assets in Argentina, such as factories making ceramics, disposable diapers, bottled gas and welded products, candies and sweets, cables and industrial oils, and more recently in private pension funds that began to function in 1994 and in which Chilean firms have several years of experience.

In 1993, Chilean investors also began to become interested in Peru. There, as in Argentina, the most profitable deals have been linked to the privatization of public enterprises and new opportunities generated by economic liberalization, such as the private pension funds being created.

The Changing Nature of External Liabilities

With the development of new forms of capital flows, the traditional measurement of external debt has lost some of its meaning. It is a phenomenon similar to what happened with the standard measurement of the debt during the 1970s, which did not include private debt with creditor banks nor short-term debt. Both components skyrocketed, leading to an ever-larger underestimation of external indebtedness (Ffrench-Davis, 1982). A similar phenomenon has been taking place in the 1990s, although now implying a different composition, with a rise in the share of external liabilities related to portfolio and FDI flows.

For this reason, international financial institutions seek to measure external liabilities more precisely by broadening definitions. Table 4.5 measures Chile's international liabilities for certain years, including the peak year of the traditional measurement, 1986.

Macroeconomic Equilibria, Development, and Capital Inflows

Capital movements can significantly affect exports and macroeconomic equilibria through their impact on the exchange rate and on aggregate

Table 4.5   External Liabilities of Chile
(billions of U.S.$)

	1980	1986	1990	1993
Traditional debt	11.1	19.5	17.4	19.2
Long-term debt	9.4	17.8	14.0	15.7
Public	4.7	14.4	9.8	8.6
Private	4.7	3.4	4.2	7.1
Short-term debt	1.7	1.7	3.4	3.5
Public	0.3	1.4	2.0	0.5
Private	1.3	0.3	1.4	3.0
International reserves				
Central Bank[a]	4.0	1.8	5.4	9.8
Financial system assets	0.6	0.5	0.5	0.5
Foreign investment				
Foreign direct investment[b]	1.0	2.1	2.8	4.9
Investment with external debt notes[c]	—	0.3	3.3	3.2
American Depositary Receipts[d]	—	—	0.1	2.2
Investment funds[d]	—	—	0.5	1.6
Investment abroad (Chapter XII assets)	0.0	0.1	0.2	1.2
Undistributed profits[e]	n.a.	n.a.	1.6	3.2

Sources: Traditional debt and international reserves: Central Bank of Chile; foreign investment and undistributed profits: estimations of authors.

Notes: [a]Gross international reserves, net of use of IMF credits.

[b]Sum of the nominal net flows of risk capital under DL 600 and Chapter XIV of CNCI; excludes directly capitalized debt under Chapter XIX and undistributed profits. Loans associated with FDI are included in long-term private debt.

[c]Redenominated value (net of capital withdrawals) of Chapter XIX investment plus direct capitalizations.

[d]Stock at market prices.

[e]Conservative estimate of undistributed profits and increases in nominal value of the stock of FDI and Chapter XIX.

demand. The current development strategy assigns a central role to the expansion and diversification of exports. The level and stability of the real exchange rate are key determinants of export behavior. The Chilean economy has been highly unstable in macroeconomic terms, due to external shocks in terms of trade and external financing. For example, the 15 percent plunge in GDP in 1982 and the 10 percent rise in 1989, each the most pronounced in Latin America in those two years, were linked with external shocks.

Generally speaking, recent macroeconomic policy has been relatively successful in offsetting the appreciation of the peso and the impact of capital flows on the rate of expansion of aggregate demand and inflation. To achieve that, the economic authorities have resorted to compensatory intervention policies or sterilization at three levels. First, capital inflows were discouraged by restricting and taxing the entrance of (mainly) short-term capital and by increasing the uncertainty of interest rate arbitrage. Second, the exchange rate has been actively sustained by accumulating considerable international reserves. Third, the monetary effects of the accumulation of reserves have been effectively sterilized.

Macroeconomic Policy and the Character of Capital Movements

When the debt crisis broke out in 1982, the exchange rate was fixed and monetary policy was passive, which, as a consequence of the external shocks, gave rise to an automatic sharp drop in domestic spending for consumption and investment (Table 4.6, lines 2, 3, and 4). In order to narrow the external gap, the main policy variable was an extremely strong reduction in aggregate demand. The adjustment spread to the external sector, reducing imports and increasing exportable supply (line 6).

This endogenous reallocation was also subsequently supported by a series of substantial real devaluations of the exchange rate and increased import tariffs and surcharges (see Ffrench-Davis, Leiva, and Madrid, 1992). However, the effects of demand-reducing policies were notably stronger than those of switching policies, as can be concluded from the fact that the adjustment did more to shrink demand than to reallocate demand and supply. This led to a high rate of underutilization of productive capacity, which is partially reflected in line 1 of Table 4.6.[19] Over the course of time, given exchange rate and tariff incentives for the production of tradables, economic activity and investment gradually recovered, although very mildly, led by dynamic export growth.[20]

From 1988 onward, thanks to an improvement in the terms of trade (Table 4.6, line 7), especially due to a sharp rise in the price of copper between 1986 and 1988 and new flows of foreign capital (line 8a), the Chilean economy began to face a radically different conjuncture.

Among the more important effects of the new flow of foreign capital have been, on the one hand, its positive impact on the level of economic activity and investment, and on the other, a pressure on the money supply to expand and the currency to appreciate. To offset the effect on the exchange rate, Chilean authorities undertook a series of measures to prevent an appreciation such as the one in the previous period of capital inflows (1978–1981), and its negative effects on the sustainability of macroeconomic equilibria and the expansion and diversification of exports.

The perception that large deficits on the current account of the balance of payments are not sustainable over the long term as well as the lessons learned from the debt crisis led the authorities to give priority attention to the level of the real exchange rate. The Central Bank decided to intervene actively to keep the real exchange rate at a level consistent with sustainable

Table 4.6 Per Capita Production, Investment, and External Shocks: Chile, 1980–1993
(percentages of 1981 per capita GDP)

	1980	1981	1982	1983	1984	1985	1986	1987	1988	1989	1990	1991	1992	1993	Average 1983–1989	Average 1990–1993
1. GDP	95.7	100.0	85.0	81.2	84.5	84.7	88.1	91.5	96.7	104.6	105.1	109.6	119.1	124.6	90.2	114.6
2. Domestic expenditure	102.1	112.8	85.1	77.6	82.7	78.6	81.4	85.9	92.0	101.4	99.8	102.5	114.1	123.1	85.7	109.9
3. Consumption	79.2	86.5	73.9	69.0	68.1	66.7	68.0	69.3	74.3	77.9	77.2	79.9	85.8	91.1	70.5	83.5
4. Gross fixed capital formation	16.9	19.4	11.7	9.8	11.5	12.4	13.1	14.9	16.2	19.3	20.3	19.8	23.4	28.0	13.9	22.9
5. Domestic saving[a]	16.5	13.5	11.0	12.2	16.4	18.1	20.0	22.2	22.4	26.7	27.9	29.8	33.3	33.5	19.7	31.1
6. Nonfinancial current account[b]	-6.4	-12.8	-0.1	3.6	1.8	6.2	6.7	5.7	4.7	3.2	5.3	7.1	5.0	1.5	4.5	4.7
a. Exports	22.6	20.3	20.9	20.5	20.7	22.8	24.6	26.3	27.5	31.3	33.1	36.8	40.7	41.8	24.8	38.1
b. Imports	29.0	33.1	21.0	17.0	18.9	16.6	17.9	20.7	22.8	28.1	27.8	29.7	35.7	40.3	20.3	33.3
7. Terms-of-trade effect	1.9	0.0	-1.7	-1.2	-2.5	-3.7	-3.3	-2.2	0.9	0.2	-2.3	-1.7	-2.0	-4.7	-1.7	-2.7
8. Net transfers of funds	4.5	12.8	1.9	-2.4	0.7	-2.4	-3.4	-3.5	-5.6	-3.4	-3.0	-5.4	-3.0	3.2	-2.9	-2.1
a. Capital movements	12.0	17.5	4.0	1.6	7.6	3.8	2.9	2.6	3.3	4.0	9.1	3.0	9.2	8.0	3.7	7.3
b. Net profit and interest payments	-3.4	-5.0	-6.8	-6.5	-7.4	-7.0	-7.6	-6.5	-6.9	-6.5	-5.5	-5.7	-5.8	-4.4	-6.9	-5.3
c. Unrequited transfers	0.4	0.5	0.6	0.5	0.6	0.4	0.5	0.5	0.6	0.7	0.7	1.1	1.3	1.2	0.5	1.1
d. Subtotal	9.0	13.0	-2.3	-4.4	0.8	-2.7	-4.3	-3.4	-3.0	-1.9	4.2	-1.5	4.7	4.9	-2.7	3.1
e. Changes in international reserves	4.6	0.2	-4.1	-2.0	0.1	-0.3	-0.9	0.2	2.6	1.5	7.2	3.9	7.7	1.7	0.2	5.1

Sources: Calculated on the basis of data from the Central Bank of Chile: for 1980–1985. Final Official National Accounts of the Central Bank in 1977 pesos for 1974–1985; for 1986–1992, coupled in 1985 with rescaled provisional figures in 1977 for pesos for 1985–1992; for 1993, rate of growth in 1986 pesos of the Quarterly National Accounts of the Central Bank, August 1994.

Notes: All the figures have been adjusted for population growth and are expressed as percentages of 1981 GDP. Thus, the comparison of any figure in a given line with its 1981 value indicates the per capita percentage change in the respective period.

[a]Calculated as the difference between GDP and consumption.

[b]Includes trade of goods and nonfinancial services. Unrequited transfers are included in line 8.

macroeconomic equilibria, protecting the development of tradables sectors and directing investment resources toward these sectors.

Ultimately, the authorities sought to determine if the forces affecting foreign trade, FDI, and access to international capital markets were transitory or permanent. The objective was to avoid volatility in a key price for an open economy in order to avoid generating uncertainty among investors, particularly those in tradable sectors.

The impact of capital inflows on stability and formation of relative prices has been a cause of concern for the monetary authorities in Chile (Zahler, 1992). Inflows affect the country's level and structure of relative prices in two basic ways: first, by encouraging an exchange-rate appreciation, lowering the costs of imports, and generating greater demands on producers of tradables; and second, through the monetary effect of foreign exchange operations, which, if not sufficiently sterilized, can lead to either excessive demand and inflation or to recessions that hinder investment and technological innovation.

Expectations can play a strong role over the short term. For example, favorable expectations can provide incentives for a strong inflow of funds, which in turn generates expectations of appreciation, which then leads to an additional inflow.

The Chilean authorities opted to regulate the market in order to influence the real exchange rate over the short term, so that it would match better with the long-term trend. That option, purposely to make the fundamentals prevail, was based on the asymmetry of information between the market and the monetary authorities, assuming that the latter: (1) have a better knowledge of the prospects of the different components of the balance of payments and their probable effects on the economy, and (2) have a longer planning horizon than agents who operate intensively in short-term markets. However, faced with uncertainty about what will happen in reality, the authorities used, rather than a unique price, an exchange-rate band centered on a reference price; this is linked to a basket of three currencies, in which the U.S. dollar, the deutsche Mark, and the yen are represented with fixed weights associated with their share in Chilean trade.[21]

There are crucial policy implications for two key variables that affect the allocation and volume of investment resources: the exchange rate and the interest rate. Fiscal policy can also play a key role in shaping market trends and the short term. The policy dilemma is how to reconcile three objectives simultaneously: low price inflation; a stable real exchange rate, in order to provide a reasonable incentive to the tradables sector; and the achievement of sustained development with social equity.

The goal is to have the exchange rate, interest rates, and fiscal policy sending proper medium-term signals to economic agents in order to promote an efficient development of production. To do so, the inevitable short-term problems must be dealt with by an appropriate policy mix. Too much dependence on one policy tends to lead to an overadjustment of its tool and therefore a distorted resource allocation.

The Evolution of Exchange Rate Policy

Exchange rate policy has experienced substantial change over time. At the beginning of the military regime, there was an attempt to offset the impact of trade liberalization with real devaluations. Subsequently, beginning in 1976, the nominal exchange rate began to be used to fight inflation. This was because inflation stubbornly refused to slow down in reaction to the deep economic recession, which also caused a surplus on current account. The real revaluation that usually results from this policy culminated in 1979, when the rate was fixed at 39 Chilean pesos per U.S.$1, a nominal parity that was maintained until the crisis of 1982; a significant real appreciation took place during these years. After a period of experimentation with successive policy changes, a "crawling-peg" exchange rate was again adopted, and was maintained from 1983 to 1988. Basically, the Central Bank fixed a benchmark price for the dollar on the official market (called the "agreed" exchange rate), with a floating band of ±2 percent (expanded to 3 percent in 1988). The "official" rate was devalued daily, in line with the differential between domestic inflation and an estimate of external inflation. On a number of occasions, discrete real devaluations were added, helping to achieve the notable depreciation following the 1982 crisis (119 percent from 1981 to 1988).

Because various exchange controls remained in force (except for a few weeks in 1982), there also operated a parallel, illegal exchange market. This was legalized as the "informal" exchange market only in April 1990, under the provisions of the Central Bank Autonomy Act issued by the end of the Pinochet government.

In 1988, revaluations, together with tax and tariff reductions, managed to reconcile a reduction in inflation with a rise in economic activity. The recovery was completed in 1989, with economic activity then climbing up to the production frontier. This was achieved through an accelerated increase in aggregate demand, sustained by tax reductions and exchange-rate appreciation in 1988 and the additional income generated by a sharp increase in the price of copper in 1987–1989. The improvement in the terms of trade in 1988 with respect to 1986 was equivalent to 7 percent of GDP (New National Accounts of the Central Bank). A considerable increase in imports and in the current-account deficit (which rose to 10 percent of GDP, if the current account is recalculated using the normalized price of the Copper Stabilization Fund, which is discussed below) led the Central Bank to reverse earlier drops in interest rates and, in particular, to depreciate the exchange rate.

In fact, by mid-1989, the dollar floating band was widened further to ±5 percent. The Central Bank's action was accompanied by a shift in the foreign exchange market expectations, which led the market to move quickly to the ceiling of the band. Thus, without any great trauma, a significant depreciation was achieved without modifying the official rate. For about a year—which included the return to a democratic regime, presidential elections (in December 1989), and the inauguration of President Aylwin (in March 1990)—the observed exchange rate remained at the top of the band. This occurred despite the fact that the adjustment process was tightened in January 1990 to control a jump in inflation (which had reached an annualized rate of about 31 percent in the five preceding months). The adjustment was based on a sharp rise in interest rates, led by a Central Bank ten-year paper offered at the high real annual rate of 9.7 percent.

The changes taking place in global markets, the high interest rates in Chile, and the fact that the uncertainty stemming from the 1988 plebiscite and from the induction into office of President Aylwin was quickly dispelled stimulated a growing inflow of capital to Chile (also, imports slowed down as a result of the domestic adjustment). These events were quickly reflected in a real appreciation of the market exchange rate. Beginning in July 1990, the observed exchange rate was on the floor of the band. Even during the Iraq crisis in September 1990, the observed rate stayed on the floor, despite the fact that Chile was then importing 85 percent of its oil consumption. Chile reacted to this crisis by drastically raising the domestic price of fuel (together with reducing nonsocial fiscal expenditure), which caused an inflationary shock in September and October. The CPI, whose inertial component implied a rise of about 2 percent monthly at the time, jumped to 4.9 percent and 3.8 percent, respectively, in those months. The speed and close coordination with which the Central Bank and the government reacted to external events may explain why in the foreign exchange market pressures continued to be toward an appreciation.

The strong inflow of capital continued. In October 1990, the Central Bank had to buy U.S.$620 million worth of surplus foreign exchange, equivalent to 27 percent of monthly GDP. Recurrent runs on the dollar in favor of the peso were reinforced with expectations of a revaluation (and drops in domestic interest rates), which hampered monetary policy.

In early 1991, the strict crawling peg system that had been followed by the monetary authorities was modified and, in order to introduce "exchange rate noise," which would discourage short-term flows, the rate was moderately revalued on three occasions and then, in compensation, devalued in the following months. Thus, at the end of each of these moves, the official rate returned to its initial real level. The real devaluations within each move made it more costly for short-term funds to enter the country, and thus served as an effective tool for temporarily stemming the excess supply of foreign exchange. However, the measure could not be repeated too often because the market would then anticipate the revaluation and the policy would lose its effectiveness—what actually happened in the third move. Nevertheless, during nearly one semester the authorities gained time to design a policy to enable them to act efficiently in a more prolonged transition period. The policy was based on the perception that short-term factors affecting the current account—such as the high price of copper, the incentive of high domestic interest rates, and the temporary depressed level of imports—would tend to change in the near to medium term.

It was recognized, however, that part of the observed improvement in the current account—a considerably improved nonfinancial services account, a more vigorous nontraditional exports sector, and a reduction in the external debt burden—was more structural or permanent. In June 1991, in reaction to this mix of factors (some of which were regarded by the authorities as temporary and others as permanent), in addition to a small (2 percent) revaluation of the official rate and a drop in the import tariff from 15 to 11 percent, a reserve requirement of 20 percent was established on external credits, whose effect was concentrated on short-term credits. In parallel, a tax on domestic credit at an annual rate of 1.2 percent on operations of up to one year was extended to apply to external loans. Both the reserve requirement and the tax had a zero marginal cost for operations of more than one year. The reserve requirement, in turn, was more burdensome for operations of less than ninety days because that was the minimum period that the cash reserve had to be kept in a non–interest-bearing account (Central Bank, 1992, pp. 13–19).[22] The authorities estimated the financial burden of the two measures, at the time they were taken, as an equalizer of the cost of external (from the U.S. market) and domestic funds.[23]

Pressures on the foreign exchange market continued in the ensuing months, although short-term capital inflows remained at low levels in response to the regulatory policies that had been adopted and to a reduction in domestic interest rates. It should be noted that the stages of the business cycle in Chile and in its "financial center" (the United States) coincided during most of 1991, although this was no longer true by the end of 1991 and in 1992.

The pressure on the market in 1991 stemmed from long-term inflows, but mainly from a very favorable current account; exports continued to surge, including a notable increase in tourism from Argentina; the price of copper remained abnormally high; the coefficients of remittances of profits and interest payments were also low; and the recovery of imports was very slow and lagged behind the economic upturn. The net result was a (small) current-account surplus.

Many observers began to hold the view that a modification of exchange rate policy with a significant revaluation was inevitable. Consequently, the official rate began to lose its allocative capacity. In January 1992, the official exchange rate was revalued by 5 percent and the floating band in the formal market was expanded to ±10 percent.

The observed rate abruptly appreciated by 9 percent in the market, a little less than the sum of the appreciation of the official rate and the lowering of the floor of the band. There followed an overwhelming wave of expectations of more revaluations, fed by capital inflows in the formal and informal markets. These flows were encouraged by the certainty that the Central Bank, under its own rules, could not intervene within the band. Thus, in a market persistently situated near the floor, it intervened only by buying at the bottom price. The market's expectation was that if something changed, the floor exchange rate would be revalued, as in fact it was in January 1992.

For a long time the proposal had been circulating in the Bank that a "dirty" or regulated float should be initiated within the band; proponents of this view argued that the prevailing rules, with a pure band, an increasingly active informal market, and a more porous formal market, would lead to an observed exchange-rate leaning toward either extreme of the band (on the ceiling in 1989–1990; on the floor later). The sudden revaluation of the observed rate by nearly 10 percent between January and February 1992 contributed to the Bank taking the decision to initiate the dirty floating in March of that year. The observed rate has fluctuated since then within a range of 1 to 8 points above the floor (i.e., normally not on the floor itself), with the Bank continuing to make active purchases but also frequent sales.

The widening of the band in itself apparently meant that the Central Bank had renounced the attempt to deter pressures to revaluate in defense of the export strategy, allowing the market, dominated by the more "short-termist" segment, to determine the observed rate within a very wide range. To the contrary, the establishment of the dirty float gave back to the Central Bank a greater management capacity, enabling it to strengthen long-term variables in determining the exchange rate for producers of exportable and importable goods and services.

In the ensuing months, U.S. interest rates continued to decline, exerting pressure on the Central Bank. However, the Chilean economy was booming, and its GDP growth rate had risen well into two digits (about 15 percent over twelve months). Consequently, for reasons of macroeconomic equilibrium, the Central Bank wanted to raise rather than lower domestic interest rates. To avoid encouraging arbitrage, it decided to raise the reserve requirement rate on capital inflows. In May 1992, reserve requirements on external credits were raised to 30 percent and the period of deposit was fixed at one year.

Finally, in July of the same year, the dollar-peg of the official rate was replaced by a peg to a basket of currencies (of which the dollar represented 50 percent, the deutsche Mark 30 percent, and the yen 20 percent) as the new benchmark exchange rate. The purpose of these measures was to make arbitrage of interest rates between the dollar and the peso less profitable and to introduce greater exchange rate uncertainty in the short term, given the daily instability of the international prices among these three currencies. The replacement of a peg to the dollar for a basket of currencies also tended to give greater average stability to the peso values of proceeds from exports. Indeed, unlike financial operations that are largely dollar-denominated, trade is fairly diversified in geographic terms with the United States representing only one-fifth of the total, and actually it also operates with a more diversified basket of currencies.

Since 1991 an attempt has been made to ease or anticipate capital outflows as a way of alleviating downward pressures on the exchange rate. For example, the minimum time periods for repatriating capital or remitting profits for investments under Chapter XIX (debt-equity swaps) were liberalized, under some options after paying a commission on the original investment or on the capital gain or subsidy received by the swapper. In addition, the private pension fund administrators (AFPs) were gradually authorized to invest abroad up to 6 percent of their assets by late 1994. The national banks were also permitted to finance intra–Latin American trade to firms in other countries of the region, and to buy low-risk financial assets abroad. Additionally, exporters who must return their proceeds by the formal foreign exchange market within a given period have been allowed longer periods to return their proceeds and to retain for their free use in foreign currency a growing share (10 percent of exports by 1993 and, after successive raises, 50 percent since the end of 1994). Lastly, as discussed earlier, investment abroad was liberalized through both foreign exchange markets.

It is unlikely, in the prevailing foreign exchange market climate, that these measures would have the desired impact on the real exchange rate because the rate of return on financial assets has been considerably higher within Chile than outside; this has discouraged banks or pension fund administrators from making large investments abroad.[24] There are even signs that foreign investors have been reinvesting a bigger than "normal" share of their profits in Chile instead of repatriating them. Evidently, exporters have scarcely made use of their option to retain proceeds abroad or to operate via the informal market,[25] and in general have rushed to transfer funds to Chile as quickly as possible due to their larger profitability in the domestic market. On the other hand, direct and portfolio investments in countries of the region have indeed been significant, a fact that is associated with the capital gains that could be obtained in several Latin American stock markets and in the purchase of privatized firms.

A distinction should be drawn between short-term and permanent effects of the liberalization of capital outflows. In a situation of "orderly" market conditions and an abundant supply of foreign exchange, as in Chile, and with the prevailing low interest rates in the financial center, measures to ease the outflow of capital (or of profits, dividends, or interest) in the short run may have an effect contrary to the one desired and may act as an incentive instead to more inflows (Williamson, 1992; Labán and Larraín, 1993). Moreover, in the long run, too many doors will probably be left open for outflows, which are used in case the market gets nervous and shifts to devaluatory expectations. An unthoughtful financial liberalization may pose significant obstacles to exchange-rate policy and macroeconomic management, generating sources of instability.

As can be seen in Figure 4.3, the real (observed) exchange rate depreciated sharply from its low point in April 1982 until reaching a peak in early 1988. After fluctuating without any particular trend until the first quarter of 1991, it began a decline that continued until April 1992. The appreciation in this last period was 17 percent.

Since that time and up to early 1994, the strong pressures for a real currency appreciation eased, in part owing to the above-mentioned deterioration in the prices of Chile's principal exports and (as predicted by supporters of avoiding additional revaluation) a strong increase of imports in

Figure 4.3   Real Exchange Rate Index
            (base 1986 average = 100)

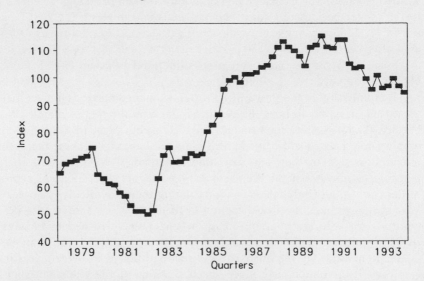

Source: Central Bank of Chile.

1992–1993. The trade surplus that had prevailed since the 1982 crisis turned into a deficit of around U.S.$1 billion and the current-account balance fell from a slight surplus in 1991 to a deficit of more than U.S.$2 billion in 1993 (5 percent of GDP). Nevertheless, the balance of payments continues to show a surplus (see Table 4.2).

If policies toward foreign capital and regulation of its effects on the economy during the current episode are compared with those adopted in similar circumstances in 1978–1981, it may be concluded that macroeconomic policies that have been followed since 1991 have been, on the average, much more pragmatic and have yielded positive results.

As for the impact of capital flows on the exchange rate, the policies that have been followed since the beginning of the new foreign exchange boom have met their objective of moderating a real appreciation that otherwise would have been more significant. In contrast, a policy was implemented in 1978–1981 that involved a substantial exchange-rate appreciation, parallel to the effects of a radical trade liberalization that culminated with the uniform tariff of 10 percent in 1979. The appreciation turned out to be extremely damaging to the production of tradables. In contrast to that episode, ever since foreign capital again became abundant, an attempt has been made to keep appreciation within reasonable limits and to promote the predominance of FDI and long-term credits in capital inflows. The differences between the two episodes are even more marked in terms of domestic saving because this appears to have undergone a crowding-out by external saving in 1978–1981, whereas now there seems to be evidence of a crowding-in (see Table 4.6).

Monetary and Fiscal Policies

This section focuses only on the aspects that are most closely related with exchange-rate policy and capital movements. Other topics of considerable interest include the implications of different ways of carrying out open-market operations, and policy concerning the interest rate yield curve.

The Central Bank's intervention in the foreign exchange market was reflected, inter alia, in a large accumulation of international reserves from 1989 to 1992 (Table 4.2 and Table 4.6, line 8e). The counterpart of foreign exchange purchases in the market was an increase in money supply. This frequently meant a greater increase in liquidity than was consistent with official targets for economic activity and inflation.

The monetary authority has managed to successfully sterilize the monetary effects of the above-mentioned capital inflows and the ensuing accumulation of international reserves. The Central Bank, in order to prevent a monetary expansion, issued domestic debt paper to sterilize the effect of the purchase of foreign exchange. Sterilization may have two feedback effects. First, the issue of debt paper puts pressure on the domestic interest rate, preventing it from dropping to the international level and creating incentives to a greater inflow of capital. Second, it may entail a deficit to the Central Bank because it has to borrow domestically at a higher cost than the returns it can obtain from international reserves. This situation becomes unsustainable in the long run, especially if the amounts involved are huge. In such a case, the policy self-defeats because it creates expectations of a revaluation and thus increases the expected profitability of arbitrage.

Sterilization and macroeconomic balances. The need for sterilization varies according to the prevailing macroeconomic situation. In the period 1976–1979, the Chilean economy was in recession, operating well below its production capacity (Marfán, 1992). The first inflows of capital and the resulting expansion of the monetary base contributed to a recovery of aggregate demand for both tradables and nontradables, which was met by a supply that was able to react owing to increased financing for imports and the available production capacity. The economic conjuncture did not require an active sterilization.

As production capacity began to be used, as early as 1979, growing capital inflows tended to create an increase in aggregate demand that was manifested in a rapid expansion of the current account deficit, a rise in the relative price of nontradables, and a weakness in exportable supply (Ffrench-Davis and Arellano, 1981; Morandé, 1988).[26] A passive monetary policy had been adopted deliberately, however, within the monetary approach to the balance of payments. It was assumed that the economy would automatically make an efficient adjustment.

Following the 1982 crisis, the economy again stood well below the production frontier. In addition, during an initial stage, the need to depreciate the national currency caused a sharp drop in incentives for arbitrage between external and domestic funding. Figure 4.4 shows that the spread for arbitrage between the international and the domestic interest rates, measured ex-post[27] and without taking into account the country risk, showed negative values, on average, for the four-year period 1983–1986.

Capital flows were concentrated on short-term trade credit, involuntary loans from creditor banks, and funds from international financial institutions to the Treasury and the Central Bank. The growing, voluminous debt swaps did not have direct monetary or exchange rate effects, although they did influence the secondary paper market and the parallel foreign exchange market.

Only later did the spread for arbitrage become positive and begin to attract external funds, but still in smaller amounts than debt service. The recovery of the Chilean economy continued until 1988. There was therefore no need for active sterilization.

Figure 4.4   Domestic Interest Rates and London Inter-Bank Offer Rate (LIBOR) (annualized quarterly rates)

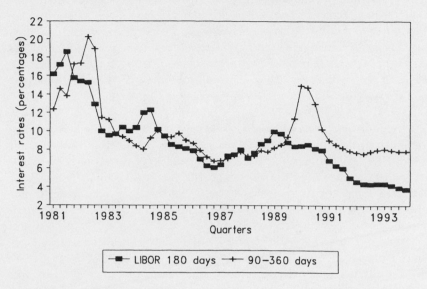

Source: Based on data of the Central Bank of Chile.

In 1988–1989 the dilemma began to arise concerning the difficulty, in the absence of active policies, of simultaneously maintaining macroeconomic equilibria, the complementarity between external and domestic saving, and a stable real exchange rate (see Figure 4.5). Active sterilization has clearly become a necessity in the 1990s, with a macroeconomic environment hovering around the production frontier and a surplus foreign exchange market. Unlike 1985, when a mini-adjustment was made because of excess demand against a binding external constraint, in 1990 and 1992 two mini-adjustments were made because of a primarily domestic constraint (a tendency to exceed the production frontier on both occasions).

Interest rates and the quasi-fiscal deficit. Sterilization can help to stabilize the real exchange rate and short-term macroeconomic balances. However, it has other effects as well on domestic interest rates, aggregate supply and demand, and the reserve position of the Central Bank.

Net sales of bonds have kept domestic interest rates higher than they would have been otherwise. That is, if domestic absorption had increased in response to exchange rate revaluations and more intensive spending on tradables, lower domestic interest rates, tending to converge with the corresponding external rates, would have resulted. Investment is still low, especially in comparison to the levels reached by the most dynamic developing

**Figure 4.5   Changes in Monetary Base
              (thousand million pesos)**

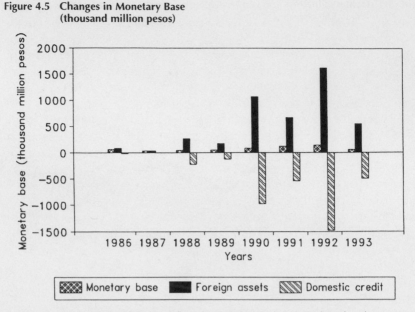

Source: Central Bank, *Assets and Liabilities* (annual changes in balances), various issues.

economies; lower real domestic interest rates would give it a boost (although this result may be more than offset by the discouraging effect of the corresponding exchange rate appreciation on the demand for tradables).

If the supply and cost of external credits were to stay as favorable indefinitely as they were in 1990–1993, the appropriate policy would be to allow domestic interest rates to fall to the external level and to revalue the exchange rate. The pending policy issue would solely concern the relative gradualness of these measures. However, the authorities have operated on the assumption that significant components of the current abundance of external funds are only transitory; this approach has a solid support in the specialized literature (see Calvo, Leiderman, and Reinhart, 1993; ECLAC, 1995, chapters 9–11; Reisen, 1993b; World Bank, 1993; and Chapter 7 in this volume). Therefore, in the current macroeconomic circumstances, it would be advisable to implement policies that maintain a positive gap between domestic and external rates.

The immediate financial cost of monetary sterilization has been high: the interest rates the Central Bank must pay on its notes are much higher than those it obtains on its loans in foreign currency. It is estimated that in 1992, the Central Bank's losses on this score amounted to approximately 0.5 percent of GDP.[28]

These costs are not necessarily permanent. If the intervention stabilizes an "equilibrium" exchange rate, it should be profitable for the Central Bank in that the Bank would sell higher than it buys; nonetheless, losses would be incurred because of the differential in interest rates, which would always tend to be higher than in the creditor financial center. The longer the surplus phase in a clean-float regime, the greater the financial cost incurred because of this differential; dirty floating tends to lower this cost. In the end, the net financial effect of sterilization on the Central Bank's balance sheet could be either positive or negative.

When the final inevitable result is a significant revaluation, this cost is added to that of the interest differentials. However, it must be borne in mind that it seems essential for Chile to maintain some level of international reserves. It is clear, too, that Chile's reserves were in need of replenishment at the end of the last decade; indeed, in early 1990 the Central Bank had U.S.$3 billion in international reserves and U.S.$5 billion in short-term foreign-currency liabilities "with residents." The costs of accumulating reserves and of the monetary sterilization this may require do not, then, appear to be exclusively attributable to stabilizing foreign exchange and monetary policies. Additionally, if a drastic revaluation is unavoidable over time, a phasing-in of the change in relative prices may be efficient—which can be achieved with a flexible stabilization policy and a mix of stepwise revaluations. Therefore, part of the financial cost of sterilization could represent an investment in the country's transition to more efficient resource allocation and greater stability.

The domestic capital market and fiscal policy. It is argued commonly that a tighter fiscal expenditure policy could obviate the need for revaluation. This latter approach seems to overestimate the effect on the foreign exchange market of saving by cutting fiscal expenditure and/or by replacing public expenditure (intensive in nontradables) with private expenditure (intensive in tradables).[29] At the same time, it underestimates the importance of government spending on social services, on infrastructure, and on modern institutions for developing production. Chile still shows a severe deficit in this regard.

Fiscal policy has supported efforts toward macroeconomic and exchange rate stabilization in two ways. On the one hand, it has generated growing savings in the nonfinancial public sector. Increased spending has been more than offset by a stronger rise in revenues as a result of a tax reform adopted in 1990 (at the beginning of the democratic government), improved collection, and faster-than-expected economic growth (an effective average of 6.3 percent versus the 5 percent projected at the beginning of that administration).

Fiscal policy has given priority to the objectives of maintaining domestic stability and, at the same time, increasing social spending, especially on health and education. Since the inflow of capital began, the Treasury has maintained a significant and growing savings rate and surplus.

The public sector current account balance has been positive, at or above 5.5 percent of GDP since 1990 (5.6 percent in 1990, 5.5 percent in 1991, and 6.6 percent in 1992). The robust increase in aggregate demand has also led to a cautious government expenditure policy. In recent years, instead of increasing disbursements in proportion to the growth of government revenues, the administration has used part of its surplus to prepay its large debt with the Central Bank (which originated in the bail-out of the private banking sector after the crisis of 1982). In fact, the overall surplus (including the capital account) was 1.5 percent of GDP in 1990, 1.7 percent in 1991, and 2.8 percent in 1992 (ECLAC, 1994).

A central factor in the Chilean monetary situation, in addition to the disciplined management of public finances, was the establishment of a fund to stabilize the price of the country's main export, whose production is primarily in the hands of the state (Romaguera, 1991).

The Copper Stabilization Fund accrues whenever the price of copper exceeds the "base" level. The fund is deposited in the Central Bank. In 1988 and 1989, nearly all of these resources were used as prepayments of the Treasury's debt with the Central Bank (see Table 4.7). The policy of using resources from the fund to prepay fiscal debt has continued in part, so that the undisbursed balance is only one-fourth of total deposits. This implies that during upswings in copper prices, the fund has helped to moderate the expansive cycle; having transferred funds to the Bank, the Treasury will be unable to operate symmetrically, and with similar intensity, in the event of a contractive cycle.

Table 4.7   Copper Stabilization Fund Flows
(millions of U.S.$)

Period	Deposits	Withdrawals	Balance
1987	26.4	—	26.4
1988	496.0	439.5	82.9
1989	1,202.9	1,260.1	25.7
1990	785.1	256.2	554.6
1991	289.7	200.0	644.3
1992	134.6	—	778.9
1993	9.8	39.0	749.7
Total	2,944.5	2,194.8	749.7

Source: Romaguera (1991) and Central Bank of Chile.

The Central Bank has been able to resort to the financial market to regulate the flood of liquidity that emerged in response to the flow of capital, partly because of a reform of the pension system and the fiscal effort that made it viable.[30]

One of the basic features of Chile's social security reform is individual capitalization, through which growing volumes of financial resources have been accumulated. This has led to a substantial increase in the participation of these institutional investors in the market for financial instruments they are authorized to operate. The pension funds are majority participants in the market for several instruments, such as mortgage bills, corporate bonds, and Treasury securities. They also purchase a significant proportion of Central Bank notes (Iglesias and Acuña, 1991).

By virtue of fiscal discipline and a relatively well-developed financial market, the Central Bank has been able to regulate the money supply by intervening in the foreign exchange and money markets. Discipline in public sector finances and deposits by the Government and pension funds in the Central Bank's financial instruments have helped to regulate the money supply.

This effect can be seen in Figure 4.5, which shows variations in the monetary base, and disaggregates them into Central Bank foreign exchange operations and domestic credit. Notice that the changes in domestic credit are closely (and negatively) correlated with foreign exchange operations. This shows that domestic credit was used extensively to counteract the buying and selling of foreign currency. The differences between the two components are related to changes in the demand for money, which in Chile is highly sensitive to variations in the cost of maintaining liquidity (the nominal interest rate) and to the stage of the cycle in which the economy is situated.

Effects on Investment

Domestic investment was markedly depressed in the first half of the 1980s and did not begin to recover significantly until the end of that decade. The recovery of investment has affected all components. Taking 1981 as a base year, by 1993 gross fixed investment per capita had increased by 45 percent (Table 4.8). A good part of these very significant improvements took place in the last two years. Up to 1989, the increases in the investment ratio in Chile can be considered to have been purely a recovery from the very low levels reached in 1983 and 1984. Only in 1993 did the ratio of fixed investment to GDP surpass the peaks reached in the 1960s. In view of the strong upsurge during the second half of the 1980s in investment in exportables, particularly those related to foreign investment, the weak performance of overall investment seems to indicate that, with the exception of exports related to raw materials, investment in most of the other sectors (including manufacturing) experienced setbacks throughout the 1980s.

Table 4.8   Investment Indicators, 1981–1993

Year	Gross Fixed Investment (% of GDP)		Real Per Capita Gross Fixed Investment[a] (1981 = 100)	Real Per Capita Imports of Capital Goods[c] (1981 = 100)
	Old National Accounts[a]	New National Accounts[b]		
1981	19.4	23.2	100.0	100.0
1982	13.8	15.8	60.7	49.7
1983	12.1	13.7	50.7	28.3
1984	13.6	16.3	59.2	40.4
1985	14.6	17.7	64.0	45.3
1986	14.8	17.1	67.4	46.4
1987	16.3	19.6	77.0	62.5
1988	16.8	20.8	83.9	69.9
1989	18.4	23.5[d]	99.6	93.2
1990	19.3	23.1[d]	104.8	94.2
1991	18.0	21.1[d]	102.1	81.2
1992	19.6	23.9[d]	120.8	106.6
1993	22.5	26.5[d]	144.6	121.5

Sources: Calculated on the basis of data from the Central Bank of Chile: for 1980–1985. Final Official National Accounts of the Central Bank in 1977 pesos for 1974–1985; for 1986–1992, coupled in 1985 with rescaled provisional figures in 1977 for pesos for 1985–1992; for 1993, rate of growth in 1986 pesos of the Quarterly National Accounts of the Central Bank, August 1994.

Notes: [a]In 1977 pesos.
[b]In 1986 pesos.
[c]Rescaled coupling of the "old" and "new" classification of imports of capital goods, deflated by the Index of External Prices of Chile.
[d]Provisional figures.

The General Impact of Capital Flows

It is difficult to assess the extent to which capital flows have contributed to boost investment. Five main effects can be distinguished: (1) the direct and positive effect of FDI; (2) a possible impact through the relaxation of the balance-of-payments restriction, which led to a normalization of effective demand and increased the country's capacity to import capital goods; (3) if investment was constrained by a lack of access to credit (in other words, if the interest rate did not, in itself, clear the credit market), the increased liquidity produced by capital inflows and the ensuing accumulation of reserves may have promoted investment; (4) the appreciation of the exchange rate as one of the effects of capital inflows may have discouraged investment in tradables, but also may have provided an incentive for investment by lowering the price of capital goods, most of which are imported; and (5) the effects on the macroeconomic environment that potential investors face.

The effects of capital flows on the distribution of investment between tradables and nontradables may have been significant. When the appreciation of the peso exceeds net increases in productivity, it tends to have net adverse effects on investment in tradables (particularly exportables, which have fueled Chile's recovery of economic growth since the mid-1980s) by adversely affecting their profitability. The impact may be particularly significant for marginal projects related to exports of manufactures, the most dynamic of Chile's export sectors. These depend heavily on the maintenance of a favorable exchange rate, as their high price elasticities show (ECLAC, 1995, chapter 4). Exchange rate appreciation also has an expansive effect on economic activity in the short term (by raising real income). Consequently, the acceleration effect would tend to increase investment in the short term and to decrease it in the medium term.

As argued earlier, the abundance of foreign exchange in the Chilean economy is attributable to a variety of factors, the most important of which has been the previous positive change in the current account (see Table 4.2), starting with a sharp increase in the price of copper since 1987. With respect to the private sector's access to credit, external conditions undoubtedly have become more favorable in recent years, since Chilean borrowers, particularly banks and some large firms, have been able to return to international credit markets. If there was a credit squeeze that operated through channels other than the interest rate, the resumption of voluntary loans to Chilean banks and firms may have helped to ease it. Additionally, all firms, including those that did not have access to the international capital market, have benefited from an effective demand, which, for the first time in two decades, has been located close to the production frontier for five years. This is a strong determinant of the good behavior of investment.

The most important impact of flows apparently has been via FDI. As noted above, a significant share of these investments has gone toward increasing the capacity to produce exportables.

Exchange Rate, Investment in Exportables, and Imports of Capital Goods

It is particularly interesting to study the indirect effect of capital inflows on investment in exportables, especially manufactures, via its influence on the exchange rate. Unfortunately, information disaggregated by sector of economic activity is lacking, as are data on investment in producing exportables. Chile's economic development over the past two decades has been closely linked to the expansion and diversification of exports. Exports of raw materials other than copper and of semimanufactured products associated with them have performed most dynamically. Exports of manufactures as such have also grown fast, but from very low initial levels. The exchange rate is the basic variable that explains the behavior of the supply of exportables (Moguillansky and Titelman, 1993). The only subperiod in which the volume of manufactured exports contracted (while exports of nonmining resource-based products grew much more slowly) was 1979–1983. Interestingly, as already noted, in 1979–1982 a massive exchange-rate appreciation took place, which was associated with the previous episode of heavy inflows of bank loans.

This explains why the authorities have given such high priority to moderating exchange rate appreciation, at least up to early 1994, in spite of its implications for inflation.

In a small, open economy such as that of Chile, appreciation affects not only the allocation of resources between tradable and nontradable sectors, but also the long-term growth rate.[31] The growth of the nontradable sector (like that of import-substituting sectors) is bounded by narrow limits determined by the size of the domestic market. The expansion of exports generally is not subject to these limitations, especially when it is accompanied by a process of diversifying products and markets to which they are exported. Moreover, producers are more likely to reap economies of scale and the benefits of *learning by exporting* than by producing solely for the domestic market.

The exchange rate can also affect investment through its impact on the cost of capital goods, most of which are imported in a small economy like Chile's. This effect and that associated with investment in exportables may be of opposite signs: the more depreciated the real exchange rate, the higher the replacement costs of capital goods, which, in turn, could discourage investment. However, even if an exchange rate depreciation adversely affects investment through the effect on the price of capital goods, it may still increase total investment by leading to a higher growth rate of exports and GDP (income effect of depreciation). What must be determined is the relative importance of the effects.

Assael and Rojas (1993) have examined disaggregated import demand functions, and have found that the cointegration equation for imports of capital goods shows a negative elasticity of 0.24 in relation to the real exchange rate, and a positive elasticity of 1.15 in relation to gross fixed capital formation (which is the scale variable used by the authors). Since a cointegration ratio is obtained, an error-correction model is estimated. In this model, the elasticity with respect to the exchange rate is negative, at 0.32 in the short term. Thus, both calculations show an effect that has the expected sign, but is of a relatively low magnitude.

Solimano (1990) sheds additional light on the determinants of investment with a model of three simultaneous equations for investment, Tobin's *q* (approximated by the real share price index), and real income. The results obtained using this model show that investment is affected by the level of credit to the private sector, but the effect is not very significant in quantitative terms. However, the exchange rate's impact on investment is complex. In the short term, exchange rate appreciation can encourage investment by reducing the cost of replenishing capital goods, thereby giving rise to an expansion of investment that is, however, concentrated in the "wrong" (i.e., nontradable) sectors. In the longer term, the impact of real depreciation tends to be positive because it raises the value of installed capital in the tradable sector, and this effect eventually outweighs that of increased costs of investment insofar as the tradable sector of the economy takes on greater relative importance and investment becomes less intensive on imported capital goods.

As noted previously, the effects of a real depreciation of the exchange rate on exports are significant and positive, although they vary by sector (Moguillansky and Titelman, 1993). This, in turn, has a positive effect on economic growth, which should be reflected in an increase in total investment, and ultimately in larger imports of capital goods. Consequently, a real depreciation by positively affecting exports and import-substituting sectors is likely to have a net positive effect on investment through its effects on aggregate demand, despite the fact that it raises the price of capital goods.

Concluding Remarks

Chile's experience shows that achieving the simultaneous goals of bringing in capital, maintaining some control over exchange rate and monetary policies, and increasing national savings usually calls for a high degree of sterilized intervention and regulation of inflows of short-term capital. The success of this strategy is rooted in macrofinancial factors that are within the competence of the Central Bank and the Ministry of Finance.

The Chilean experience highlights the importance of taking a pragmatic approach to the regulation of capital movements. In general, regulations have been modified with a view to maintaining incentives that attract capital while minimizing the temporary undesirable side effects these inflows may cause on macroeconomic stability and the allocation of resources.

One expression of this pragmatism is a gradual approach that reflects an intention on the part of the economic authorities to identify whether the inflow of external financing constitutes a transitory or permanent external shock. This allows them to minimize the costs and maximize the benefits of receiving such resources. The combination of policy tools used for these purposes has involved regulating speculative short-term movements through reserve requirements, quotas, and fees; intervening in the foreign exchange market through dirty floating, with an enlarged band, around a reference value pegged to a currency basket; and sterilizing the monetary effect of the larger supply of foreign exchange.

It is unlikely that the current abundance of external funds is exclusively attributable to domestic economic policy. This situation is common to countries with different policies. Important external factors are effectively diverting international capital toward Latin America (Calvo, Leiderman, and Reinhart, 1993), and Chile is a major recipient of that capital. The recovery of international economic activity and interest rates may cause significant reversals of capital flows, regardless of Chile's domestic policies.

Most of the foreign capital that has actually flowed into Chile in recent years has consisted of FDI. The first important factor has been the "replenishment" of FDI stocks, whose levels were unusually low in the mid-1980s. But additional flows are related to the favorable conditions the Chilean economy offers to foreign investment, particularly in exportables in which Chile has natural comparative advantages.

Another important component of capital flows in recent years is so-called speculative, or hot, money. Because this concept is difficult to define, alternative definitions were discussed in this study. The definition chosen is closely related to movements of short-term private capital. Under "normal" circumstances, these flows are strongly influenced by the differential between domestic and international interest rates, corrected by expectations of devaluation.

Basically, two structural changes explain the evolution observed in short-term capital flows since 1987. The first is the debt problem, which was at its worst between 1982 and mid-1987. In mid-1987, copper prices rose sharply, and also Chile was able to reach an agreement with foreign bank creditors to reschedule its debt. In addition, the pressure of external debt was being lessened by the debt-equity swap program. The second structural change concerns the exchange rate measures adopted to discourage international arbitrage of interest rates, in particular the introduction of reserve requirements for short-term external credits and the increased uncertainty about the price of the dollar owing to the widening of its flotation band, along with the initiation of a dirty-float regime, and the use of a currency basket to determine the midpoint of the band. These policies, adopted in 1991, have markedly reduced short-term capital flows, which had been stimulated by the maintenance of domestic interest rates that were much higher than international ones.

Thus, far from exemplifying liberalization with perfect mobility of capital, a fixed exchange rate, and lack of control over aggregate demand, Chile's case has involved a flexible pragmatic intervention to regulate the inflow of capital and to act in money and foreign exchange markets as a means of managing domestic liquidity and regulating aggregate expenditure.

The Central Bank and the Ministry of Finance have acted in concert to implement this strategy. Their role has consisted of using the domestic capital market—deepened as a result of the pension system reform—as an area in which to sterilize the monetary effects of the accumulation of reserves so as to avert an unwanted appreciation of the real exchange rate. This approach, in turn, has required savings on the part of the public sector and, ultimately, a disciplined fiscal policy in which positive shocks to the prices of state-owned copper exports are duly saved for use during periods of negative shocks.

The differences between the first period of large capital inflows (1978–1981) and the period 1987–1992 have been studied. The main difference is that during the first period monetary policy was essentially passive and allowed the flows to be monetized and the exchange rate to appreciate strongly, whereas in the second the monetary authorities have effectively sterilized a good proportion of the capital inflow and implemented effective policies to moderate revaluatory pressures. This has caused interest rates to rise higher than they would have in the absence of sterilization, and has required the use of the above-mentioned exchange-rate measures and cost restrictions to forestall an even larger flow of speculative capital. In compensation, this contributes to a more sustainable macroeconomic balance and to sounder productive development linked to the dynamism of exports.

The capital account has increased a great deal, whereas total investment has shown more modest growth. This may reflect two complementary phenomena: (1) despite the increase in the investment coefficient of the economy as a whole, in tradable sectors not associated with natural resources, which have not received FDI, it remains weak; and (2) a significant but difficult-to-quantify proportion of foreign funding has been used to invest abroad or to finance the purchase of existing assets (such as the case for investment funds and secondary ADRs). It is evident that it is FDI, directly associated loans, and multilateral sources that comprise the bulk of the foreign supplement in domestic capital formation.

Even though there are no systematic figures on the sectoral distribution of investment between tradables and nontradables, available empirical research for several countries (see ECLAC, 1995, chapter 4) shows that the exchange rate is a crucial variable for maintaining the dynamism of exports, particularly with respect to nontraditional products. Chile's economic growth is increasingly rooted in the steady expansion of the supply of exportables, which has risen considerably as a share of GDP. As a result of this structural change, exchange-rate depreciation has an increasingly positive effect on investment. This is partly due to the fact that the capital stock in exportables has grown, so that depreciation raises the value of the economy's installed capital (an effect discussed by Solimano, 1990).

Moreover, the larger the exportable sector, the greater the positive impact of a real depreciation on investment. As the export sector grows, the increases in investment caused by the effect of depreciation on relative prices of tradables become greater than the decreases in investment in nontradable sectors. In turn, the multiplier effect of export growth on the economy as a whole could be exerting a positive *income* effect, even on nontradable and import-substituting sectors.

These considerations explain the authorities' effort to contain the real appreciation of the peso in response to foreign private capital inflows in recent years. For Chilean development it is especially important to avoid additional real exchange rate appreciations in the near future.

One of the reasons so much emphasis has been placed on stabilizing the exchange rate is that the authorities have few alternative tools. The trade liberalization undertaken by Chile nearly twenty years ago, and the country's uncritical adherence to neutral incentive policies, made it difficult to design fiscal or financial measures to support the process of diversifying and expanding Chile's supply of exportables. The exchange rate has fluctuated and appreciated, despite the efforts of the monetary authorities, with greater intensity than what appeared to be their preference. This outcome can be attributed to two policy-induced features (1) the growing leakages of the reserve requirements on capital inflows, the larger leakage being that posed by the secondary ADRs; and (2) the gradual erosion of the boundaries between the formal and informal foreign exchange markets. More pragmatic policies could make the exchange rate follow closer the fundamentals rather than short-run outliers, thus contributing better to the development of the Chilean economy.

Notes

The authors are grateful for the comments of Guillermo Calvo, Vittorio Corbo, Rodrigo Vergara, and Joaquín Vial, and for the valuable contributions of Alvaro Calderón and Daniel Titelman.

1. The real exchange rate is defined as the nominal price of the dollar multiplied by the quotient between the relevant external and domestic inflation rates. The latter is measured by the consumer price index (CPI). External inflation is calculated using the wholesale price index (WPI), expressed in U.S. dollars, of Chile's principal trading partners, weighted by their relative importance in Chile's trade (excluding petroleum and copper). See Feliú (1992).

2. The Central Bank published new national accounts in 1994 (based on the year 1986); these present investment ratios that have fluctuations similar to those in the accounts of base year 1977 but with considerably higher levels than in the previous series (see Table 4.8). In this chapter we shall be working with the earlier national accounts.

3. Effective FDI includes net capital inflows under Decree Law (DL) 600 and Chapter XIV of the Central Bank's *Compendio de Normas de Cambios Internacionales* (CNCI). To these can be added the net credits associated with DL 600. Here, external debt capitalization and debt-equity swaps under Chapter XIX of the CNCI are classified separately (see Table 4.1).

4. For an analysis of the management and impact of capital inflows in 1978–1982, see Ffrench-Davis and Arellano (1981), Ffrench-Davis (1985), Hachette and Cabrera (1989), Mizala (1985), Morandé (1988), and Ramos (1988).

5. The depressed international situation caused a drop in prices for the main export products. In the case of copper, for instance, by December 1993 the price had dropped by 25 percent with respect to the average of 1991–1992, the price of pulp had declined by 35 percent, and that of fishmeal by 19 percent. In 1994 there was a notable recovery of export prices.

6. In the balance-of-payments capital account, investments made with external debt notes are recorded as capital inflows. However, they are also registered as special amortizations of debt represented by those notes.

7. This is true if total foreign investment is taken to include (1) net capital inflows under DL 600 and Chapter XIV (effective FDI); (2) credits associated with DL 600; (3) direct capitalization of external credits; and (4) debt-equity swaps.

8. Evaluations of the debt reduction mechanism can be found in Desormeaux (1989), Ffrench-Davis (1990), and Larraín (1988).

9. Their face value reached U.S.$3.2 billion—roughly 15 percent of Chile's external debt at the time the conversion program began. Another mechanism (Chapter XVIII) was more important. See Desormeaux (1989), Ffrench-Davis (1990), and Larraín (1988).

10. Act. No. 18.657, an annex of DL 600, has authorized and regulated the functioning of foreign capital investment funds in Chile since September 1987. The act may be applied to entities organized as FICEs that raise money outside the national territory by placing shares on a foreign stock market (public investment funds), or that bring into the country capital contributed directly by foreign institutional investors (private funds) for the purchase of securities offered publicly in Chile. Originally, funds could be retired only five years after their entry.

11. These firms include Endesa, with 13 percent of the funds' total assets, Compañía de Teléfonos (10 percent), Andina (8 percent), Enersis, and Copec.

12. These funds are in the process of dissolving; they paid a 3 percent commission, which allows investors to retire their contributions through the informal foreign exchange market without having to comply with the waiting period initially set for repatriating capital brought in through debt swaps (twelve years for investment funds). By the end of 1993 only U.S.$30 million of the original investment remained in Chile.

13. However, more recent placings, for instance in July 1994, have been sold with a discount (15 percent in the case of Embotelladora Andina and 10 percent for Chilquinta) with respect to the previous domestic price.

14. Issues of new shares on the Chilean stock market continue to be notably low. In 1992 and 1993 the equivalent of only U.S.$60 million and U.S.$95 million, respectively, were issued and sold on the Santiago stock market.

15. Since voluntary credit dried up, credits were mostly from multilateral financial institutions and medium-term new money from international banks granted to the Central Bank and the Treasury as part of debt restructuring. Unlike other Latin American debtor countries, Chile received significant net transfers from

multilateral creditors, which facilitated the strong structural adjustment of the economy (Damill, Fanelli, and Frenkel, 1992; Ffrench-Davis, 1992).

16. It must be recalled that other borrowers abroad paid the Central Bank an equivalent financial surcharge instead of making a noninterest deposit or reserve requirement.

17. The legal mechanism through which this kind of operation has been carried out is Chapter XII of the CNCI. This legal instrument established that remittances of foreign exchange used for investment abroad had to be carried out exclusively in the formal market and with the authorization of the Central Bank. That clause was changed in April 1991 to allow also the purchase of foreign exchange in the informal market and subsequently informing the Central Bank. In 1991–1992 most of the outflows were channeled by the informal market. However, more recently Chileans preferred the formal market because Chile and Argentina signed an agreement on double taxation that applies solely to investment via the formal market.

18. In March 1992, 60 percent of the shares of Central Puerto was sold to the Chilean firms Chilgener (49.5 percent) and Chilectra Quinta Región (10.5 percent) for U.S.$92 million. In May 1992, 60 percent of Central Térmica Costanera was sold to the consortium formed by the Chilean enterprises Endesa (30 percent and operator of the plant), Enersis (9 percent), Chilectra (3 percent), the Argentinean company Pérez Compac (15 percent), and the U.S. company Public Services of Indiana (3 percent) for U.S.$90 million. In July 1992, 51 percent of the distributor EDESUR was sold for U.S.$511 million to the same consortium that won the bid for Central Térmica Costanera. But because this was another deal altogether, distinct from electricity generation, the largest Chilean shareholders were Enersis and Chilectra, holding 20 percent between them, which together with the 5 percent share of Endesa, brought the Chilean presence to 25 percent.

19. Estimates of the gap between effective demand and the production frontier are found in Ffrench-Davis and Muñoz (1992) and in Marfán (1992).

20. Per capita GDP in 1988 was still 3 percent less than in 1981, and surpassed it by 25 percent in 1993 (Table 4.6, line 1). Investment began to show signs of recovery only in 1987, and did not exceed its 1981 per capita level until 1989; in 1993 it was 45 percent above the 1981 level.

21. A comparative analysis of bands in Chile, Israel, and Mexico is presented in Helpman, Leiderman, and Bufman (1993).

22. By law, the reserve requirement could not be applied to "buyers' advances" or imports for collection, which are not considered credit operations. Deposits in foreign currency in June 1991 were still bound by a 4 percent (demand deposits) and 10 percent (time deposits) reserve requirement, which applied to all deposits. These rates were raised to that of the reserve requirement for external credits in January 1992.

23. For further information on calculation methods, see Central Bank (1992), tables 4 and 5.

24. There has not been much investment by banks in low-risk foreign assets because the rate of return in Chile is higher; the same is true so far in the case of the pension funds. On the other hand, trade credits have indeed moved because the banks were able to take advantage of a high spread. Within a short time, however, situations of insolvency of creditors, involving losses to domestic banks, caused the Central Bank to suspend new operations.

25. By the first semester of 1994 only 2–3 percent of export proceeds made use of the option.

26. Nevertheless, capital inflows increased until 1981, attracted by the gradual currency appreciation and a manifest short-term horizon.

27. It is evident that investors' decisions are affected by exchange rate expectations. However, in view of how difficult it is to measure such expectations, and for purposes of the graph, we have estimated the spread using the actual devaluation observed during that period. The term "ex-post" is used in this sense.

28. The Central Bank estimates that in 1992 it lost 130 billion Chilean pesos because of differences in rates of return between its assets and its liabilities (Central Bank, 1992, p. 51). This is equivalent to U.S.$359 million, or approximately 1 percent of GDP. About half of these losses are attributable to differences in rates of return between foreign-currency reserves and the notes the Bank had to issue to sterilize the monetary effects of accumulating them.

29. See, for example, Arrau and Quiroz (1992) for a study that supports the thesis of overestimation.

30. The public sector remains responsible for the pensions of those already retired as well as a recognition bond to all those affiliated with the old system who joined the new one. Meanwhile, the flow of revenue was transferred from the public sector to private administrators. The fiscal burden of this operation is estimated to rise from an equivalent of 1.2 percent of GDP at the starting date (1981), to a maximum of 4.8 percent of GDP by the early 1990s, and then smoothly decline to 2.4 percent by 2010 (Arrau, 1992).

31. We are referring here to appreciation that is not sustained by factors that affect the level of exchange-rate equilibrium in the long term. It is normal for the exchange rate to appreciate as an economy develops in relation to the rest of the world, because of a systematic improvement in the productivity of factors that tend to be biased in favor of tradables.

References

Agosin, M., R. Fuentes, and L. Letelier (1993), "Los capitales extranjeros en las economías latinoamericanas: El caso de Chile," *Working Paper* 146, IDB, Washington, D.C.

Akyuz, Y. (1993), "Financial liberalization: The key issues," in Y. Akyuz and G. Held (eds.), *Finance and the real economy: Issues and case studies in developing countries*, ECLAC/UNCTAD/UNU/WIDER, Santiago.

Arrau, P. (1992), "El nuevo régimen previsional chileno," Seminario Internacional de Reformas al Régimen Previsional, Bogotá, May 20–21.

Arrau, P., and J. Quiroz (1992), "Ahorro fiscal y tipo de cambio real," *Cuadernos de Economía*, no. 88, Santiago, December.

Assael, P., and P. Rojas (1993), *Un análisis econométrico de la demanda por importaciones desagregadas en Chile: 1960–1992*, Banco Central de Chile, September, unpublished.

Bianchi, A. (1992), "Overabundance of foreign exchange, inflation and exchange rate policy: The Chilean experience," in C. Bradford (comp.), *Mobilising international investment for Latin America*, OECD, Paris, November.

Budnevich, C., and R. Cifuentes (1993), "Manejo macroeconómico de los flujos de capitales de corto plazo: La experiencia de Chile," *Colección Estudios CIEPLAN*, no. 38, Santiago, December.

Calvo, G., L. Leiderman, and C. Reinhart (1993), "Capital inflows and real exchange rate appreciation in Latin America: The role of external factors," *Staff Papers*, vol. 40, no. 1, IMF, Washington, D.C., March.

Central Bank of Chile (1992), *Evolución de la economía en 1992 y perspectivas para 1993*, Santiago, September.

——— (1993), *Evolución de la economía en 1993 y perspectivas para 1994*, Santiago, September.

——— (1994), "Series trimestrates del origen y gasto del PIB: 1986–94," *Boletín Mensual,* no. 798, August.

Corbo, V., J. De Melo, and J. Tybout (1985), "What went wrong with the recent reforms in the Southern Cone," *Discussion Paper*, The World Bank, Washington, D.C., July.

Damill, M., J. M. Fanelli, and R. Frenkel (1992), "Shock externo y desequilibrio fiscal. La macroeconomía de América Latina en los ochenta, Chile," ECLAC, Santiago, August.

Departamento de Economía, Universidad de Chile (1993), *Comentarios sobre la situación económica*, Santiago, December.

Desormeaux, J. (1989), "La inversión extranjera y su rol en el desarrollo de Chile," *Documento de trabajo*, no. 119, Universidad Católica de Chile, Santiago, July.

ECLAC (1994), *Economic survey of Latin America and the Caribbean 1992: Chile*, United Nations, Santiago, January.

——— (1995), *Policies to improve linkages with the global economy*, United Nations, Santiago.

Feliú, C. (1992), "Inflación externa y tipo de cambio real: Nota metodológica," *Serie de Estudios Económicos*, no. 37, Banco Central de Chile, Santiago.

Ffrench-Davis, R. (1982), "External debt and balance of payments in Latin America: Recent trends and outlook," in *Economic and social progress in Latin America. 1982 report*, IDB, Washington, D.C.

——— (1985), "The external debt, financial liberalization and crisis in Chile," in M. Wionczek (ed.), *Politics and economics of external debt crisis*, Westview Press, Boulder, Colorado.

——— (1990), "Debt-equity swaps in Chile," *Cambridge Journal of Economics*, vol. 14, no. 1, March.

——— (1992), "Adjustment and conditionality in Chile, 1982–88," in E. Rodríguez and S. Griffith-Jones (eds.), *Cross-conditionality, banking regulations and Third World debt*, MacMillan, London.

Ffrench-Davis, R., and J. P. Arellano (1981), "Apertura financiera externa: La experiencia chilena en 1973–80," *Colección Estudios CIEPLAN*, no. 5, Center for Economic Research on Latin America (CIEPLAN), Santiago, July.

Ffrench-Davis, R., P. Leiva, and R. Madrid (1992), "Trade liberalization in Chile: Experiences and Prospects," *Trade Policy Series*, no. 1, UNCTAD, United Nations, New York.

Ffrench-Davis, R., and O. Muñoz (1992), "Economic and political instability in Chile: 1950–89," in S. Teitel (ed.), *Towards a new development strategy for Latin America*, IDB/Johns Hopkins University Press, Baltimore.

Fischer, B., and H. Reisen (1992), "Towards capital account convertibility," *Policy Brief*, no. 4, Development Centre, OECD, Paris.

Fontaine, J. A. (1988), "Los mecanismos de conversión de deuda en Chile," *Estudios Públicos*, no. 30, Centre for Public Studies (CEP), Santiago.

Hachette, D., and A. Cabrera (1989), "The capital account liberalization in Chile, 1974–82," *Documento de Trabajo*, no. 120, Pontificia Universidad Católica de Chile, Santiago.

Hanson, J. (1992), "Opening the capital account. A survey of issues and results," *Policy Research Working Papers*, no. 901, World Bank, Washington, D.C., May.

Held, G. (1993), "Bank regulation, liberalization and financial instability in Latin American and Caribbean countries," in Y. Akyüz and G. Held (eds.), *Finance and the real economy: Issues and case studies in developing countries*, ECLAC/UNU-WIDER/UNCTAD, Santiago, September.

Helpman, E., L. Leiderman, and G. Bufman (1993), "A new breed of exchange rate bands: Chile, Israel and Mexico," mimeo, Tel Aviv University, Tel Aviv, September.

Iglesias, A., and R. Acuña (1991), *Sistema de pensiones en América Latina. Chile: Experiencia con un régimen de capitalización 1981–1991*, S.R.V. Impresos, Santiago.

Labán, R., and F. Larraín (1993), "Can a liberalization of capital outflows increase net capital inflows?" *Documento de Trabajo,* no. 155, Pontificia Universidad Católica de Chile, Santiago.

Larraín, F. (1988), "Debt-reduction schemes and the management of Chilean debt," World Bank, Washington, D.C., December.

Marfán, M. (1992), "Reestimación del PGB potencial en Chile: Implicancias para el crecimiento," *Cuadernos de economía*, no. 87, Santiago, August.

Mizala, A. (1985), "Segmentación del mercado de capitales y liberalización financiera," *Notas técnicas*, no. 69, CIEPLAN, Santiago, March.

———— (1992), "Las reformas económicas de los años setenta y la industria manufacturera chilena," *Colección Estudios CIEPLAN*, no. 35, special edition, CIEPLAN, Santiago, September.

Moguillansky, G., and D. Titelman (1993), "Estimación econométrica de funciones de exportación en Chile," *Estudios de economía*, vol. 20, no. 1, Santiago.

Morandé, F. (1988), "Apreciación del peso y entrada de capitales externos: ¿cuál viene antes? Chile, 1977–82," in F. Morandé and K. Schmidt-Hebbel (eds.), *Del auge a la crisis de 1982: Ensayos sobre liberalización financiera y endeudamiento en Chile*, ILADES, Santiago.

Ramos, J. (1988), "Auge y caída de los mercados de capitales en Chile: 1975–1983," in F. Morandé and K. Schmidt-Hebbel (eds.), *Del auge a la crisis de 1982: Ensayos sobre liberalización financiera y endeudamiento en Chile*, ILADES, Santiago.

Reisen, H. (1993a), "The impossible trinity in South East Asia," *International Economic Insights*, Institute for International Economics, Washington, D.C.

———— (1993b), "Capital flows and their effect on the monetary base," *CEPAL Review*, no. 51, December.

Repetto, A. (1992), "Políticas macroeconómicas y tipo de cambio real en Chile, 1980–91," CIEPLAN, Santiago, December, unpublished.

Romaguera, P. (1991), "Las fluctuaciones del precio del cobre y su impacto en la economía chilena," *Notas técnicas*, no. 143, CIEPLAN, Santiago, October.

Solimano, A. (1990), "Inversión privada y ajuste macroeconómico: La experiencia chilena en la década del 80," *Colección Estudios CIEPLAN*, no. 28, CIEPLAN, Santiago, June.

Uthoff, A. (1992), "Estabilización y precios relativos, el desafío de reducir la inflación a un dígito," Joint ECLAC/UNDP regional project, *Finance policies for development*, Santiago.

Valdés, S. (1993), "Ajuste estructural en el mercado de capitales: La evidencia chilena," in D. Wisecarver (ed.), *El modelo económico chileno*, Universidad Católica de Chile/International Center for Economic Growth, Santiago.

Williamson, J. (1992), "Acerca de la liberalización de la cuenta de capitales," *Estudios de Economía*, vol. 19, no. 2, Department of Economics, University of Chile, Santiago, December.

World Bank (1993), *A decade after the debt crisis*, World Bank, Latin America and the Caribbean Regional Office, Washington, D.C., September.

Zahler, R. (1992), "Monetary policy and an open capital account," *CEPAL Review*, no. 48, Santiago, December.

5

Capital Movements in Argentina

José María Fanelli & José Luis Machinea

Exogenous factors seem to play a determinant role regarding capital movements in Latin America. The most important among these factors are the evolution of international interest rates, changes in financial regulations and forms of operations in foreign capital markets, and the level of the current U.S. account deficit (see Chapters 1 and 7; Calvo, Leiderman, and Reinhart, 1993; Damill et al., 1993). Even though the recently achieved greater degree of macroeconomic stability and the implementation of market-friendly policies in many countries of the region can be considered important factors influencing the availability of external financing, their contribution to fostering capital inflows seems to be much less relevant. They do not seem to be able to account for the striking change in the direction and the quantity of capital inflows in recent years. To support this argument, the experiences of Chile and Brazil are often cited. Chile has succeeded in stabilizing its economy and has consistently implemented profound structural reforms since the mid-1970s; it nevertheless did not receive a significant amount of private capital inflows during the 1980s.[1] On the other hand, there has recently been a marked increase in capital inflows in Brazil, a country that has neither stabilized its economy nor succeeded in implementing market-oriented structural reforms.

This chapter analyzes capital movements in Argentina; consequently, international factors will be considered exogenous. But even if everything could be explained by external factors alone—which we believe is not the case—we would still have a task ahead of us. This task is to identify and analyze the effects of a sudden and exogenous change in the amount and characteristics of capital inflows on macrostability and in the financial and real structures of the domestic economy.

Indeed, the analysis of these effects would be important even if capital inflows were endogenously induced by domestic reforms. If there is a specific kind of reform (and not others) capable of ensuring a significant amount of capital inflows, a valid question asks whether such a reform can also ensure stability and sustainable growth. For instance, if financial liberalization were a sine qua non condition, would a free financial regime coupled with massive capital inflows be compatible with the level of the real exchange rate and the interest rate needed for assuring growth?

The analysis of past experiences in financial and capital account liberalizations is a valuable source for the identification of stylized facts regarding the interactions between capital movements and internal equilibria. This is specially true in the case of Argentina. Between 1979 and 1981 there was an integral attempt at liberalizing the financial structure that presented some similarities with the policies that are now being implemented. That policy package had profound consequences on short-run stability and induced long-lasting effects on savings, investment, and financial intermediation.

Financial and Exchange Rate Policies in the 1970s and 1980s

The first program to open the capital and current accounts in the context of a liberalized domestic financial market was implemented in December 1978. The experience ended in a complete failure in the first quarter of 1981 when there was a speculative attack against the peso fed by capital flight. The collapse of the program was followed by several maxidevaluations and the complete reversal of the reforms: imports and external financial transactions were put under tight control.

The Architecture of the Liberalization Program

The liberalization program reduced the restrictions on capital movements to a minimum,[2] some—but not all—quantitative restrictions on imports were eliminated, and import tariffs were markedly cut.[3] In order to ensure macrostability during the liberalization process, a stabilization plan was launched in December 1978. The program was based on a modified version of the monetary approach to the balance of payments and its core was the preannouncement of the future nominal exchange rate.[4] It was assumed that, in a context of increasing integration with foreign markets and with the future value of the nominal exchange rate fixed, purchasing-power parity would ensure an increasing convergence between domestic and international inflation rates. When the preannounced devaluation rate reached zero, the domestic inflation rate would equal the international one.

On the monetary side, it was expected that the liberalization of capital flows would render the money supply endogenous and deprive the Central Bank of an independent monetary policy, which could introduce a wedge between domestic and international interest rates.[5] To preserve international reserves, the rate of expansion of domestic credit was set in accordance to the preannounced devaluation rate. The policy regarding secondary expansion within the banking system, however, was not as tight as the one related to the expansion of the monetary base. The minimum reserve requirements on bank deposits were significantly reduced.[6] The purpose was to induce an expansion of the credit supply that would favor the private sector because the "repression" on the financial system had been eliminated by the financial reform, which had been implemented in 1977, before the opening of the capital account. Under the new regime, allocation of credit and interest rates were both determined by the market.[7]

The Evolution of the Economy
Under the Liberalization Program

Immediately after the liberalization of the capital account and the preannouncement of the devaluation rate, there was a substantial increase in private capital inflow (Table 5.1).

Table 5.1   Selected Indicators of the 1978–1981 Program

Period	Autonomous Capital Flows (millions of U.S.$)			Risk Premium (annual %)	Real Exchange Rate[a]	Credit (in real terms)[b]
	Total	Private	Public			
Total 1978	1,366	–83	1,449		100.0	100.0
First quarter 1979	1,029	866	163	1.1	76.8	100.0
Second quarter 1979	1,033	773	260	1.2	73.1	108.8
Third quarter 1979	1,335	973	362	2.7	66.6	123.3
Fourth quarter 1979	1,517	1,027	491	2.5	64.2	159.3
Total 1979	4,915	3,639	1,276			
First quarter 1980	1,126	398	728	1.8	61.3	183.8
Second quarter 1980	–793	–1,439	646	2.2	57.4	193.8
Third quarter 1980	1,455	1,103	352	3.6	53.6	224.0
Fourth quarter 1980	465	–805	1,270	3.1	48.6	244.0
Total 1980	2,253	–743	2,997			
First quarter 1981	–1,236	–3,797	2,561	4.2	48.7	231.6

Source: Elaborated on the basis of Central Bank data.
Notes: [a]Deflated by the consumer price index.
[b]Nominal domestic credit deflated by the wholesale price index.

The upward trend of private capital inflows, however, reverted later on. After reaching a maximum in the last quarter of 1979, private flows became negative for the first time under the program in the second quarter of 1980. In the first quarter of 1981, the outward flow of private funds reached the unprecedented amount of U.S.$3.8 billion. As a consequence, there was a rapid depletion of Central Bank reserves, which ultimately led to the collapse of the program. The lack of international reserves obliged the authorities to abandon the preannouncment of the future nominal exchange rates.

The public sector's behavior followed a "countercyclical" pattern. In the period in which the inward flow of private funds was high, the demand for external credit by the public sector stagnated, but when private capital outflows began to increase, the authorities tried to compensate private outflows by raising their foreign credit demand (Table 5.1). In a context of mounting uncertainty, the liberalization of the capital account resulted in higher public indebtedness and capital flight.

The credibility in the authorities' capacity for maintaining the anticipated devaluation rate played a key role in determining the direction of private capital movements. At the beginning of the program, credibility was strong because the Central Bank held a significant amount of international reserves and the economy had been showing substantial current account surpluses in the previous years. In such a context, the preannouncement of the devaluation rate acted like a free exchange-rate insurance for the private sector and, consequently, this sector was able to reap the benefits resulting from the difference between domestic and international interest rates without incurring in additional costs in terms of risk bearing. As time elapsed, however, credibility in the announced exchange rate eroded, giving way to a growing level of uncertainty, in spite of the tablita. The mounting level of uncertainty was reflected in a continuous increase in the country risk premium, as seen in Table 5.1.[8] Two main factors, endogenously generated by the program, were behind the gradual increment of uncertainty: (1) the widening of the current account disequilibrium and (2) the "credit cycle" triggered by both capital inflows and domestic financial liberalization.

The increase in the current account disequilibrium was caused by a booming demand for imports. Imports in 1980 were 2.7 times higher than in 1978, and hence the trade account showed a surplus of U.S.$2.6 billion in 1978 and a deficit of U.S.$2.5 billion in 1980. The primary causes of this spurt in imports were the rapid liberalization of external trade and the appreciation of the domestic currency provoked by the fact that the internal inflation rate was systematically greater than the sum of the international inflation rate and the devaluation rate. Table 5.1 shows that the program induced a remarkable distortion in the structure of relative prices of the economy.

The sharp and sudden increase in capital inflows that followed the deregulation of foreign exchange and financial markets, in a context of weak supervision of the financial institutions by Central Bank authorities, gave way to a marked expansion of credit. The monetary authorities not only acted passively by failing to sterilize the increased flows but also made the monetary impulse stronger by reducing the reserve requirement ratio. Real interest rates actually became negative at the beginning of the program.

The easy-credit phase, nonetheless, tended to exhaust rapidly. First, real interest rates began to show an upward trend at the end of 1979 pari passu with the weakening of the credibility in the preannounced exchange rate. Second, given the high speed of credit expansion and the private banks' lack of experience in a free system, the quality of the banks' balance sheets worsened. A good part of the new credit supply was allocated to the acquisition of real estate and to speculative stocks of goods. Third, the weakness of the Central Bank's supervision allowed a disproportionate expansion of the "groups" related to some domestic banks. Fourth, the level of financial fragility of the system was accentuated by shrinking profits in those sectors competing with imports and by the incipient recession.

Even though the financial reform increased the economy's monetization level, it was unable to extend the maturity term of domestic deposits. Almost all of the existing term deposits showed a maturity of less than one month. This facilitated the rapid reallocation of the private sector's portfolio. When credibility weakened, U.S. dollars were increasingly substituted for pesos. The counterpart of the higher demand for foreign exchange was the reduction in domestic bank deposits. To maintain the equilibrium between their assets and liabilities, the banks should have reduced the existing stock of credit pari passu with the decline in deposits. Private firms, however, were unable to cancel their existing bank loans as quickly as the decline in bank deposits.

In such a context, monetary policy proved to be completely ineffective. When international reserves began to fall, the authorities tried to use monetary restraint—mainly via an increase in reserve requirements—to stop the depletion of international reserves,[9] but this accentuated the lack of liquidity that capital outflows were producing and further aggravated the weak situation of commercial banks. To avoid a deepening of the financial crisis, the Central Bank had to act as "lender of last resort," and the money supply began to be endogenously determined by the financial crisis.

In Argentina, the financial crisis of 1980–1981 anticipated the "debt crisis" that the countries of the region would experience beginning in 1982. Indeed, for Argentina, the debt crisis meant that the rationing of foreign credit, which the private sector had begun to face as a consequence of the domestic financial crash in 1980–1981, would be extended to the public sector as well. And when this happened, the government was unable to continue increasing public foreign debt in order to sustain the fiction of an "open" capital account. In 1982 the authorities were obliged to "close" the economy again in order not to run out of international reserves.[10]

Some Lessons from the Liberalization Experience

There are relevant lessons that can be extracted from this liberalization experience. First, private capital flows show a high degree of volatility. This volatility seems to be greater in periods of deregulation of the capital account. The negative effects of volatility on domestic markets can barely be offset by resorting to the available short-run macroeconomic tools. Even though there is a positive correlation between capital inflows and internal monetization, this does not necessarily mean that there will be a lengthening in the maturity of domestic deposits.

Second, capital movements have important macroeconomic effects. The transmission mechanisms are domestic currency appreciation and the triggering of internal credit cycles. This tends to generate unsustainable disequilibria in the current account and to increase domestic financial fragility.

Third, the magnitude of the inward flow of capital tends to be excessive compared to the size of the national capital market. The domestic financial system is usually unable to efficiently intermediate a sudden and high increase in the supply of loanable funds, and it cannot smooth out the volatility of such funds either. These facts are aggravated if the Central Bank's authorities act passively regarding both the sterilization of capital inflows and the supervision of private banks' balance sheets.

Fourth, when there exists a severe deterioration in the financial system's position that seriously threatens the payment and credit systems, the government is forced to act in a compensatory way. The authorities are de facto obliged to act as lender of last resort through the Central Bank in order to preserve stability. If this fact is internalized by the private sector, it may give rise to the existence of a "moral hazard" problem. The private sector behaves as if there were an implicit and free private deposit and/or exchange rate insurance.

Last, the schemes based on a fixed or preannounced nominal exchange rate when inflation is still uncurbed can "buy" some credibility in the short run but at the cost of increasing uncertainty in the medium run. Regarding this, it is worthwhile to mention that the current Chilean policy of augmenting the short-run exchange rate uncertainty while ensuring a stable level for the long-run real exchange rate seems to be a wiser choice. This may greatly help discourage short-run speculative capital inflows and provide firm incentives for real investment in the tradables sector.[11]

Capital Movements During the "Debt Crisis" of the 1980s

The behavior of capital flows during the 1980s showed noticeable differences with the period just analyzed and with the current situation as well. Beyond the "endogenously" generated crisis that the Argentine economy was undergoing in 1982, capital movements were strongly determined by two exogenous changes that occurred in the international setting in the early 1980s: the marked increase in interest rates and the increasing rationing in foreign credit markets.

The impact of the negative shock was first felt in the external sector because the country was obliged to generate unsustainable trade surpluses to compensate for the increased deficit in the financial services account. However, this shock readily propagated to the whole economy. The effect was of unprecedented magnitude, not only because of the size of the external shock but also because of the occurrence of the shock in the context of the macroeconomic, fiscal, and financial crisis produced by the collapse of the liberalization model. In spite of adjustment efforts, the Argentine economy could reach an acceptable degree of stability only after foreign credit rationing was relaxed in the present decade.

A few figures will show the magnitude of the external gap during the 1980s. In the 1982–1990 period, Argentina generated an accumulated trade surplus of U.S.$34 billion (Table 5.2). That is, the country effected an external transfer equivalent to 3.5 percent of each year's GDP. The reduction in the domestic absorption associated with such trade surpluses, however, was not enough to compensate for the increment in the services on the foreign debt. Between 1982 and 1990, Argentina accumulated a current account deficit that amounted to U.S.$16 billion. Contrasting with the liberalization period, there were continuous current account deficits in spite of the substantial generation of trade account surpluses induced by the successive adjustment efforts.

During this period, the net result of autonomous capital movements was negative.[12] As a consequence, the deficit in the capital account added U.S.$5 billion[13] to the borrowing requirements originating in the current account deficit, as can be seen in Table 5.2.

The net result of the autonomous capital account, however, conceals different patterns of behavior of the private vis-à-vis the public sector. Table 5.3 shows that the account corresponding to the private sector registered a net capital outflow of U.S.$12 billion. All the items that correspond to the private sector are systematically negative, with the exception of that corresponding to foreign direct investment. The public sector's account, on the contrary, records a surplus of U.S.$7 billion. To a certain extent, this behavior of the public and the private sectors reproduces the pattern observed during the collapse of the liberalization attempt. The net

outflow of private funds is partially offset by the inflow of public external credit. The task of closing the external gap was faced exclusively by
the government.

However, given the existence of credit rationing, the authorities were
unable to raise the funds needed to close the external gap by resorting only
to voluntary sources of finance in the international markets. Consequently,
"compensatory" finance played a key role in financing the disequilibrium
in the current account. A good part of the "compensatory" funds. however,
consisted of payments of services on the foreign debt that were in arrears.

Table 5.2   Sources and Destination of Foreign Funds, 1977–1993
(millions of U.S.$)

Period	Trade Account Surplus (1)	Current Account Deficit (2)	Changes in Foreign Reserves (3)	(3) + (2) = (4) + (5)	Compensatory Capital Movements (4)	Autonomous Capital Movements (5)
1977	1,488	−1,290	2,226	936	−253	1,189
1978	2,566	−1,833	1,998	165	−1,201	1,366
1979	1,100	537	4,442	4,979	65	4,915
1980	−2,529	4,768	−2,796	1,972	−281	2,253
1981	−287	4,714	−3,521	1,193	38	1,155
1982	2,287	2,358	−715	1,643	5,451	−3,808
1983	3,331	2,461	1,684	4,145	4,256	−111
1984	3,983	2,391	99	2,490	1,843	647
1985	4,582	953	2,017	2,970	2,573	397
1986	2,128	2,859	−514	2,345	1,561	784
1987	540	4,238	−1,274	2,964	2,826	138
1988	3,810	1,572	1,961	3,533	3,342	191
1989	5,374	1,292	−1,559	−267	5,326	−5,593
					1,937[a]	−2,204[a]
1990	8,275	−1,789	2,751	962	2,072	−1,110
1991	3,703	2,803	1,880	4,683	6,566	−1,883
					1,109[b]	3,574[b]
1992	−2,637	8,311	4,337	12,648	1,185	11,463
					1,293[c]	11,355[c]
1993[d]	−3,696	8,300	3,808	12,108	−3,151	15,259
Total, 1982–1990	34,310	16,335	4,450	20,785	25,861	−5,076
Total, 1991–1993	−2,630	19,414	10,025	29,439	4,600	24,839

Source: Elaborated on the basis of Central Bank data.

Notes: [a]Net of operations of consolidation of public debt. Under the Bonex Plan, a proportion
of the domestic financial assets held by the private sector was converted into foreign assets
(Bonex) issued by the government. The difference between this figure and the one above it in the
table is the outward flow of funds associated with the issue of Bonex (U.S.$3,389 million).

[b]Net of operations of consolidation of public debt. The difference between this figure and the
one above it is the issue of government bonds (U.S.$5,457 million).

[c]Net of operations of consolidation of public debt. The difference between this figure and the
one above it in the table is the outstanding debt amortized by the Treasury (U.S.$108 million).

[d]Estimated.

This kind of financing should be considered "forced" rather than "compensatory." The continuous outflow of private capital and the systematic use of compensatory finance proved to have marked consequences on macrostability and on the financial structure.

Throughout this period there was a direct relationship between the availability of compensatory finance and the real exchange rate: the lower the supply of foreign financing, the greater the trade surplus needed to close the external gap, and hence, the higher the "equilibrium" real exchange rate. Given that the correction of the real exchange rate level meant an upward shift of the nominal exchange rate that tended to fuel inflation, the uncertainty regarding the equilibrium real exchange rate affected not only the expected devaluation rate but also the expected rates of both inflation and nominal interests.

The existence of a permanent deficit in the private capital account, together with a high rate of inflation, on the other hand, induced a systematic tendency for the domestic financial system to become smaller. The use of the U.S. dollar as a means to denominate contracts was generalized during this period. In this sense, "dollarization" and demonetization are alternative names for the same phenomenon.

In addition to exchange rate uncertainty and financial deintermediation, a third factor generating instability was the public sector's marked financial fragility. The financial deterioration of the public sector had one of its important roots in the debt crisis, which, in turn, gave rise to the appearance of the "domestic transfer" problem (Fanelli, Frenkel, and Taylor, 1992). The inability of the public sector to resolve this problem implied that throughout the decade there would be substantial government deficits in spite of the strong reduction in government expenditures (especially in public investment).

The persistence of the disequilibria in the balance of payments and in the government budget determined the failure of the successive stabilization packages that were to be launched during the decade. In the late 1980s, when political uncertainty originating in the change of administration added to the existing economic uncertainty, the country experienced two short periods of hyperinflation. Indeed, macroeconomic instability was dramatically reduced only in the present decade after the implementation of the so-called Convertibility Plan in April 1991, when a new and sharp change in the international setting made the stabilization package viable.

Capital Flows in the 1990s

The dynamics of capital movements greatly changed in the 1990s because of the changes on the international and domestic fronts. Regarding the

Table 5.3   Autonomous Capital Movements, 1977–1993 (millions of U.S.$)

Period	Autonomous Capital (1)=(2)+(7)	Private (2)=(3)+(4)+(5)+(6)	Privatization and FDI (3)	Bonds and Loans (4)	Trade Credit (5)	Other (6)	Public[a] (7)=(8)+(9)	Bonds and Loans (8)	Loans to Public Enterprises (9)
1977	1,189	216	52	393	−81	−149	973	5	968
1978	1,366	−83	295	514	−398	−494	1,449	624	825
1979	4,915	3,639	235	3,543	772	−912	1,276	585	691
1980	2,253	−743	739	3,886	−86	−5,283	2,997	1,016	1,981
1981	1,155	−3,469	927	3,112	−3,386	−4,122	4,624	2,695	1,929
1982	−3,808	−4,017	257	−521	−2,720	−1,032	209	481	−272
1983	−111	−2,514	183	−1,831	−411	−456	2,403	2,249	154
1984	647	−1,558	269	−2,674	500	347	2,205	2,210	−5
1985	397	−894	919	−1,733	−812	732	1,291	1,098	193
1986	784	420	574	−459	−539	844	364	318	46
1987	138	−695	−19	−24	−492	−160	833	421	412
1988	191	393	1,147	−228	−693	167	−202	−305	103
1989	−5,593	−5,242	1,028	111	−2,228	−4,153	−351	−391	40
	−2,204[b]	−1,853	1,028	111	−2,228	−764	−351	−391	40
1990	−1,110	−1,361	1,141	92	451	−3,045	251	255	−4
1991	−1,883	−2,636	2,439	345	1,758	−7,178	753	647	105
	3,574[c]	2,821	2,439	345	1,758	−1,721	753	647	105
1992	11,463	11,620	2,283	611	3,190	5,536	−157	55	−212
	11,355[d]	11,512	2,283	611	3,190	5,428	−157	55	−212
1993	15,259	11,707	3,164	3,318	386	4,839	3,522	3,567	−15

(continues)

Table 5.3   continued

Period	Autonomous Capital (1)=(2)+(7)	Private (2)=(3)+(4)+(5)+(6)	Privatization and FDI (3)	Bonds and Loans (4)	Trade Credit (5)	Other (6)	Public^a (7)=(8)+(9)	Bonds and Loans (8)	Loans to Public Enterprises (9)
Total 1982–1990	−5,076	−12,079	5,499	−7,267	−6,944	−3,367	7,003	6,336	667
	−1,687^e	−8,690	5,499	−7,267	−6,944	22	7,003	6,336	667
Total 1991–1993	24,839	20,691	7,886	4,274	5,334	3,197	4,148	4,269	−122
	30,188^e	26,040	7,886	4,274	5,334	7,546	4,148	4,269	−122

Source: Elaborated on the basis of Central Bank data.

Notes: ^{a}Includes the use of the "trade credit facility."

^{b}Net of operations of consolidation of public debt. In 1989, under the Bonex Plan, a proportion of the domestic financial assets held by the private sector was converted into foreign assets (Bonex) issued by the government. Consistently, column (6) disaggregates in: −4,153 = −764 −3,389; where the latter figure (U.S.$3,389 million) represents the outward flow of funds associated with the issue of Bonex. Consistently, the private capital account net result can be disaggregated as: −5,242 = −1,853 −3,389. When this operation is deducted, the overall result of the autonomous capital account becomes U.S.$−2,204 million.

^{c}Net of the operations of consolidation of public debt. In 1991, there was an operation of consolidation of public debt that affected the figures recorded in the balance of payments. In that year, there was an issue of government bonds for U.S.$5,457 million. When this operation is deducted, the private and autonomous capital accounts show a surplus of U.S.$2,821 million and U.S.$3,574 million, respectively.

^{d}Net of the operations of consolidation of public debt. In 1992, the Treasury amortized U.S.$108 million of its outstanding debt. This amount was recorded under the item "other private capital movements" with a positive sign and under "other compensatory capital movements" with a negative one. If both records are eliminated, the net results of the private capital account falls from U.S.$11,620 million to U.S.$11,512 million, while the surplus corresponding to the autonomous capital account declines from U.S.$11,463 million to U.S.$11,355 million. To preserve accounting consistency, the net result corresponding to compensatory capital must be corrected upward, from U.S.$1,185 million to U.S.$1,293 million. It must be mentioned, on the other hand, that the debt-equity swaps associated to the privatization process have been eliminated. These operations of conversion amounted to U.S.$895 million in 1990 and to U.S.$1,819 million in 1992.

^{e}Figures in this row are not of the operations of consolidation of public debt.

international setting, the most significant changes were, on the one hand, the relaxation of the existing credit rationing, and, on the other, the marked reduction in international interest rates. Both the income and substitution effects induced by the falling interest rates contributed to deactivating the debt crisis. The income effect weakened the external constraint by reducing the deficit in the financial services account. Likewise, two other facts are connected with this effect. First, there was, ceteris paribus, an overall increase in the national income. Second, given that the public sector held more than 90 percent of the outstanding foreign debt, the primary beneficiary of the increase in national income induced by the falling interest rate was the public sector. In this way, the pressure exerted by the "domestic transfer" became much weaker than it had been during the 1980s.

The substitution effect was no less important. The deterioration in the rate of return on financial assets abroad heavily contributed to inducing a reversion in capital flight. Besides, the reduction in the return rate on financial assets per se acted in favor of investment in real assets. Indeed, the higher rate of return perceived on real assets greatly helped Argentina's stabilization and structural reform by enabling a massive process of privatization to take place that could not have been possible without the participation of foreign investors.

On the domestic side, the most relevant facts were the increasing success of the Convertibility Plan from the beginning of 1991 on, and the deepening of the structural reform process oriented toward market deregulation and liberalization put into practice by the new administration, which took office in July 1989.

Internal Factors and Capital Movements: Reforms in the Economic, Institutional, and Legal Frameworks

From the point of view of capital flows, the most influential elements of the structural reform package were the new rules governing monetary policy, the deregulation of both the financial system and the stock exchange market, and the public sector's structural reform.

Among the normative changes that directly influenced capital flows, one of the most relevant was the *Ley de Emergencia Económica* (Economic Emergency Law), instituted in August 1989, which establishes equal treatment for national and foreign capital invested in productive activities. This law eliminated the requisite of previous approval for foreign direct investment (the only exception being investment projects related to defense); it gave foreign firms free access to the domestic credit market; it abolished the tax on the repatriation of foreign capital; and it instituted a common tax rate on profits of foreign and national companies. To eliminate obstacles in the repatriation of flight capital, the *Ley de Olvido Fiscal* (Amnesty Tax Law) was promulgated in April 1992. It established a special regime for individuals declaring their real and/or financial investments abroad or their holding of foreign currency within the country.

The development of a dollarized segment in the domestic financial system (the so-called argendollars) was greatly reinforced by a series of norms dictated by the Central Bank (Comunicación "A" 1493 in July 1989 and "A" 1820 in March 1991). The dollarization of the portfolio was also greatly helped by the liberalization of the foreign exchange market (Comunicación "A" 1589 in December 1989 and "A" 1822 in April 1991) and the establishment of a fixed exchange rate and free convertibility of domestic currency by means of the *Ley de Convertibilidad* (Convertibility Law). Additionally, this law instituted the validity of contracts denominated in any currency. In this way, deregulation of the foreign exchange market was complete. There are now no restrictions on buying and selling foreign currencies. Indeed, the lack of controls is so marked that there are even no reliable records of operations that take place in the foreign exchange market. In such a context, there is practically no cost for entering and exiting the market.

The main objective of the aforementioned measures was to serve as a signal that there would be unrestricted respect for monetary stability and currency convertibility. To stress this fact, in September 1992 a new law regulating the Central Bank's behavior was promulgated (the *Ley de Carta Orgánica del Banco Central*). In addition to instituting the independence of the Central Bank, the law prohibited the monetary financing of the fiscal deficit and established severe limits on both rediscounts and the government's open market operations. This significantly reduced the lender-of-last-resort role of the monetary authorities and its autonomy in managing monetary policy as well. The possibility of establishing a scheme to guarantee domestic bank deposits was also virtually eliminated. Under this new regime, the lack of instruments in the hands of authorities could lead to a situation of serious financial instability if the level of financial fragility of large—or even medium—financial institutions should reach a critical point. Central Bank regulations have improved during 1993, especially in relation to capital requirements of commercial banks. However, as in past experiences, there is still no tight supervision of balance sheets by the Central Bank.

In this new setting of absolute financial deregulation, by the end of 1993 the Central Bank lifted the only significant remaining restriction: the nonauthorization of new entries into the financial system, a policy that had been in effect for more than ten years. The reform also comprises the stock market. In November 1991, the *Decreto de Desregulación* (Deregulation Decree) was issued. This decree suppressed the tax on the transfer of equities, eliminated the "stamp" tax that affected contracts in capital markets, and freed brokerage fees. There were, in addition, modifications in the legal framework, regulating the institution in charge of supervising the transactions in the stock market. To increase the size of the market, the entry of new enterprises was encouraged and new forms of operations were introduced by law (*Ley de Obligaciones Negociables* of July 1991).

The reform of the public sector has had an important effect on capital movements. The *Ley de Reforma del Estado* (Law for the Reform of the State) was especially relevant because it set the bases for the privatization process and for debt-equity swaps.

In addition to the aforementioned measures, which were oriented toward structural reform, the Convertibility Plan greatly helped to stimulate capital inflows to the extent that it succeeded in ensuring a much greater degree of macroeconomic stability, and hence, improved the economic climate perceived by foreign investors.

The explicit objective pursued by the Convertibility Plan was to reduce dramatically the inflation rate and to protect the existing stock of international reserves from a new speculative attack that could put into motion a new hyperinflationary episode. The plan succeeded regarding both objectives. The huge increase in the trade account surplus in the previous year played a crucial role in making this possible.

The program combined strictly "orthodox" measures regarding fiscal and monetary policy (implicit in the Convertibility Plan and in the law regulating the Central Bank's behavior) with "heterodox" ones such as prohibiting the indexation of contracts and freezing public prices and wages.[14] At the same time, several trade barriers were lifted and tariffs were reduced.

At first sight, the program appears to be similar to others implemented during the 1990s that made use of certain key variables (especially the nominal exchange rate) as nominal anchors. The program, however, has shown important differences. First of all the opening up of the economy in the context of an overvalued real exchange rate has exerted a significant downward pressure on the prices of tradable goods. Second, the prohibition of resorting to monetary financing of the fiscal deficit was strictly enforced.[15] Third, the fixing of the nominal exchange rate by law had the expected effect in terms of enhancing the credibility of the exchange rate regime and turned out to be a key element favoring capital inflows. Unlike the Mexican case, in which the exchange rate stability at the beginning of the *Pacto de Solidaridad* was based on the strong reserves position of the Central Bank, the main factor guaranteeing the sustainability of the fixed exchange rate in the Argentine case was the huge surplus in the trade account recorded in 1990.[16] A further element that acted in favor of credibility was the depth of the structural public sector reform via privatization and reductions in the number of public employees.

The Magnitude and Composition of Capital Inflows
Under the Convertibility Plan

The strict credit rationing faced by Argentina in the 1980s provoked a strong decline in domestic absorption while the stock of international reserves was reduced to a minimum. When the quantitative restrictions weakened, there was a sharp expansion in the use of foreign savings. In the 1991–1993 period, the accumulated deficit in the current account reached U.S.$21.4 billion. If the funds used for accumulating international reserves are added, the total demand for foreign finance was U.S.$29.4 billion. This represented 40 percent more than the total net flow of funds received between 1982 and 1990 (see Table 5.2).

Unlike in the 1980s, the increment in the current account deficit was not explained by an upward trend of interest payments abroad—the financial account deficit tended to decline pari passu with the international interest rate—but rather by the mounting level of the trade deficit. This was primarily the result of domestic expansion of activity level. Likewise, the growth rate of imports tended to be greater than the domestic global demand mainly because of trade liberalization and the decline in the real exchange rate. The latter was a consequence of the fact that the nominal exchange rate was fixed in a context in which the "residual" rate of inflation in the poststabilization period was far from zero. Imports increased from U.S.$4.1 billion in 1990 to around U.S.$16 billion in 1993. Following this increase in imports, the trade account surplus of U.S.$8.3 billion in 1990 became a deficit of U.S.$2.6 billion in 1992 and it is estimated at U.S.$3.7 billion in 1993.

In the capital account, the relationship between autonomous and compensatory finance also showed an abrupt change. In sharp contrast with what had happened in the 1980s, capital inflows were led by the private sector. Between 1991 and 1993, the net result corresponding to private capital was U.S.$26 billion (see Table 5.3).

A closer look reveals that the first signs of a reversal in capital flows appeared before the implementation of the convertibility regime. Table 5.4 shows that the private capital account recorded a surplus for the first time in the last quarter of 1990. This surplus is associated to the high domestic interest rate registered from March 1990 on. Nonetheless, due to the turbulence in the foreign exchange market that preceded the convertibility in the first quarter of 1991, net private capital flows again became negative in the first and second quarters of 1991. The sign of private flows once more reverted in the third quarter of 1991, reflecting an increasing degree of credibility in the new policy package.

However, the balance-of-payments classification according to the public or private character of capital inflows is ambiguous. In effect, on the one hand, the account corresponding to private flows includes the funds

Table 5.4   Autonomous Capital Movements, 1990–1993

Period	Total	Private	Private According to Destination	Private According to Origin
First quarter 1990	−195	−187	−187	−227
Second quarter 1990	−68	−27	−27	−125
Third quarter 1990	−1,276	−1,530	−1,694	−1,560
Fourth quarter 1990	429	383	−261	344
Total 1990	−1,110	−1,361	−2,169	−1,568
First quarter 1991	−206	−163	−290	−165
Second quarter 1991	−25	−29	−362	−119
Third quarter 1991	616	236	−670	591
Fourth quarter 1991	3,189	2,777	2,169	2,954
Total 1991	3,574	2,821	847	3,261
First quarter 1992	2,967	3,073	2,212	3,062
Second quarter 1992	2,165	2,344	2,616	2,265
Third quarter 1992	2,177	2,045	1,809	2,147
Fourth quarter 1992	4,046	4,050	3,040	4,088
Total 1992	11,355	11,512	9,671	11,562
First quarter 1993	3,288	1,679	1,377	1,739
Second quarter 1993	2,495	1,745	1,745	2,272
Third quarter 1993	4,402	4,086	2,135	4,361
Fourth quarter 1993	4,874	3,997	3,707	4,737
Total 1993	15,259	11,707	9,164	13,109

Source: Elaborated on the basis of Central Bank data.

originating in privatization that finance the public sector, and, on the other hand, excludes government bonds, which are flows of funds that originate in the private sector. In order to consider this, Table 5.4 includes two new columns corresponding to the private sector.

Private funds according to destination includes the amount directed to finance the private sector and, consequently, excludes funds stemming from privatization. As can be seen, the private sector received a positive net flow of credit from the fourth quarter of 1991 on, after this flow had became positive for the government. Notice that the reversal of flows is very sharp: in the third quarter of 1991, this private sector received a net negative flow of U.S.$670 million, but in the fourth quarter it received a positive flow of U.S.$2.2 billion.

The last column of Table 5.4 includes the total amount of inflows originating in the private sector without considering whether these funds went to finance the public or the private sector. In this case, there are no important qualitative differences with the balance-of-payments records.

The net result of capital flows is positive for the first time in the last quarter of 1990, then becomes negative, and then changes its sign again in the third quarter of 1991. An important conclusion that can be drawn from this is that capital inflows associated with the privatization process have "led" the movements of private capital, and consequently, the divestiture of public property has had a favorable effect on the expectations of foreign investors.

The Allocation of Foreign Capital Inflows

Due to lack of data, it is very difficult to address the question of the domestic allocation of capital inflows. In spite of this fact, we will make an effort to analyze the allocation of capital inflows on the basis of available data.

Table 5.5 reclassifies the flow of foreign funds. The objective is to see whether these funds financed the public or the private sector and which kinds of expenditures were financed. The table shows that under the Convertibility Plan, if the items corresponding to the nonfinancial public sector and to the Central Bank were consolidated, the net flow of foreign capital received by the public sector would total U.S.$9.8 billion, whereas the private sector would receive U.S.$20.0 billion.

From this total of U.S.$29.8 billion, U.S.$9 billion were allocated to reserves accumulation and the rest covered the borrowing needs originating in the current account. Given that the primary cause of the increase in the current account deficit was the upward trend of the trade deficit, it follows that there was a continuous expansion in domestic absorption. When such an expansion is analyzed at a more disaggregate level, it is clearly seen that consumption growth played an important role: in the 1990–1993 period it increased 29 percent. On the other hand, from 1990 to 1993, investment grew 85 percent, although the investment rate of 1990 was the lowest of at least the last forty years.

The public sector. Undoubtedly, the most important source of financing for the public sector has been the funds stemming from privatization. From the aforementioned total of U.S.$9.8 billion received, U.S.$6.2 billion originated in the divestiture of public enterprises and U.S.$3.6 billion represented inflows of autonomous and compensatory finance. These figures, however, underestimate the actual change in the position of the government because the effects of debt-equity swap schemes are excluded. Table 5.6, based on alternative sources of data, shows the total amount received by the public sector from privatization.

In the 1990–1993 period, as a consequence of the divestiture of public enterprises, there was a reduction in the nominal stock of public debt of

Table 5.5   Allocation of Foreign Funds to the Private and Public Sectors (excluding debt-equity swaps associated with privatization; millions of U.S.$)

	89	90	1991[a]					1992[a]					1993[a]					Plan[b]
			Total	I	II	III	IV	Total	I	II	III	IV	Total	I	II	III	IV	
Private sector	-1,853	-2,169	847	-290	-362	-670	2,169	9,671	2,110	2,147	1,912	3,502	9,819	1,426	1,781	2,137	4,475	20,627
Export credit	-717	1,411	70	1,100	213	-641	-602	-2,175	-72	-409	-1,007	-687	1,032	149	48	313	522	4,928
Import credit	-1,511	-960	1,688	-48	157	656	923	5,365	919	1,239	1,790	1,417	3,318	251	710	1,047	1,310	4,242
Firms	111	92	345	32	52	-10	271	611	317	56	88	150	621	130	219	123	149	1,475
FDI	1,028	333	465	53	107	76	229	442	59	112	47	224	4,848	896	804	654	2,494	9,982
Others	-764	-3,045	-1,721	-1,427	-891	-751	1,348	5,428	887	1,149	994	2,398						
Public sector	1,586	3,131	3,836	-205	951	1,627	1,463	2,977	640	742	1,192	403	2,944	2,776	-2,341	1,912	597	9,962
Privatization	0	808	1,974	127	333	906	608	1,841	963	197	133	548	2,543	302	0	1,951	290	6,231
Autonomous																		
Capital	-351	251	753	-43	4	380	412	-157	-106	-179	132	-4	3,552	1,609	750	316	877	4,191
Others	-3,389	0	-5,457	0	0	0	-5,457	108	0	108	0	0	0	0	0	0	0	-5,349
Compensatory finance	5,326	2,072	6,566	-289	614	341	5,900	1,185	-217	616	927	-141	-3,151	865	-3,091	-355	-570	4,889
Arrears	2,927	1,912	1,788	440	825	312	211	884	215	222	181	266	68	68	0	0	0	2,300
Others[c]	2,399	160	4,778	-729	-211	29	5,689	301	-432	394	746	-407	-3,219	797	-3,091	-355	-570	2,589
Total	-267	962	4,683	-495	589	957	3,632	12,648	2,750	2,889	3,104	3,905	12,763	4,202	-560	4,049	5,072	30,589

Source: Elaborated on the basis of Central Bank data.

Notes: [a] I = first quarter; II = second quarter; III = third quarter; IV = fourth quarter.
[b] The Convertibility Plan, from second quarter 1991 to fourth quarter 1993.
[c] Includes the operations of consolidation except for the regularization of arrears during the second quarter 1993.

Table 5.6   Financial Results of the Privatization Process, 1990–1993 (millions of U.S.$)

Sector	Form of Transference	Cash	Amortization of Foreign Debt (market value)	Transferred Liabilities	Total	Amortization of Foreign Debt (nominal value)
Telecommunications	Sale of stocks	2,271	1,257	—	3,528	5,000
Airlines	Direct sale	260	483	—	743	1,610
Railways	Concession	—	—	—	—	—
Electricity	Direct sale	524	1,681	1,071	3,276	3,362
Harbors	Concession/direct sale	14	—	—	14	—
Roads	Concession	—	—	—	—	—
Television and Radio	Concession	14	—	—	14	—
Petroleum	Sale of stocks	2,041	—	—	2,041	—
YPF (petroleum company)	Concession	3,040	—	—	3,040	—
Gas	Direct sale	300	1,541	1,110	2,951	3,082
Water and sewage	Concession	—	—	—	—	—
Industry						
Petrochemical	Sale of stocks	545	28	—	573	140
Ships	Direct sale	60	—	—	60	—
Steel	Direct sale	143	22	—	165	42
Public real estate	Direct sale	184	—	—	184	—
Others	Direct sale/concession	65	2	—	68	12
Total		9,460	5,015	2,181	16,657	13,248

Source: Ministry of Economy.

U.S.$13.2 billion. The market value of the amortized debt was U.S.$5 billion. Likewise, in the privatization process, U.S.$2.2 billion in commercial liabilities held by public companies were transferred to the private sector together with such enterprises. The cash payments received by the public sector, on the other hand, amounted to U.S.$9.5 billion. Consequently, the overall revenues stemming from privatization were U.S.$16.7 billion (U.S.$9.5 billion in cash, U.S.$5 billion in debt swaps, and U.S.$2.2 billion in transfers of commercial liabilities) (see Table 5.6). The participation corresponding to foreign investors represented 60 percent of this amount (U.S.$9.8 billion).

Data regarding the estimated rate of return on the privatized assets are unavailable. However, it is estimated that this rate declined after the sale of the public telecommunications company (Entel). Indeed, the privatization process has undergone three well-defined stages. In the first, privatization had the primary objective of inducing a change in private-sector expectations. This stage was comprised of the worst-designed privatizations, in which there were high rates of return and poorly defined regulatory frameworks. In the second stage, the main objective pursued was to close the fiscal gap by resorting to the revenues originating in the privatization process. In the third and present stage, as from 1992, the rate of return has been lower and there has been much more concern regarding consumers' interests. In this third stage, the sale of the state petroleum company (YPF) was made in a manner that reflected the administration's need to fulfill political aims, and consequently it has had some common characteristics with the first stage.[17]

The second item of government financing in order of importance was "forced" credit originating in interest payment arrears (see Table 5.5). The relevance of this kind of credit, however, had been steadily declining until it completely disappeared after the authorities signed an agreement to refinance the outstanding debt with foreign commercial banks in March 1993 under the Brady Initiative. When the funds coming from privatization and arrears are excluded, the remaining amount of foreign credit received by the public sector is very low, U.S.$1.3 billion.[18]

It is not possible, however, to trace the actual utilization of foreign funds by considering only the balance of payments. The funds originating in foreign sources could have been devoted to canceling the existing domestic public debt and/or augmenting the stock of domestic assets held by the public sector. It is necessary, then, to examine the government balance sheet.

Table 5.7 shows the fiscal budget measured on cash bases. In 1990–1991, the public sector ran a deficit, whereas it showed a surplus in 1992–1993. In 1990–1991 a part of public expenditures was financed by the proceeds from privatization. In 1992 and 1993, in contrast, the capital

Table 5.7   National Public Sector Overall Surplus
(as a percentage of GDP)

	1990	1991	1992	1993
(1) Current revenues	14.41	15.86	17.15	17.85
(2) Current expenditures excluding interests	11.99	14.3	14.96	15.15
(3) Current savings (1)–(2)	2.42	1.56	2.19	2.7
(4) Cash interest payments	–1.12	–2.12	–0.38	–1.18
(5) Current surplus (cash) (3)–(4)	1.3	–0.56	1.81	1.52
(6) Investment	1.42	1.05	0.81	0.78
(7) Surplus of the Central Bank	–0.75	–0.36	–0.14	0
(8) Cash surplus (5)–(6)–(7)	–0.87	–1.97	0.86	0.74
(9) Unpaid interests	–2.98	–0.92	–0.68	–0.08
(10) Surplus (8)+(9)	–3.85	–2.89	0.18	0.66
(11) Proceeds from privatization (cash)	0.45	1.21	0.79	1.00
(12) Overall surplus (10)–(11)	–3.4	–1.68	0.97	1.66
Overall surplus excluding arrears	–0.42	–0.76	1.65	1.74

Source: Ministry of Economy.

inflows generated by the sale of public companies were channeled to canceling government debt.[19]

The private sector. Table 5.5 shows that during the period of the Convertibility Plan 24 percent of private capital inflows represented commercial credit, 7 percent was foreign direct investment (excluding funds originating in privatization process) and 21 percent was credit directly received by firms operating in the domestic market. The remaining 48 percent appears under the heading of "others" and, consequently, represents unidentified inflows.

The net amount of commercial credit received during the Convertibility Plan totaled U.S.$4.9 billion. This amount is the result of a negative flow of U.S.$3.2 billion in export credit and a positive one to finance imports of U.S.$7.1 billion.[20]

Therefore the expansion in imports after the implementation of the Convertibility Plan is a primary factor explaining the increase in the availability of external loanable funds. However, given the short-run character of commercial credit, the fall in the rate of growth of imports during 1993 produced a drop in the net flow of commercial credit. This led to added demand for other kinds of foreign credit because the current account disequilibrium persisted.[21]

When the funds connected to privatization are excluded, it is clear that foreign direct investment has not been a significant component of capital inflows. Foreign direct investment amounted to U.S.$1.5 billion during the convertibility period, and almost all of this was a reinvestment of profits.

After a long period of credit rationing, many financial and nonfinancial Argentine corporations were able to place U.S.$4 billion in Euronotes and bonds in foreign markets in 1991–1993. As Table 5.8 shows, 41.9 percent of this amount was placed by domestic banks, 16.4 percent by firms producing services, 24.8 percent by petroleum companies, and 16.9 percent by leading firms pertaining to the industrial sector. This allocation pattern is due to two reasons: first, it reflects the ability of different firms to generate profits and consequently to sustain a significant investment rate, and second, it reveals the fact that the firms with greater net worth and repayment capacity in Argentina belong to the banking, petroleum, and services sectors. Only a few leading firms in the industrial sector have access to the international credit markets. In the particular case of services, owing to the privatization process, there are currently many enterprises with fluent access to international capital markets; not only because of their size, but also because of the participation of foreign investors in the ownership of a significant part of the shares.

Table 5.8   Issues of Euronotes and International Bonds
(1991–1993)

	Issues	
Sector	Millions of U.S.$	Percentage of Total
Industry	679.5	16.9
Petroleum	1,000.0	24.8
Services	660.0	16.4
Banks	1,692.5	41.9
Total	4,032.0	100.0

Source: Elaborated on the basis of *Prensa Económica* data.

As was stated earlier, the item "others" in Table 5.5 represents almost 50 percent of capital inflows recorded in the capital account. The growth in domestic dollar deposits (argendollars) was a very important channel for these capital inflows. It must be taken into account, however, that the increase in argendollar deposits is recorded as a capital inflow in the balance of payments only when they are loaned and to the extent that the borrower purchases pesos with the proceeds from the credit in the foreign exchange market or makes a payment abroad. But, given that internal transactions using U.S. dollars as a means of exchange are unimportant, it can be argued that the bulk of the expansion of the argendollar segment was reflected in the balance of payments as an inflow of foreign capital under the heading of "other movements."[22] In this respect, it is worthwhile noting that the expansion of the argendollar segment is higher than the amount recorded in the item "other movements."

The increment in argendollar deposits since the implementation of convertibility has amounted to U.S.$14.6 billion (Table 5.9). This increase in deposits gave way to an expansion of the banks' lending capacity of U.S.$12.4 billion.

We can deduce, therefore, that residents and nonresidents alike have been employing the argendollar segment as a channel for capital inflows. In that way foreign investors and residents repatriating capital have tried to protect their financial investment in the domestic market from the devaluation risk. It seems, consequently, that investors believe that they can take advantage of the positive differential between the domestic and foreign interest rates while avoiding the devaluation risk. The belief that they are assuming the country risk but not the devaluation risk, however, may not be justified. By placing their funds in Argentine banks, investors are sharing the banks' investment decisions, which are reflected in credit policies, and banks are assuming significant devaluation risks. In order to clarify this we must make a brief reference to the domestic credit market situation.

An analysis based on the fifty major debtors of each bank shows that 67 percent of the outstanding credit is in dollars, whereas only 43 percent of the total amount of credit in dollars has been loaned to firms producing tradable goods (primary products and industrial goods).[23] It is clear, then, that repayment capacity of bank debtors would be severely affected by a real devaluation, as would the banks' financial positions. Moreover, if a devaluation was accompanied by a recession—as is typically the case in Argentina due to the reduction in domestic absorption—the repayment capacity of firms producing nontradables would deteriorate further. From this it follows that placing funds in dollar-denominated deposits to bypass a potential devaluation is not risk free.

Capital Inflows and Transformations in the Domestic Capital Market

The reversion in capital movements has had important effects on the structure and evolution of both the financial system and the stock market.

Changes in the financial system. The sharp increment in capital inflows caused, in the first place, a significant remonetization of the economy. As Table 5.10 shows, the hyperinflationary episodes of 1989 and 1990,

Table 5.9   Evolution of the Argendollar Segment
(millions of U.S.$)

	Dollar Deposits				Lending Capacity	Dollar Deposits as a Percentage of Total Deposits	Dollar Term Deposits as a Percentage of Term Deposits[a]
	Sight Deposits	Savings Deposits	Term Deposits	Total			
Total 1988	12		1,219	1,231	0	0.10	0.11
Total 1989	22		1,200	1,222	331	0.12	0.13
Total 1990	231		1,480	1,711	1,280	0.29	0.36
December 1990	597		2,246	2,843	2,591	0.28	0.30
March 1991	853		2,536	3,389	3,180	0.40	0.40
June 1991	661	506	3,432	4,599	4,068	0.43	0.50
September 1991	716	868	4,139	5,723	5,036	0.46	0.54
December 1991	782	1,137	4,642	6,561	5,746	0.45	0.54
March 1992	879	1,505	5,516	7,900	6,900	0.46	0.55
June 1992	852	1,536	6,670	9,058	8,017	0.43	0.52
September 1992	836	1,674	7,834	10,344	9,205	0.44	0.53
December 1992	839	1,868	8,231	10,938	9,703	0.45	0.54
March 1993	543	2,406	9,282	12,231	11,543	0.43	0.51
June 1993	555	2,679	10,298	13,532	11,832	0.44	0.53
September 1993	601	3,824	12,488	16,913	14,636	0.47	0.56
December 1993	616	4,151	13,264	18,031	15,583	0.47	0.58

Source: Elaborated on the basis of Central Bank data.
Note: [a]Excludes sight deposits.

together with the so-called Bonex Plan, by which there was a compulsory substitution of long-run government bonds for bank deposits in January 1990, induced a strong demonetization of the economy. Although there was a slight recovery of the monetization level in 1990, it only began to change markedly in the period following the implementation of the Convertibility Plan, when the capital flight process began to revert and there was a sharp and permanent fall in the inflation rate.

Table 5.10 Monetary Aggregates in Pesos
(millions of U.S.$)

	Bills and Coins	Sight Deposits	Savings	Term Deposits	M1	M2	Deposits in Pesos
Total 1988	1,711	1,508	1,261	8,605	3,219	13,085	11,374
Total 1989	1,504	1,241	798	7,344	2,745	10,887	9,383
Total 1990	1,644	1,520	1,636	1,014	3,164	5,814	4,170
December 1990	3,521	2,063	2,632	2,706	5,584	10,922	7,401
March 1991	2,350	1,429	1,804	1,933	3,779	7,516	5,166
June 1991	3,209	2,114	1,594	2,312	5,323	9,229	6,020
September 1991	3,790	2,353	1,619	2,719	6,143	10,481	6,691
December 1991	4,761	3,160	1,789	3,066	7,921	12,776	8,015
March 1992	5,028	3,577	2,039	3,622	8,605	14,266	9,238
June 1992	5,529	4,396	2,542	4,912	9,925	17,379	11,850
September 1992	5,843	4,612	2,768	5,778	10,455	19,001	13,138
December 1992	6,783	4,909	2,758	5,998	11,692	20,448	13,665
March 1993	6,997	4,995	3,639	7,474	11,992	23,105	16,108
June 1993	7,580	5,472	3,998	7,600	13,052	24,650	17,070
September 1993	8,378	6,648	4,268	8,350	15,026	27,644	19,266
December 1993	9,254	7,403	4,323	8,455	16,657	29,435	20,181

Source: Elaborated on the basis of Central Bank data.

One particular trait of the postconvertibility remonetization process, which stands out from similar processes that had occurred in the past after the implementation of a stabilization package, was the financial system's deepening dollarization. Table 5.9 shows that the proportion of dollar-denominated deposits rose from 10 percent of total private deposits in 1988, to 28 percent at the end of 1990, and to 43 percent in June 1991, following an 80 percent devaluation of the domestic currency in the first quarter of that year. From then on, the proportion has been fluctuating around that level, although it increased slightly at the end of 1993. If sight deposits in pesos are excluded, however, the share of total deposits accounted for dollar deposits is higher. After almost three years of currency convertibility (December 1993), the ratio of dollarized deposits to total deposits (in both cases excluding sight deposits) has reached 58 percent (see

Table 5.9). This dollarization process has greatly changed the structure of the banks' balance sheets. In June 1993, 47 percent of the banks' total assets and 48 percent of their aggregate liabilities were denominated in dollars.

A significant proportion of the credit capacity created by the expansion of dollar deposits was allocated to finance firms producing nontradable goods. As noted before, this implies that the banks' financial positions could become unduly fragile if a real devaluation occurred. It should be mentioned, however, that not all banks are running the same "devaluation risk." In particular, the financial position of government-owned banks seems to be much riskier than the one corresponding to private banks. In effect, while the percentage of dollarized credit allocated to the tradable sector is 43 percent for the financial system as a whole, the percentage corresponding to public banks is only 20 percent.[24]

A greater degree of monetization has resulted in an expansion of credit available not only for firms but also for individuals. After a long period during which the availability of loanable funds for financing consumption expenditures was practically nil, there has been a remarkable increase in the supply of such funds. Especially important was the expansion of credit for purchasing automobiles and consumer durables. Individuals also benefited from an expansion in mortgage availability. Because an important part of credit to individuals is denominated in U.S. dollars, it seems clear that growth in the argendollar segment of the domestic financial system has contributed to financing not only production (especially of nontradables) but also consumption.

The economy's remonetization also affected the temporal path of interest rates. Table 5.11 shows that the deposit rate has followed a declining trend since the implementation of the Convertibility Plan. Two factors are crucial in explaining the downward trend of both nominal and real interest rates: reduction in the country-risk premium and a sharp decrease in the devaluation risk perceived by investors. The country-risk premium can be measured as the difference between the rate of return of the Bonex and the London Inter-Bank Offer Rate (LIBOR).[25] Table 5.11 shows the evolution of this variable.

As can be seen, the country-risk premium fell noticeably with the launching of the Convertibility Plan and continued to fall afterwards. The sharp drop in the expected rate of devaluation[26] seems to have played the most prominent role in reducing the deposit rate: after having reached a striking level in the years prior to the implementation of convertibility, expected devaluation was only 4.5 percent per annum at the beginning of 1993 and around 1 percent at the end of that year.

This deposit rate evolution contrasts sharply with what was observed in other experiences in the past, particularly in the tablita period. In the

Table 5.11   Evolution of Annual Interest Rate, Risk Premium, and
Expected Devaluation (%)

Period	Domestic Interest Rate[a]	Rate of Return of Bonex	LIBOR U.S.$	Estimated Risk Premium	Estimated Expected Devaluation	Observed Devaluation
Fourth quarter 1981	127.58	18.38	14.66	3.25	92.24	465.17
Fourth quarter 1982	151.10	20.15	9.96	9.27	108.99	331.69
Fourth quarter 1983	407.77	22.22	9.79	11.32	315.45	526.99
Fourth quarter 1984	1,269.48	19.11	9.73	8.55	1,049.79	477.42
Fourth quarter 1985	72.47	17.78	8.10	8.95	46.43	52.75
Fourth quarter 1986	138.62	14.34	6.10	7.76	108.70	208.39
Fourth quarter 1987	198.93	23.73	7.73	14.85	141.60	267.98
Fourth quarter 1988	215.52	23.69	9.15	13.32	155.09	5,955.42
First quarter 1989	434.38	36.12	10.23	23.49	292.58	11,739.88
Second quarter 1989	29,473.47	33.27	9.58	21.61	22,091.10	3,340.69
Third quarter 1989	301.49	25.36	8.79	15.23	220.26	774.77
Fourth quarter 1989	298.36	32.35	8.29	22.21	201.00	470.14
First quarter 1990	3,934.55	45.98	8.48	34.57	2,663.80	171.48
Second quarter 1990	239.56	29.85	8.65	19.51	163.67	94.52
Third quarter 1990	270.68	23.06	8.21	13.72	201.18	73.70
Fourth quarter 1990	135.90	25.15	7.87	16.02	93.12	85.70
First quarter 1991	240.47	25.16	6.81	17.18	185.24	19.05
Second quarter 1991	22.09	17.21	6.37	10.19	4.16	0.45
Third quarter 1991	22.62	15.01	5.96	8.54	6.62	−0.20
Fourth quarter 1991	17.08	10.51	4.90	5.09	5.95	0.10
First quarter 1992	15.43	10.85	4.40	5.19	4.13	0.80
Second quarter 1992	16.17	9.85	4.17	5.45	5.75	0.00
Third quarter 1992	14.80	10.56	3.50	6.80	3.84	0.00
Fourth quarter 1992	17.24	12.20	3.61	8.29	4.49	0.00
First quarter 1993	16.75	11.53	3.28	7.99	4.60	0.00
Second quarter 1993	11.62	8.36	3.31	4.89	3.00	0.00
Third quarter 1993	10.27	7.55	3.55	3.93	2.45	0.00
Fourth quarter 1993	7.93	6.95	3.50	3.20	0.91	0.00

Source: CEDES.
Note: [a]On thirty-day deposits.

present situation, in spite of an increase in the current account disequilibrium that could have had a negative influence on devaluation expectations, there is no tendency for the deposit rate to increase.

It should be mentioned, nonetheless, that during the Convertibility Plan there was a sizable gap between the rate paid on dollar deposits and the one paid on deposits in pesos, although the difference has been quite small during the last months. One consequence of this gap was that banks that have managed to increase the proportion of dollar deposits in their portfolios have gained a competitive advantage over those who have not. In this respect, private banks have shown a much better performance than their public peers. For the financial system as a whole, the proportion of dollar-denominated deposits was 46 percent in August 1993, but that

proportion in the case of public banks was only 31 percent. Indeed, an uneven distribution of dollar deposits can also be found in private banks.
Dollar deposits are concentrated primarily in foreign banks (65 percent of
their total deposits) and national banks located in Buenos Aires (58 percent). Small-sized banks located in the provinces show a much lower proportion of dollar deposits (48 percent).

Besides having a higher share of total dollar deposits, small financial
intermediaries (cooperative banks and nonbank financial institutions) have
to pay higher interest rates in order to attract depositors. Small banks have
no fluent access to other sources of loanable funds, such as foreign credit
or the domestic capital market, which are cheaper and of longer maturity.

These factors have contributed to the segmentation of the financial
market and hence to a differentiation in the cost of funds faced by each
type of bank. In this context, the actual cost of funds for a given institution
depends heavily upon both its size and the origin of the resources. This
further deteriorates the competitive position of small banks, which are already handicapped by the fact that they show higher operational costs per
unit of deposits.[27] It is not surprising, then, that both the spread between
lending and borrowing rates and the real rate are higher for loans denominated in pesos and intermediated by small banks operating outside the city
of Buenos Aires.

As Table 5.12 shows, it is not unusual that the interest rate on loans in
pesos be more than 3 percent per month in a context in which the monthly
inflation rate is around 0.3 percent. One important consequence of this
high level in the real interest rate is that the quality of the existing stock of
credit tends to deteriorate. This represents a threat to the financial (and
even macroeconomic) health of the economy.

In the context of the increasing financial deepening in recent years,
large enterprises have had much easier access to both domestic and international credit markets. But this was not the case for small- and medium-
sized businesses, which have continued to be rationed in the international
credit markets and have had limited access to financing from large domestic banks.[28] Therefore they have had to resort to small banks—which
charge a higher interest rate on loans—to fulfill their borrowing needs. In
a situation in which the opening of the economy calls for a deep restructuring of the productive capacity, small- and medium-sized businesses
cannot count on a fluent supply of credit at reasonable rates for financing
either working capital or investment.[29]

Regarding term maturity of domestic financial instruments, the present process of financial deepening has not shown substantial differences
from the liberalization experience of the late 1970s and early 1980s. Although there was a certain lengthening of deposit maturity as compared to
the immediate posthyperinflationary period, the average maturity in both

Table 5.12 Monthly Lending Rates (%)

Institution	June 1991		December 1991		June 1992		December 1992		August 1993	
	Pesos	U.S.$	Pesos	U.S.$	Pesos	U.S.$	Pesos	U.S.$	Pesos	U.S.$
National public banks	1.65	n.d.	2.17	n.d.	1.79	0.66	1.45	0.39	1.17	
Provincial public banks	3.07	n.d.	3.01	n.d.	2.77	1.07	1.99	1.16	1.54	
Total public banks	2.17	n.d.	2.94	n.d.	2.56	0.94	1.95	0.94	1.41	0.93
Private banks	4.91	n.d.	4.76	n.d.	2.85	1.14	4.41	1.23	2.67	1.14
Foreign banks	3.13	n.d.	3.91	n.d.	2.72	0.83	3.95	1.02	2.21	0.91
Cooperative banks	6.43	n.d.	5.23	n.d.	4.27	1.43	4.55	1.58	3.34	1.49
Total private banks	4.74	n.d.	4.67	n.d.	3.33	1.04	4.33	1.19	2.70	1.09
Nonbanking institutions	5.33	n.d.	4.46	n.d.	3.74	1.62	4.31	1.66	2.62	1.66
Aggregate financial system	2.71	n.d.	3.77	n.d.	3.07	1.05	3.23	1.17	2.07	1.06

Source: Central Bank.
Note: Import credits are included in dollar credit. n.d. = not determined.

pesos and dollars is still too short (around forty and ninety days for pesos and dollar deposits, respectively). The average maturity of bank credit, on the other hand, is longer than that of deposits.[30]

To summarize, the domestic financial system has channeled an important part of the capital inflows during the postconvertibility period. Particularly important was the role of the argendollar segment. More than 50 percent of the credit created was channeled to finance the nontradable sector and has also contributed to financing consumption expenditures, particularly of durable-consumption goods. At the same time, the reduction in both the country-risk premium and the expected rate of devaluation induced a sharp fall in domestic nominal and real interest rates. Large enterprises were the primary beneficiaries of the downward trend in interest rates, and this undoubtedly fueled investment expenditures. Because of the persistence of the credit-rationing phenomenon affecting small- and medium-sized businesses, however, the benefits of the fall in interest rates have not been distributed evenly.[31]

These recent financial developments could potentially create solvency problems in certain segments of the banking system. Two factors are worth mentioning: (1) a good part of the lending capacity has been allocated to firms producing nontradables, and (2) the borrowing rate is still too high, which opens the question of the proportion of credit repayment that will be observed in the future. This is especially relevant in the case of small banks in the interior of the country.

It should be taken into account that according to the new *Carta Orgánica,* which regulates the Central Bank, if there were a deterioration in the financial situation, the Central Bank could not act as lender of last resort. It has been established that the maximum term to maturity of rediscounts cannot exceed thirty days and that their amount cannot be greater than the value of the net worth of the bank receiving the funds. Equally important is the fact that although the stock of international reserves held by the Central Bank equals the stock of monetary base, the ratio M2/monetary base is 2; and if dollar deposits are added to M2, this ratio reaches a level of 3. This means that in addition to the legal restrictions that constrain the Central Bank's behavior, there are strict economic limits to the capacity of the Central Bank to help the financial system should solvency and/or severe liquidity disturbances arise.

The stock market. The increase in capital inflows has also had a marked influence on the domestic stock market. Table 5.13 shows the evolution of total market capitalization in the Buenos Aires stock exchange market. Total capitalization went from U.S.$5.3 billion in the first quarter of 1991 to U.S.$25.5 billion in the second quarter of 1992. After that, total capitalization declined as a consequence of falling prices until the sale of the

Table 5.13 Evolution of the Buenos Aires Stock Market

Period	Amount of Transactions[a]	Market Capitalization[a]	Stock Price Index[b]
1990			
First quarter	56.6	2,593	1,045
Second quarter	58.0	3,241	1,511
Third quarter	67.2	3,360	1,858
Fourth quarter	44.1	3,620	1,599
1991			
First quarter	173.6	5,272	3,680
Second quarter	132.9	5,501	5,091
Third quarter	595.6	11,995	9,991
Fourth quarter	660.5	18,644	12,272
1992			
First quarter	1,071	25,746	15,088
Second quarter	2,147	25,524	18,186
Third quarter	1,252	18,210	11,350
Fourth quarter	1,328	18,435	10,023
1993			
First quarter	1,322	18,769	10,215
Second quarter	4,305	26,733	10,228
Third quarter	7,172	31,178	12,076
Fourth quarter	9,819	42,931	15,381

Source: Research Institute of the Buenos Aires Stock Market.
Notes: [a]In millions of U.S. dollars.
[b]In pesos.

stock of the state petroleum company (YPF) in June 1993. From then on it increased until reaching a value of U.S.$43 billion by the end of 1993.

From the beginning of the convertibility program, the primary cause of the increment in total market capitalization was the increase in the price of existing stocks rather than a rise in the quantity of shares. In the 1991–1993 period, the most important issue in new shares was associated with the privatization of the telephone and state oil companies.

Although there are no reliable data to support this, it seems that institutional investors have not had a relevant role in the recovery of the demand for shares. It seems that the resources from these investors have been basically channeled toward purchasing shares of privatized public utilities, which offer "secure" profits in the medium run. The role of foreign investors was particularly important in the case of the privatization of the state petroleum company, YPF.

In conclusion, although the Argentine stock market was classified as "emergent" because of the positive evolution shown during the period under analysis, the present situation is far from consolidated, especially because—as can be seen in Table 5.13—there have been sharp fluctuations in stock prices, indicating that the level of uncertainty is high. Likewise, excluding the issues associated with the privatization process, there has been a very low number of new entrants or of issues of new stocks by existing firms oriented toward the expansion of their capital. It seems that private enterprises have privileged external credit and domestic funds coming from banks or bond markets as a means to finance investment.

Capital Flows, Stability, and Growth

As we have seen, the reversal of capital flows induced a series of changes in the domestic side of the economy. At the macroeconomic level, growing availability of foreign savings gave support to the ongoing stabilization and permitted a sharp increase in domestic absorption. On the financial side, foreign savings induced a higher degree of monetization, together with a consolidation of the dollarization process.

As a general rule, economic policy has passively adapted to the accrued inflows of capital. From the point of view adopted by the Argentine authorities, an activist policy regarding capital inflows was unnecessary: in the short run because the Convertibility Plan guaranteed macroeconomic stability, and in the long run because capital inflows would finance the increases in investment and productivity. These issues undoubtedly are at the core of the question of stability and growth.

Macroeconomic Stability and Capital Flows

Under the Convertibility Plan and the new *Carta Orgánica* of the Central Bank, monetary policy was completely passive, and therefore net capital inflows induced a strong increase in the money supply. The economy's financial deepening was additionally helped by the expansion of domestic dollar-denominated deposits. The counterpart of this, as was mentioned, was a strong expansion in the supply of domestically generated credit.

The expansion of credit produced concomitant growth in effective demand. In the context of a fixed exchange rate and trade liberalization, the upward shift of effective demand has had differential effects on the components of overall supply. Stylizing the facts, it can be said that tradables (imports) adjusted via "quantities" and nontradables adjusted via "prices." Given that the Argentine economy is small and open, the increased demand for imports was met by a supply that can be considered highly elastic, whereas the higher demand for nontradable goods exerted an appreciable pressure on prices because the supply could be expanded only by increasing marginal costs.

These differential features of the adjustment process have had two important macroeconomic consequences. First, they strongly affected the trade account. Between the surplus of 1990 and the deficit of 1993, there is a difference of more than U.S.$11 billion. Second, since the first signs of the recovery of capital inflows, there has been a systematic trend for the real exchange rate to appreciate and for the relative price of nontradables to increase.[32]

One indicator of the increasing distortion of relative prices is the differential evolution of consumer and wholesale indices. After the implementation of the plan, the inflation rate in terms of consumer prices was 54 percent, but in terms of wholesale prices it was 8 percent. The main cause of this divergence is that the weight of tradables in the wholesale index is much more important than in the consumer one. It is worthwhile noting that when the indices are disaggregated, the items showing higher increases are those whose exposure to international competition is lower. For example, the items of the consumer index that recorded the highest increases are private services (72 percent) and food—fruit and legumes (84 percent) and meat (68 percent). The lifting of trade barriers and reduction of tariffs are clearly related to these results.

Besides the rise in global demand, there are "structural" factors that explain the dynamics of relative prices. On the one hand, the deflationary shock, although successful in sharply curtailing inflation, left a small but persistent residual "inertial inflation." On the other hand, the increase in the tax burden—because of the reduction in tax evasion—pushed up the price of nontradables.

In addition to the divergence between the consumer and wholesale prices, the differential path of other key relative prices can be seen in Table 5.14. It shows, for example, that taking 1986=100, the value of industrial goods in relation to private services was only 35 in December 1993, and the value corresponding to agricultural (primary) products was 29.[33]

This evolution of the economy shows, among other things, that the relationship between macroeconomic stability and capital flows is not a simple one. On the one hand, the distortion of relative prices in a context of liberalization of the capital account presents close similarities to the period of the tablita. But, on the other hand, it is also true that the relaxation of the foreign credit constraint vastly helped the stabilization effort of the posthyperinflation period. The greater availability of foreign exchange allowed the nominal exchange rate to be fixed and hence heavily contributed to anchoring nominal prices.

Beyond the first stages of stabilization, however, it seems that an excess supply of foreign loanable funds tends to act against macrostability. It is a well-known fact that programs based on deindexation of contracts and a fixed nominal exchange rate are especially apt to deactivate a process of high inflation, and even hyperinflation. But it is also an established fact that if the period of fixed nominal exchange rate is excessively extended,

Table 5.14 Evolution of Key Relative Prices
          (%, 1986=100)

| | Real Exchange Rate[a] | | Wholesale/ Consumer | Industry/ Private Services | Industry/ Total Services | Primary/ Private Services |
	U.S.$	Basket				
1980	39.5	46.2	87.1	90.2	87.0	85.4
1981	47.9	51.8	88.3	90.5	88.3	78.3
1982	82.4	83.9	116.9	139.4	129.9	141.7
1983	97.4	93.6	126.1	146.3	147.1	153.4
1984	90.7	80.7	119.0	131.7	134.6	131.0
1985	105.7	89.4	114.6	120.0	120.0	89.5
1986	100.0	100.0	100.0	100.0	100.0	100.0
1987	103.0	110.6	94.9	99.7	97.1	96.6
1988	98.3	109.5	109.6	126.7	122.0	113.9
1989	133.1	146.6	124.3	155.1	152.8	143.6
1990	90.1	107.1	94.6	85.9	87.0	70.4
1991	67.1	96.3	67.6	61.0	59.5	45.4
December 1991	65.8	81.0	61.8	54.2	53.9	42.3
June 1992	62.6	77.0	57.8	49.4	49.0	38.7
December 1992	61.6	79.1	54.3	38.7	44.2	32.8
March 1993	61.1	80.4	53.3	37.9	43.5	32.2
June 1993	60.9	79.5	52.2	37.0	42.9	32.3
September 1993	60.8	77.9	52.0	36.3	41.6	32.7
December 1993	61.3	—	50.6	35.3	40.6	29.3

Source: Elaborated on the basis of Central Bank data.
Note: [a]Deflated by a combined index of wholesale and consumer prices.

there will be a tendency for the economy to generate unsustainable external disequilibria. In the particular case of Argentina at present, the distortion in relative prices is generating a growing imbalance in the current account. Nonetheless, there is no pressure on the exchange rate because the fluid supply of external credit has provided the required financing.

In such a context, authorities are facing a policy dilemma that is not easy to solve. If the exchange rate regime were modified to induce a correction in relative prices, it might act in favor of medium-run stability to the extent that the current account disequilibrium would tend to be closed. But given the strong emphasis on the fixed exchange rate as a "structural" component of the new economic policy, a correction in the nominal exchange rate would have a deleterious effect on credibility. Furthermore, if the deterioration in credibility induced a shift in the private sector's portfolios in favor of foreign assets, ceteris paribus, the required correction in the real exchange rate should be both greater and more rapid. In this sense, there is a paradoxical situation: given the inflationary and contractionary effects of devaluation, the incentive for the authorities to induce a "preventive" upward correction in the existing exchange rate will always be weak, provided that there are no interruptions in capital inflows. But, if an interruption of capital inflows does not take place, given the passive character of the economic policy, it is likely that the current account disequilibrium will continue to grow.

Obviously, one could conceive of alternatives to devaluation. A sharp fall in the activity level could induce a decline in imports and in the price of nontradables strong enough to eliminate the current account imbalance. This alternative, however, does not seem to be feasible. The required recession would be so far-reaching and would last for so long that its effects on macroeconomic stability would not be much different from the consequences of a devaluation. Besides, from the empirical point of view, there is evidence regarding the downward inflexibility of the overall price level. On the other hand, the passivity of economic policy implies that the occurrence of a recession-cum-deflation could take place only if there were a massive reversal of capital inflows. The government does not have the necessary policy tools to achieve such a result by other means.

The changes induced in the financial structure by the recent upsurge of capital inflows pose an additional problem. Unlike in the tablita period, the remonetization of the economy has taken the form of a growing dollarization of the domestic financial system, led by the increase in the demand for dollar-denominated term deposits. A good part of the new credit generated in this way has been allocated through the domestic financial system to productive activities related to nontradable goods. Either deflation or devaluation would induce a strong increase in the real value of the debt burden for sectors producing nontradables. In such a situation, there would be a marked deterioration in the quality of the banks' balance sheets with subsequent effects on the stability of the argendollars segment of the domestic financial system. If the change in relative prices were induced by a strong recession, deterioration of private agents' financial positions would likely be greater. It is worthwhile mentioning, on the other hand, that an important fall in the activity level would also have a significant impact on the government budget because tax collection has become much more dependent on the activity level following the recent tax system reform.

Aware of this, the government is trying to reduce costs through deregulation of certain activities and reducing or eliminating taxes on production.[34] The viability of that strategy will depend on the strength of fiscal accounts and basically on the ability to reduce tax evasion even more.

For this strategy to succeed, however, it needs to be accompanied by a discrete jump in the economy's productivity level. It could happen only if the investment rate continues to increase above the still low levels. If the increase in productivity were to take place in the production of nontradable goods, the real exchange rate would improve by means of deflation induced by an improvement in productivity, providing such improvement is not passed on to wages.

The current dependence on capital inflows can be a source of instability for another reason. Because current capital inflows are led by the private sector, the participation of private firms in the outstanding stock of foreign debt is increasing. In contrast to the experience of the 1980s, the public sector has succeeded in lowering its degree of external financial exposure, while the overall deficit of the private sector is becoming the primary cause of growth in the stock of foreign debt. This increase in the private debt impeded a further reduction in Argentina's financial fragility indicators, which are still too high. The current ratio between foreign debt (around U.S.$75 billion) and exports, for instance, is around 6.

In addition, financial exposure of domestic firms in terms of argendollars is also high. The stock of private debt denominated in argendollars is currently U.S.$16 billion (6 percent of GDP). This increase in domestic indebtedness was also a consequence of the accrued inflow of funds. It can be expected, then, that creditors in the domestic financial system will behave like "true" foreign investors concerning portfolio decisions if some signs of instability appear.

The similarities between the present economic situation and the Argentine experience of 1978–1981 are quite obvious. Among them are the important capital inflows, the large expansion in domestic credit, the appreciation of the exchange rate, the growing deficit in the balance of trade, and the fragility of the financial system.

There are, however, some significant differences as well. The most important is the situation of international financial markets. Interest rates are now much lower than they were at the beginning of the 1980s. Other significant differences are a better fiscal situation, which is the result not only of the receipts from the privatization process but mainly from the reduction in tax evasion; and the fact that the private sector has a larger participation in the investment process. Therefore, there is likely to be a more efficient allocation of resources. Nonetheless, in assessing the probable relevance of this fact in fostering growth, it should be considered that the investment rate is lower than it was in 1979–1981, mainly because of extremely low public investment. Another difference is that over the last thirty months there has been a persistent reduction in the country risk, which, together with a reduction in international interest rates, has produced an impressive decline in the interest rates of domestic deposits. And finally, although there has been active speculation in real estate and capital markets, signs of the possible generation of a bubble in those markets are not clear. After an initial increase, prices in both markets are lower now than they were eighteen months ago, even though they are substantially higher than at the beginning of the stabilization process.

In spite of their importance, none of these differences concerning the domestic side of the economy seems to be important enough to change the premise that basic similarities exist between the present experience and the one of 1978–1981. Indeed, it is the modified international setting (particularly the present low level of interest rates) that accounts for the main differences between the present situation and the previous liberalization experience. It not only reduces the solvency problems of the public sector, but also reduces the required expected return of any physical investment and renders more likely an important supply of foreign resources for the coming years. In other words, what the situation in the international markets is telling us is that there are more incentives to invest and there is more time to carry out the adjustment process.

But more time and more incentives to invest in physical assets do not guarantee long-run sustainability of reform, especially if the existing distortion in relative prices leads to the accumulation of a larger disequilibrium in the current account instead of setting the economy on a new equilibrium path. A knowledge of the future evolution of exports is essential to answering this question.

Given the important role that the evolution of both national savings and investment will have in determining the macroeconomic viability of the program, it is worthwhile to take a closer look at the path followed by these variables after the reversal of capital flows.

Growth, Foreign Savings, and Investment

The dramatic reduction in investment rates was one of the most damaging consequences of the debt crisis. Table 5.15 shows that between the maximum investment rate, recorded in 1980 (26.6 percent of GDP), and the minimum, following the hyperinflation period of 1989 (14.2 percent of GDP), there is a reduction in capital expenditures of more than 12 percentage points. In the 1982–1990 period, as a consequence, the investment rate was the lowest in the postwar period, its average being less than 18 percent of GDP. It is no wonder, then, that the economy stagnated during this period: in 1990, the GDP was 3.1 percent lower than it was in 1980.

The increase in interest payments during the debt crisis induced a marked reduction in national income. Between 1982 and 1990, due to the burden of interest payments, the gross national product (GNP) was on average 5 percent lower than GDP. Given that consumption expenditures as a proportion of GDP maintained their precrisis level, there was a significant drop in the national savings rate. Because this fall in savings was still more important than that in the investment rate, the economy continued to be heavily dependent on foreign savings throughout the 1980s. A good

Table 5.15   Structure of the GDP
             (%, constant prices)

Year	GDP	Imports	Global Supply	Consumption	Investment	Exports	Domestic Absorption
1980	100.0	11.9	111.9	78.3	26.6	7.0	104.9
1981	100.0	11.6	111.6	80.2	23.6	7.8	103.8
1982	100.0	6.9	106.9	78.1	20.4	8.4	98.5
1983	100.0	6.2	106.2	78.4	19.5	8.3	97.9
1984	100.0	6.3	106.3	79.9	18.5	7.9	98.4
1985	100.0	5.9	105.9	79.8	16.3	9.8	96.1
1986	100.0	6.3	106.3	80.7	17.5	8.2	98.2
1987	100.0	7.0	107.0	79.7	19.5	7.7	99.3
1988	100.0	6.3	106.3	77.5	19.5	9.3	97.0
1989	100.0	5.5	105.5	79.3	15.7	10.5	95.0
1990	100.0	5.5	105.5	78.9	14.2	12.5	93.1
1991	100.0	8.4	108.4	81.6	16.3	10.5	97.9
1992	100.0	12.6	112.6	83.2	19.6	9.7	102.8
1993	100.0	13.4	113.4	82.9	21.0	9.5	103.9

Source: Central Bank.

part of the borrowing needs, as was mentioned, was covered by forced foreign finance (i.e., interest payments arrears).

The continuous recourse to foreign savings to finance the current account, however, does not mean that the country did not effect a significant transfer abroad. There was a net transfer of resources abroad because the flows of new foreign credit were continuously less than the amount of interest that fell due. The resources required to effect the transfer were provided by a trade account, which was permanently in surplus. The counterpart of the trade surplus, in turn, was that each year's domestic absorption was about three percentage points of GDP lower than income (Table 5.15).

This evolution of the external gap greatly changed after the reversal in capital movements. As table 5.15 shows, the net transfer abroad—as measured by the difference between absorption and GDP—fell from a maximum of 6.9 percent of GDP in 1990 to −2.8 percent in 1992. To be sure, the marked reversal in capital flows permitted Argentina to effect a negative transfer abroad for the first time in eleven years.

The loosening of external constraints induced a change in the declining evolution of capital goods expenditures. Between 1990 and 1992, there was a recovery of five percentage points in the investment/GDP ratio.[35] Nonetheless, given the depressed level of investment when the recovery took place, the current amount of capital goods expenditures is still similar to the average ratio observed during the 1980s. Consequently, in order to ensure a sustained process of growth, the investment ratio should be continuously raised in the future.[36] This argument, however, does not mean to ignore the fact that the economy has grown at an average rate of 8 percent during 1991–1992 and 6 percent in 1993. On the contrary, it highlights that the ongoing recovery of the activity level is primarily associated with a growing use of idle capacity in the posthyperinflation period and not with an important expansion of the production facilities.

A second negative characteristic of the recovery process is that it was correlated with a further weakening of savings. During recovery, consumption grew at a higher rate than the one corresponding to the GDP. The ratio of consumption to GDP rose from 78.9 percent in 1990 to 83 percent in 1992–1993 (Table 5.15). The latter ratio represents a maximum in the series and is even greater than the consumption-to-GDP ratio observed during the liberalization experience of 1979–1981.[37] Certainly, the growing private capital inflows explain the fact that both consumption and investment ratios grew simultaneously in 1990–1993.

Indeed, the most important source of uncertainty for the future originates in the fact that demand for foreign savings is already high whereas the investment rate is still small. For a resumption of growth to take place under such circumstances, macroeconomic consistency requires that either the consumption rate be reduced (making room for an increase in the investment ratio without resorting to more foreign savings) or the productivity of investment be strongly improved in order to encourage growth with a given investment ratio. External consistency, on the other hand, requires that the growth rate of sectors producing tradables be greater than those producing nontradable goods. Otherwise, the dependency on foreign savings and the existing external financial exposure of the economy will not be reduced in the future. To achieve the required allocation between tradables and nontradables, and between savings and consumption as well,[38] the most important restriction that the economy is currently facing is the misalignment of relative prices.

In brief, it seems that there should be a change in relative prices; otherwise, a sustainable growth process will become more and more difficult in the future. Even if the present capital inflows persist for a long time, there still remains the question of private sector expectations of the future. It is very difficult to imagine that private investors will be eager to allocate a growing stock of funds in an economy with large current account deficits. Obviously, in addition to these constraints posed by long-run aggregated consistency, the specific short-run macroeconomic problem is still there: how to change relative prices in an economy where the fixing of the nominal exchange rate has played a crucial role in stabilizing inflation and where the dollarization of the financial system determines that a devaluation would induce strong and negative wealth effects on debtors.

Notes

1. It should be mentioned, however, that Chile received strong financial support from multilateral organizations (such as the World Bank, the IMF, and the IDB) during the process of stabilization and structural change in the 1980s. In fact, the far better performance of the Chilean economy during the 1980s compared to that in Argentina, Brazil, or Mexico could have been due to the much greater financial aid received by Chile vis-à-vis the aforementioned countries. The arguments supporting this view appear in Damill, Fanelli, and Frenkel (1991).

2. The liberalization measures eliminated the obligatory noninterest deposit for any external credit. The minimum period for debt repayment was reduced to one year and later completely eliminated. The restrictions on the purchase of foreign exchange were gradually diminished. At the beginning of the program U.S.$5,000 could be acquired without justification; this amount was later raised to U.S.$20,000.

3. Because of the active lobbying pressure of producers, the liberalization of trade did not seriously affect intermediate goods. As a consequence, the profitability of firms producing final goods was severely damaged. They were obliged to cope with international competition but did not have access to inputs at international prices.

4. The future dollar quotation—guaranteed by the government—was set by the so-called tablita cambiaria. The nominal exchange rate for the following eight months was announced at the beginning of the program and as time elapsed the tablita was consistently extended.

5. Obviously, for this to be true, domestic and foreign assets have to be close substitutes. On the effectiveness of monetary policy in a context of imperfect substitution between domestic and external assets, see Obstfeld (1982).

6. The minimum reserve requirements were 45 percent when the reform was launched in 1977. In 1978 they had been reduced to 29 percent, and at the end of 1979 they reached a level of 16.5 percent.

7. The liberalization of the financial system followed the McKinnon approach; in fact, this was the "first" McKinnon approach. In his more recent writings, McKinnon seems to be much more cautious in his analysis of the virtues of financial liberalization attempts; see McKinnon (1991) and Fanelli and Frenkel (1993). On the 1977 financial liberalization in Argentina, see Feldman and Sommer (1984), Feldman (1983), and Damill and Frenkel (1987). On the liberalization experiences in the Southern Cone, see Ffrench-Davis (1983), Machinea (1983), and Díaz Alejandro (1985).

8. Risk premium is measured as the difference between the LIBOR and the return of Bonex (a public bond). On the relationship between risk and current account disequilibrium, see Frenkel (1983). Damill and Frenkel (1987) analyze in detail the financial evolution of the economy during this period.

9. As a complement, the minimum term for foreign debt repayment was eliminated. At the cost of a reduction in the average maturity of the outstanding debt, this measure induced a short-lived reversion of capital outflows in the third quarter of 1980.

10. From April 1982 on, any operation involving foreign exchange had to be previously authorized by the Central Bank. At that point arrears in payments of the services of the foreign debt began to accumulate. The payments associated with profits and royalties abroad had to be made in Bonex instead of foreign exchange. These strict measures were made more flexible afterwards, in 1983 and 1984.

11. See Chapter 4. It should be mentioned that, in Argentina, the flaws of the liberalization experience were aggravated by the presence of a significant fiscal deficit. The public budget disequilibrium made the control of monetary aggregates more difficult. Additionally, the increment in public expenditures induced a further increment in the domestic demand for nontradables, thereby contributing to worsening the existing relative price disequilibrium.

12. We classified capital inflows following the balance-of-payments definitions. According to such definitions, the funds coming from the IMF are classified as compensatory and those from the World Bank and the IDB as autonomous. In recent years, however, much of the financing provided by the latter two institutions has been compensatory rather than autonomous.

13. This figure includes the funds associated with the consolidation of public debt. If the amount corresponding to the consolidation of public debt is subtracted, the net capital outflow is lower (U.S.$1.7 billion). On the other hand, via underinvoicing of exports and overinvoicing of imports, capital outflows have been greater. These kinds of capital movements cannot be identified on the basis of the balance-of-payments statistics.

14. There was not a generalized freezing of prices and it was announced that there would not be any control on prices in the future. In practice, however, there was a whole array of "hidden" punishments for those firms who increased their prices, such as a tightening of tax monitoring and/or access to public bank credits.

15. The issue of public bonds to finance the budget gap is not prohibited by the Convertibility Plan. Nonetheless, the government did not resort to this kind of financing because the private sector might have felt that the government was not adjusting their behavior to the spirit of the law. Two factors greatly helped the authorities to close the budget gap without resorting to money or bonds in the first stages of the Convertibility Plan: first, the proceeds stemming from the privatization process, and second, the "forced" credit provided by foreign banks via payment arrears, which amounted to U.S.$1.7 billion during the first year of the plan.

16. A "positive" consequence of hyperinflation was that it induced an overshooting in the level of the real exchange rate. This encouraged exports and provoked a fall in imports (aggravated by the decrease in the GDP). This generated an unprecedented surplus of more than U.S.$8 billion in the trade account in 1990, which allowed the country to accumulate a sufficient level of international reserves to launch the stabilization plan without waiting for the external support that would otherwise have been needed.

17. The sale of YPF was made in a very short period of time in order to partially amortize the long-term outstanding debt of the social security system. The stock price of YPF increased around 50 percent in the four months following privatization.

18. The aggregate figures do not show the credit received by the government during 1993 in order to make the cash payments related to the Brady Initiative. Most of these credits are included under autonomous capital of the public sector; the payments appear as compensatory capital.

19. This does not mean that there was a reduction in the global stock of public debt. Simultaneous with the canceling of part of the existing debt, there were important operations of consolidation of the floating debt related to the social security system and the public sector suppliers. On the basis of the available data, it is not possible to disentangle the net effect on the stock of public debt.

20. The trade credit is not open in export and import credit in 1993. Therefore, these figures do not include that year.

21. If the amount of repayments of the existing stock of trade credit is similar to the inflow of new credit because imports are not growing, there are no additional funds available, and, consequently, this item of the capital account does not contribute to financing the deficit in the current account.

22. However, if the dollar loans are used to pay imports without "passing" through the exchange market, they will be shown as import credit in the balance of payments.

23. As is well known, not all production corresponding to these sectors is strictly tradable. The estimation in the text, consequently, may overstate the proportion of credit channeled toward tradable goods.

24. These data were extracted from a sample comprising only large debtors; therefore, some bias may exist because of a greater concentration of credit in private banks.

25. This estimation of the country risk tends to be overestimated because the maturity of the Bonex averages two years. Nonetheless, to the extent that the international term structure of interest rates does not change too much, the variable that we are using can be considered a good approximation.

26. The expected rate of devaluation is measured as the difference between the domestic nominal interest rate and the internal rate of return on the Bonex.

27. The monthly costs of intermediation per unit of deposits for the whole financial system averaged 1.65 percent in December 1992. Banks with less than U.S.$29 million in deposits had an average cost per unit of deposits of 2.1–3.3 percent; those with deposits between U.S.$29 million and U.S.$67 million showed costs of 1.6–2.7 percent, and the larger banks (with more than U.S.$67 million in deposits) operated with costs that oscillated between 0.8 percent and 1.6 percent per unit of deposits. On the other hand, it must be taken into account that larger banks cover a greater proportion of their costs with the proceeds from the sale of an array of financial services and that the productivity in the provision of services is greater in larger banks.

28. Two factors seem to have played an important role in limiting their access to large-bank credit. First, during the 1980s, these banks specialized in lending to the public sector and consequently did not develop a department of project evaluation with the skills necessary for the assessment of the repayment capacity of small- and medium-sized businesses. Second, there is a high short-run uncertainty regarding the effects of opening the economy on the performance of such kinds of firms.

29. Indeed, it is possible that the high level of lending rates has accelerated capital inflows. This is a fact that is usually ignored in models explaining capital movements on the basis of interest rate differentials because such models assume only one interest rate for each country. Beyond the fact that there can be multiple interest rates because of the existence of different kinds of risks, it must be taken into account that there are always at least two rates—the lending rate and the borrowing rate. If the difference between the two is small and rates are similar between countries, this fact will not change the result of the simple models too much. However, this is not the case in Argentina, where the wedge between the lending and borrowing rates has been large as well as variable. In such a context, there can be capital movements between two countries in spite of identical deposit rates because there is a sizable difference in lending rates. A case could also occur where an investor simultaneously holds deposits abroad and takes out credit domestically. If there is a great differential between the deposit rate abroad and the domestic

lending rate, he or she could change the portfolio composition by canceling domestic credit by resorting to deposits abroad.

Regarding the recent Argentine experience, it can be argued that a part of the recent spurt in capital inflows has been caused by the huge difference between the deposit and lending rates. Firms repatriated capital to finance their working capital—or their losses induced by the opening of the economy—in order to avoid increasing their domestic indebtedness at exorbitant rates. The quantitative relevance of this phenomenon, however, is difficult to evaluate.

30. The main factors that make it possible for banks to lengthen the term to maturity of loans vis-à-vis that of deposits are foreign exchange credit, bonds placed on the domestic and international markets, and the loanable capacity generated by the banks' liquid net worth (which represents about 7 percent of the banks' total liquid assets). Deposits represent slightly more than 50 percent of the banks' total liabilities.

31. In order to soften the credit constraint of the small- and medium-sized businesses, the government has recently launched some financial measures comprised of subsidies for banks that lend to small- and medium-sized firms. The government has tried to channel some funds coming from multilateral organizations and from public banks in the same direction.

32. Indeed, when the program was launched, there already existed an overvaluation of the domestic currency provoked by the pressure exerted by the huge trade surplus of 1990 and by the incipient reversal of capital flight. The authorities were aware of this fact and at the beginning of the plan tried to induce a fall in the prices of nontradables aimed at improving the real exchange rate. However, this objective was inconsistent with a passive monetary policy that did not put limits on the strong recovery of effective demand. It is not surprising, then, that the expected deflation did not take place. In fact, just the opposite occurred. As time elapsed, the distortion in relative prices widened.

33. It could be argued that the difference is due to the fact that productivity increases more in the tradables sectors than in the services sectors. However, it is difficult to think of divergences in productivity growth of the magnitude observed, especially in the context of a stagnant economy.

34. By the end of 1993 the government announced a reduction of taxes on labor for tradables activities and the substitution of other taxes on production by consumption taxes.

35. The overall investment growth in 1991 and 1992 reached 64 percent. The item that showed the highest rate of growth was machinery and equipment (87 percent). This trend has continued during 1993, but at a slower pace (the increase seems to be around 13 percent).

36. Taking into account that the allocation of investment by public enterprises was far from efficient, it seems reasonable to expect an increment in the efficiency of investment carried out by privatized firms. However, this expected improvement in efficiency must be evaluated in light of the deterioration of the existing economic infrastructure, which calls for an investment rate well above the normal levels to ensure growth resumption.

37. During 1993 this ratio will probably show a slight reduction of around one percentage point of GDP.

38. Among other things, the lag in the exchange rate affects the consumption-to-GDP ratio because the overvaluation of the domestic currency is associated with a tendency for public consumption to increase at a higher rate than overall income.

This fact is a consequence of the high participation of nontradables in public current expenditures.

References

Calvo, G. A., L. Leiderman, and C. M. Reinhart (1993), "Capital inflows and real exchange rate appreciation in Latin America. The role of external factors," *IMF Staff Papers*, vol. 40, no 1, IMF, Washington, D.C.

Damill, M., J. M. Fanelli, R. Frenkel, and G. Rozenwurcel (1993), "Crecimiento económico en América Latina: Experiencia reciente y perspectivas," *Desarrollo Económico*, no. 130.

Damill, M., J. M. Fanelli, and R. Frenkel (1991), "Shock externo y desequilibrio fiscal. La macroeconomía de América Latina en los ochenta: Chile," *Documento Cedes*, no. 77, Buenos Aires.

Damill, M., and R. Frenkel (1987), "De la apertura a la crisis financiera. Un análisis de la experiencia argentina de 1977–82," *Ensayos Económicos*, no. 37.

Díaz Alejandro, C. (1985), "Good-bye financial repression, hello financial crash," *Journal of Development Economics*, vol. 19, September–October.

Fanelli, J. M., and R. Frenkel (1993), "On gradualism, shock treatment and sequencing," *International monetary and financial issues for the 1990's. Research papers for the Group of Twenty-Four,* vol. 2, United Nations, New York.

Fanelli, J. M., R. Frenkel, and L. Taylor (1992), "The World Development Report 1991: A critical assessment," *International monetary and financial issues for the 1990's. Research papers for the Group of Twenty-Four*, vol. 1, United Nations, New York.

Feldman, E. (1983), "La crisis financiera argentina: 1980–82. Algunos comentarios," *Desarrollo Económico*, vol. 23, no. 91.

Feldman, E., and J. F. Sommer (1984), "Crisis financiera y endeudamiento externo," Centro de Estudios Transnacionales, Buenos Aires.

Ffrench-Davis, Ricardo, ed. (1983), *Las relaciones financieras externas. Su efecto en la economía latinoamericana*, Fondo de Cultura Económica (FCE), México.

Frenkel, Roberto (1983), "Mercado financiero, expectativas cambiarias, y movimientos de capital," *El Trimestre Económico*, no. 200.

Machinea, J. L. (1983), "The use of the exchange rate as an anti-inflation instrument in a stabilization-liberalization attempt: The Southern Cone experience," Ph.D. dissertation, University of Minnesota.

Machinea, J. L., and O. Kacef (1992), "Ahorro, inversión y crecimiento. Un análisis de sus perspectivas en el caso argentino," *Documento de trabajo no. 1*, Instituto para el Desarrollo Industrial, Fundación UIA, Buenos Aires.

McKinnon, R. I. (1991), *The order of economic liberalization. Financial control and the transition to a market economy*, Johns Hopkins University Press, London.

Obstfeld, M. (1982), "Can we sterilize? Theory and evidence," *American Economic Review*, May.

6

Capital Flows:
The Mexican Case

JOSÉ ANGEL GURRÍA

During the six years following the 1982 debt crisis, most Latin American debtor countries found themselves in a radically different situation from the one they experienced in the 1970s. From being recipients of large inflows of foreign capital—mainly loans granted by commercial banks—they became net exporters of substantial amounts of capital. Nevertheless, since the second half of 1989 this trend started to change so markedly that several Latin American countries, Mexico among them, have been considered the most dynamic emerging markets of the world in terms of growth of capital inflows.

Thus, from the point of view of developing countries, the globalization of the international financial system has drawn a sizable amount of capital in the last four years. This, in turn, has challenged the ability of developing countries to manage their monetary and exchange rate policies to avoid the undesirable effects on aggregate demand and inflation. Indeed, several questions have arisen, ranging from the change in direction of international private capital flows to an understandable concern over the degree of permanence of this capital and the most appropriate way to steer economic policy to avoid a negative macroeconomic impact. Yet, it is obvious that the main concern of the developing countries lies in taking advantage of the current opportunity to finance the development of productive activities and, in the long run, to foster a continuous, sufficient, and, above all, predictable capital inflow.

Internal and external factors explain the dramatic change in the direction and the composition of capital flows. Among the former, of particular importance are the economic reforms implemented by several developing countries. Undoubtedly, the adoption of consistent macroeconomic policies and the progress achieved in stabilization have created a favorable environment for investment. The pursuit of restrictive monetary policies, in connection with stabilization programs, has resulted in high real interest rates, further stimulating capital inflows; additionally, most of the developing countries have restructured their foreign debt on a permanent basis, thus enabling them to reestablish "normal" relationships with international creditors.

Technological change has generated a permanent process of innovation of financial products and services, making possible almost instantaneous mobilization of vast amounts of capital. Moreover, the trend toward the deregulation of financial markets—in both industrialized and developing countries—has lowered the costs of transactions and broadened the scope for investment opportunities. On the other hand, the current international economic environment, characterized by recession and uncertainty in major industrialized countries by the weakening of the dollar and by historically low interest rate levels, has contributed to the sharp increase in capital flows to developing countries.

Capital Inflows to Mexico Between 1971 and 1993

Like many other developing countries, Mexico turned to external financing to meet its investment requirements due to the low rate of domestic savings. What has changed over the years is the structure of the sources of external financing. From the 1940s to the 1960s such financing came mostly from direct foreign investment and official loans. In the 1970s, the emergence and development of the Eurodollar market, coupled with the recycling of petrodollars, substantially increased the supply of external financing from private sources, whereupon foreign commercial banks, taken together, became Mexico's major creditor.

In addition, in the early 1970s certain academic experts and government policymakers in Mexico began to question the convenience of promoting direct foreign investment into the country. These concerns materialized in the restrictions set forth in the 1973 Law to Promote Mexican Investment and Regulate Foreign Investment, which reserved a number of activities exclusively to the state and to Mexican people.[1]

Thus, the inflow of direct foreign investment, which had increased at an average annual rate of 10 percent between 1959 and 1970, grew only 4 percent annually from 1971 to 1976. This contraction cannot be attributed in any way only to changes in legislation, although they were one factor.

Concurrent with the growing supply of loanable funds brought about by the boom in the Euromarkets, the Mexican government began to radically veer away from its economic policy of "stabilizing development" to a strategy of growth based on a substantial increase in public spending. Because revenues remained stagnant, the gap was covered by relying mainly on foreign debt. Between 1972 and 1982, foreign debt grew at an annual average rate of 28 percent, the highest in this century. Meanwhile, public sector deficit increased steadily, reaching 16.9 percent of GDP in 1982, compared to 4.5 percent in 1972.[2]

The real exchange rate of the peso appreciated substantially. Given a scantily developed financial system (not yet capable of offering inflation-indexed financial instruments), there followed a massive outflow of foreign currency (capital flight). It is estimated that between 1973 and 1982 Mexicans' total assets abroad increased by U.S.$26 billion.[3]

It is important to recall that between 1954 and 1976, Mexico maintained a fixed exchange rate (12.50 pesos per U.S. dollar), with free convertibility and without restrictions on capital mobility. Thus, the current account was adjusted through the following mechanisms: (1) reductions in international reserves, (2) higher effective trade protection, and (3) the introduction of tax incentives to exports.

Gradually, the economy entered into a vicious circle, leaving the Mexican government with very little room to manage its economic policy. The fiscal deficit, by expanding aggregate demand, caused an increase in the current account deficit, which was financed by a reduction in Mexico's international reserves, and that triggered more foreign borrowing and/or increases in effective protection and more fiscal incentives to exports. The reduction in international reserves gave rise to pressures against the peso, thus inducing a growing dollarization of financial assets and ultimately capital flight, which, in turn, increased Mexico's short-term foreign debt requirements, enlarging even further the public sector deficit.

The deterioration of public finances, inflation, capital flight, and the external imbalance, in addition to the sharp reduction in private investment, led to a devaluation of the Mexican peso on August 31, 1976. Between that date and November 30, 1976, a floating exchange rate policy was applied, eventually resulting in a devaluation of 80 percent. Between December 1976 and August 1982, a system of managed depreciation was adopted, although the exchange rate remained unchanged until February 1982.

Between 1978 and 1981, public investment increased considerably (doubling in real terms) due mainly to expansion in the oil sector, given the then-promising outlook regarding international oil prices. To a large extent, this investment was financed through external loans, mainly from foreign commercial banks. As a result, Mexico's outstanding external public debt grew at an average annual rate of 28 percent in that three-year period. Direct foreign investment also increased significantly, at an average annual rate of 19 percent during the same period.

Foreign investment inflows coupled with higher revenues from oil exports explain the rapid growth of foreign exchange supply. Subsequently, the government introduced important changes in its monetary policy, such as the issuance of Treasury bills (Cetes), a more practical instrument for financing the public sector deficit than reserve requirements and one that enabled the government to carry out open market operations. In the beginning, however, Cetes did not have much impact in regulating liquidity, nor, consequently, on sterilizing the considerable capital inflows that occurred between 1978 and 1981. Therefore, the main tool for controlling money supply continued to be mandatory reserve requirements on the commercial banking system. Nevertheless, since 1979 an attempt was made to introduce greater flexibility, by reviewing weekly the rates offered for peso-denominated deposits. These measures, however, were insufficient to curb the increasing appreciation of the peso against the dollar. Although real positive interest rates were maintained to compensate for the exchange rate risk, it was interpreted as a validation of an exchange rate adjustment, further feeding capital flight.[4]

As a response to the speculative crisis, the government decreed exchange controls and the nationalization of commercial banks. Paradoxically, these two measures further aggravated uncertainty and therefore capital flight. In spite of the strict regulation and surveillance of transactions carried out in foreign currencies, it is estimated that capital flight in the final quarter of 1982 alone was U.S.$2.4 billion, equivalent to 40 percent of total exports during that period.

The imposition of a controlled exchange rate turned out to be an inefficient policy to stop capital flight because most foreign exchange operations were transferred to foreign exchange houses and to U.S. banks located along the border area.

The Debt Crisis: Mexico Becomes a Net Capital Exporter

From 1983 to 1987 the main goals of the Mexican economic strategy were to curb inflation, stabilize the economy, and correct the external imbalance. Those policies were marked by the widespread economic crisis that began in 1982, the worst since the Great Depression.

Regarding the external imbalance, it was necessary to establish an orderly foreign exchange market, as well as to simplify its operation. This had to be done under macroeconomic conditions characterized by a severe scarcity of international reserves, a lack of international competitiveness, and, in particular, the external debt burden. This situation impeded the complete freeing up of the foreign exchange market in the short term. Therefore, on December 20, 1982, a dual exchange rate system started to operate, featuring a controlled and a free rate. The controlled rate would apply to the trade of goods and some services, as well as to interest payments on external debt, both public and private. The free rate would apply to all other transactions, such as tourism and border transactions. At the same time, a depreciation of 13 centavos per day was announced, equivalent to an annual 50 percent depreciation.[5]

Monetary policy sought to increase domestic savings and financial intermediation levels through positive real interest rates. Besides, it intended to avoid money creation as a source of public sector financing. Owing to the strong pressures caused by Mexico's excessive external indebtedness, the government sometimes found it necessary to apply a highly restrictive policy.

The excessive external debt burden (coupled with a drastic reduction of external financing) compelled the government to finance its deficit with high reserve requirements on commercial banks and with the creation of domestic public debt instruments. The inflation rate, which soared to unprecedented levels, and the corresponding increase in nominal interest rates, led to higher payments on the domestic public debt, thus worsening the fiscal deficit.

The stabilization efforts carried out between 1982 and 1985 were offset by two highly devastating shocks: the Mexico City earthquakes in September 1985, which required large sums of public spending for reconstruction, and the collapse in the price of oil in 1986, which made the "Mexican mix" drop from an average of U.S.$25 to U.S.$12 per barrel.

In view of these events, the government's fiscal and monetary policies became even tighter, and the real exchange rate depreciated considerably (48 percent in 1986 with respect to 1985). The remarkable improvement in Mexico's external sector in 1986–1987 (when marginal surplus was recorded in the current account), was accompanied by rising domestic prices. Consequently, interest rates remained high, putting additional pressure on public finances coming from the inflationary component of interest payments. The inflationary spiral, aggravated by frequent adjustments of wages and controlled prices, together with the October 1987 "crack" in the Mexican stock market, resulted in important capital flight. In response, the Banco de México withdrew from the exchange market, prompting a drastic devaluation of the peso and fostering greater uncertainty.

Following these events, a nonorthodox stabilization program was implemented in December 1987, in which the exchange rate was a nominal anchor for prices. The basic features of this program were the following:

- The nominal exchange rate was fixed and subsequently a crawling peg was put into effect.
- To reduce fiscal imbalances, fiscal policy focused on rigorous control of expenditures, tax reform to increase revenues, realignment

of prices of goods and services produced by the public sector, and
a comprehensive process of divestiture of public enterprises.

* A restrictive monetary policy was implemented to contribute to the
stabilization of aggregate demand.
* Import duties were reduced and the import permits system dismantled in order to consolidate the goal of a more open economy.
* A system of political consensus, called the "Pacto," was instituted,
which allowed the settlement of key prices through negotiation and
mutual agreement among the representatives of key economic
agents (unions, farmers, government, and private entrepreneurs).

The main results of these measures were a sharp fall in inflation, from
159 percent in 1987 to 20 percent in 1989; a reduction of eleven points in
the financial deficit as a percentage of GDP; an increase in the rate of
growth of economic activity from 1.8 percent in 1987 to 3.1 percent in
1989; and, finally, an environment of stability, which facilitated medium-
and long-term decisions.

The Return of Mexico to Voluntary Capital Markets

Starting in mid-1989, the country became the recipient of sizable capital
inflows. Internal and external factors explain this outcome. Among the latter, the following may be noted: a reduction in international short-term
real interest rates; the recession in industrialized countries; the deterioration of the terms of trade that exacerbated Mexico's current account
deficit, in the presence of a broad supply of external funds; and changes in
U.S. capital market regulations, reducing transaction costs for Mexican
issuers.[6]

Furthermore, the abundance of capital inflows also responded to factors in the Mexican economy itself, notably the high real interest rates, initially closely linked to the stabilization program, and later on due to the
policy of partial sterilization of such capital inflows. In addition to offering attractive real yields, progress achieved in the economic reforms begun
in 1983 had a definite influence in attracting foreign capital. In particular,
the 1989–1992 external-debt-restructuring package was a key factor in
generating greater confidence among investors, leading to the perception
of a reduced country risk (Figure 6.1).

The restructuring of Mexico's external public debt on a permanent
basis, through voluntary debt and debt service reductions, decreased almost immediately the financial requirements of the public sector, not only
because of the agreement with creditors but also because better expectations resulted in a sharp decline in domestic interest rates. Moreover, the

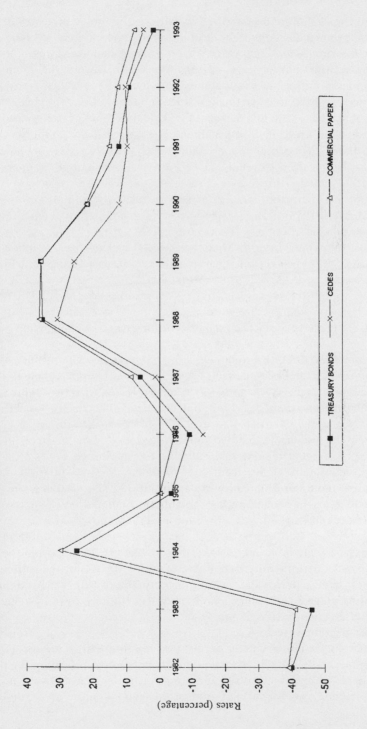

Figure 6.1 Interest Rate Differential Adjusted by Exchange Rate Nominal Depreciation, Mexico

Source: Banco de México.

government used revenues from the divestiture of public enterprises to reduce the balance of public debt, both domestic and external, thereby reversing the vicious circle in which public finances had been caught.

It is therefore not fortuitous that the return of Mexico to the voluntary international financial markets dates from the second half of 1989 onward, when the most difficult part of the negotiations with commercial bank creditors had been concluded. Thus, the capital account of the balance of payments, which recorded an accumulated deficit of U.S.$3.4 billion during the 1983–1988 period, reversed this trend, thereafter showing sizable surpluses that totaled U.S.$93 billion between 1989 and 1993. External flows have not only financed the current account deficit, they have also allowed the accumulation of a large amount of international reserves, which reached U.S.$24.5 billion in December 1993, or the equivalent of more than four months of imports (Figure 6.2).

Most capital inflows into Mexico between 1990 and 1993 were due to direct and portfolio investment and to private sector debt (Table 6.1). Of the total amount of capital inflows for 1990–1993, direct foreign investment accounted for 18 percent and portfolio investment for 54 percent (Table 6.2). Of the total amount of direct foreign investment, 10 percent came from the second auction of the debt-for-equity swap program.[7] External borrowing by the private sector accounted for 26 percent of the total. Public sector participation was rather modest, accounting for only 3 percent of the total, in comparison to the 1970–1979 period, when 70 percent of the foreign capital inflows corresponded to external credit contracted by the public sector.

The Economic Reform

The restructuring of the Mexican economy required a substantial change in the policies that had been followed until 1982. The new strategy sought two basic goals—stabilization and structural reform—through a market-oriented economy.

Stabilization of the economy. One of the cornerstones of economic reform has been the strengthening of public finances by means of the following measures: (1) the reduction of public expenditure, (2) the privatization of public enterprises, and (3) the adjustment of public revenues through tax reform and the correction of prices and tariffs of goods and services provided by the public sector.

Thus, although the public deficit was relatively high between 1983 and 1985, both the operational balance and the primary balance of the public sector reflected in a more accurate way the effort that had been made. Indeed, from 1983 onward, the primary balance (which does not include

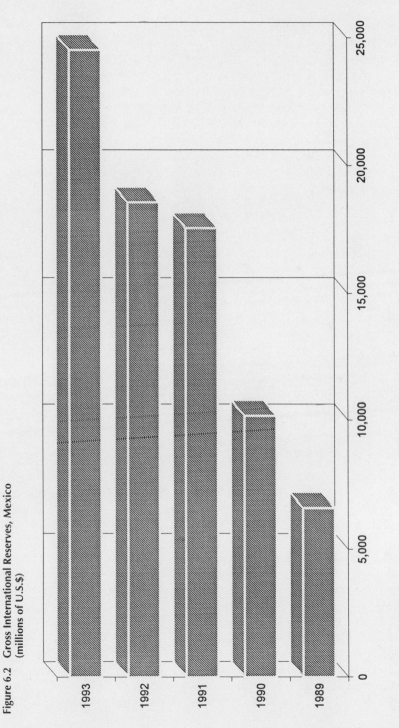

Figure 6.2   Gross International Reserves, Mexico (millions of U.S.$)

Source: Banco de México.
Note: Figures at end of period.

Table 6.1   Foreign Capital Flows, Mexico, 1970–1993
(millions of U.S.$)

	Indebtedness		Foreign Investment		Total Private Flows (2)+(3)+(4)	Total (5)+(1)	Capital Account[a]	Change in Reserves
	Public Net (1)	Private Net (2)	Direct (3)	Portfolio (4)	(5)	(6)	(7)	(8)
1970	443.0	268.6	184.6	0.0	453.2	896.2	1,244.7	102.1
1971	420.6	261.7	173.0	0.0	434.7	855.3	1,089.2	200.0
1972	149.4	460.1	156.1	0.0	616.2	765.6	1,231.2	264.7
1973	1,624.0	706.7	221.7	0.0	928.4	2,552.4	1,651.0	122.3
1974	2,921.6	1,134.6	290.0	0.0	1,425.5	4,347.1	3,262.9	36.9
1975	4,347.8	1,152.3	204.0	0.0	1,356.4	5,704.2	4,607.7	165.1
1976	5,092.2	584.6	211.8	0.0	796.4	5,888.6	2,679.4	1,004.0
1977	2,922.7	−14.1	327.0	0.0	312.9	3,235.6	2,253.5	657.1
1978	2,573.8	789.2	385.1	0.0	1,174.3	3,748.1	3,127.1	434.1
1979	3,352.2	2,058.2	782.2	0.0	2,840.4	6,192.6	5,219.5	418.9
1980	3,754.1	6,909.7	2,155.0	0.0	9,064.7	12,818.8	11,540.2	1,018.5
1981	18,282.4	9,498.6	3,835.8	0.0	13,334.4	31,616.8	17,326.6	1,012.2
1982	7,528.7	−46.8	1,657.5	0.0	1,610.7	9,139.4	2,920.9	3,184.8
1983	3,102.5	−1,982.2	460.5	0.0	−1,521.7	1,580.8	−2,300.4	3,108.8
1984	2,613.0	−2,175.7	391.1	0.0	−1,784.6	828.4	−885.4	3,200.9
1985	954.1	−2,170.6	490.5	0.0	−1,680.1	−726.0	−2,827.9	2,328.4
1986	1,646.2	−2,212.1	941.2	0.0	−1,270.9	375.3	2,373.3	985.0
1987	3,101.0	−2,554.8	1,798.0	0.0	−756.8	2,344.2	2,280.2	6,924.4
1988	−257.7	−1,937.0	1,726.5	0.0	−210.5	−468.2	−3,811.4	−7,127.0
1989	−829.4	−169.9	2,648.0	493.3	2,971.4	2,142.0	6,480.9	271.5

(continues)

Table 6.1   continued

| | Indebtedness | | Foreign Investment | | Total Private Flows (2)+(3)+(4) (5) | Total (5)+(1) (6) | Capital Account[a] (7) | Change in Reserves (8) |
	Public Net (1)	Private Net (2)	Direct (3)	Portfolio (4)				
1990	6,854.1	5,746.4	2,633.2	1,994.5	10,374.1	17,228.2	10,346.8	3,414.3
1991	1,754.3	8,967.1	4,761.5	9,870.3	23,598.9	25,353.2	21,925.9	7,821.5
1992	−1,978.3	5,808.7	5,365.7	13,553.2	24,727.6	22,749.3	23,982.3	1,161.4
1993	−3,383.1	5,013.3	4,900.5	28,430.9	38,344.7	34,961.3	29,433.2	6,083.2
Averages:								
1970–1979	2,384.7	740.2	293.7	0.0	1,033.8	3,418.6	2,636.6	139.7
1980–1989	3,989.5	315.9	1,610.4	49.3	1,975.7	5,965.2	3,309.7	388.1
1990–1993	811.7	6,383.9	4,415.2	13,462.2	24,261.3	25,073.0	17,137.6	3,750.4

Source: Indicadores Económicos del Banco de México.
Note: [a]Includes errors and omissions.

Table 6.2 Foreign Capital Flows as Percentages of Total, Mexico, 1970–1993

	Indebtedness		Foreign Investment		Total Private Flows	Total
	Public Net (1)	Private Net (2)	Direct (3)	Portfolio (4)	(2)+(3)+(4) (5)	(5)+(1) (6)
1970	49.4	30.0	20.6	0.0	50.6	100
1971	49.2	30.6	20.2	0.0	50.8	100
1972	19.5	60.1	20.4	0.0	80.5	100
1973	63.6	27.7	8.7	0.0	36.4	100
1974	67.2	26.1	6.7	0.0	32.8	100
1975	76.2	20.2	3.6	0.0	23.8	100
1976	86.5	9.9	3.6	0.0	13.5	100
1977	90.3	−0.4	10.1	0.0	9.7	100
1978	68.7	21.1	10.3	0.0	31.3	100
1979	54.1	33.2	12.6	0.0	45.9	100
1980	29.3	53.9	16.8	0.0	70.7	100
1981	57.8	30.0	12.1	0.0	42.2	100
1982	82.4	−0.5	18.1	0.0	17.6	100
1983	196.3	−125.4	29.1	0.0	−96.3	100
1984	315.4	−262.6	47.2	0.0	−215.4	100
1985	−131.4	299.0	−67.6	0.0	231.4	100
1986	438.6	−589.4	250.8	0.0	−338.6	100
1987	132.3	−109.0	76.7	0.0	−32.3	100
1988	55.0	413.7	−368.8	0.0	45.0	100
1989	−38.7	−7.9	123.6	23.0	138.7	100
1990	39.8	33.4	15.3	11.3	60.2	100
1991	6.9	35.4	18.8	38.9	93.1	100
1992	−8.7	25.5	23.6	59.6	108.7	100
1993	−9.7	14.3	14.0	81.3	109.7	100
Averages:						
1970–1979	69.8	21.7	8.6	0.0	30.2	100
1980–1989	66.9	5.3	27.0	0.8	33.1	100
1990–1993	3.2	25.5	17.6	53.7	96.8	100

Source: Indicadores Económicos del Banco de México.

interest payments on total public debt) recorded an average surplus of 4.7 percent of GDP; for its part, the operating balance (which eliminates the inflation component of interest payments in local currency on domestic public debt) was brought down to an average annual deficit of 0.8 percent of GDP during the 1983–1988 period, compared to an average deficit of 7.8 percent of GDP during 1981–1982 (Table 6.3).

In 1987, a nonorthodox stabilization program was launched. A key element was the introduction of a permanent forum (the "Pacto") in which the different economic sectors were encouraged to explicitly agree on a strategy to eliminate inflationary inertia. The program contributed to the implementation of measures of structural change and reform without producing a contraction in the level of economic activity. Indeed, between 1989 and 1992 the rate of economic growth outpaced population growth.

Table 6.3   Main Economic Indicators, Mexico, 1983–1993

	1983	1984	1985	1986	1987	1988	1989	1990	1991	1992	1993
GDP per capita (annual growth)	-6.0	1.7	0.6	-5.7	-0.2	-0.8	1.3	2.4	1.7	0.9	-1.5
Inflation	80.8	59.2	63.7	105.7	159.2	51.7	19.7	29.9	18.8	11.9	8.0
Public sector financial balance (as percentage of GDP)	-8.6	-8.5	-9.6	-15.9	-16.0	-12.4	-5.5	-3.5	-1.5	1.7	0.7
Terms of trade (1971=100)	69.4	70.8	72.4	52.9	67.0	60.5	64.5	68.8	65.1	64.0	62.1
Total external debt (as percentage of GDP)	60.2	53.6	52.0	76.3	73.9	60.2	47.7	40.0	37.8	34.6	33.0
Total external debt (as percentage of current account revenues)	310	286	303	392	332	309	257	175	177	180	176
Interest payments (as percentage of exports)	45.3	48.4	46.9	51.6	39.5	42.1	40.6	34.3	31.2	28.1	25.4

Source: Secretaría de Hacienda y Crédito Público de México.

Thus, the financial balance of the public sector, which had reached a deficit of 5.5 percent of GDP in 1989, recorded a surplus of 0.7 percent of GDP in 1993, while at the same time the economy grew at an average annual rate of 3.0 percent (Table 6.3).

The policy of structural change. Mexico began to implement measures of structural transformation in 1983 and continued to do so with greater determination following the oil shock of 1985–1986. Those efforts continued with a broader scope in the administration of President Salinas. Structural transformation was brought about by addressing six general policy areas: (1) trade liberalization, (2) the liberalization of foreign investment, (3) the privatization of public enterprises, (4) economic deregulation, (5) the transformation and modernization of the legal framework of Mexico's land tenure system, and (6) regulation of monopolistic practices through the promulgation of a new Federal Antitrust Law.

Along with these specific actions for structural change, the Mexican economy has experienced a profound macroeconomic adjustment, the most evident results being an adjustment of key prices, the strengthening of public finances, a series of concerted stabilization agreements on prices and wages, and the restructuring of Mexico's external debt.

Characteristics of Capital Inflows

In recent years, developing countries have shown a marked preference for capital inflows that are willing to share the risk of the projects financed. This contrasts with commercial bank loans, the returns of which, in principle, are disconnected from the profitability of the project. Thus, competition for capital flows is now focused on attracting both foreign direct investment and portfolio investment.

The transformation of the Mexican economy from a net exporter to a net importer of capital is the result of a policy aimed at attracting external resources to complement domestic savings, thus supporting investment and growth. The private sector's role in this process has been decisive: in recent years, the ratio of private investment to private savings has increased, whereas public finances have shown a surplus. Mexico's current account deficit during the last five years seems different from that originated in the past; currently it is attributed, among other factors, to private sector decisions leading to a growth of private investment that is above the generation of domestic savings.

Between 1988 and 1993 the current account deficit increased approximately U.S.$20 billion, whereas gross fixed private investment increased U.S.$32 billion. However, in addition to the recovery of private investment, private consumption has shown great dynamism, growing at an average annual rate of 4.7 percent between 1989 and 1993 (Table 6.4), which explains the significant expansion of imports of consumer goods. In this context two elements explain Mexico's trade balance and its current account: first, trade liberalization, and second, the massive inflow of private capital, which explains the appreciation of the real exchange rate (see Table 6.5).

Table 6.4   Aggregate Demand and Supply, Mexico, 1989–1993
             (annual growth, %)

	1989	1990	1991	1992	1993
Supply	5.1	6.1	5.1	5.1	0.6
GDP	3.5	4.4	3.6	2.6	0.4
Imports of goods and services	21.3	19.7	16.4	21.2	−1.2
Demand	5.1	6.1	5.1	5.1	0.6
Consumption	5.7	5.5	4.5	5.3	0.4
Private	6.8	6.1	4.6	5.9	0.0
Public	−0.1	2.3	3.9	2.2	3.0
Investment	6.4	13.1	8.1	13.9	−1.4
Private	7.5	13.3	12.7	20.4	0.0
Public	3.6	12.7	−4.4	−6.6	−5.0
Change in inventories	−13.3	−73.4	0.0	0.0	0.0
Exports of goods and services	2.3	3.6	5.4	0.3	3.5

Source: Secretaría de Hacienda y Crédito Público de México.

Table 6.5   Index of Prices of Tradable and Nontradable Goods
             (1980=100)

	Tradables		Nontradables		Index of Tradables as Percentage of Index of Nontradables
	Index	Rate of Growth (%)	Index	Rate of Growth (%)	
1980	100.0	—	100.0	—	100.0
1981	146.2	46.2	149.1	49.1	98.1
1982	286.1	95.7	278.4	86.7	102.8
1983	551.0	92.6	457.7	64.4	120.4
1984	908.9	65.0	684.7	49.6	132.7
1985	1,484.6	63.3	1,115.7	62.9	133.1
1986	3,029.0	104.0	2,050.7	83.8	147.7
1987	8,248.4	172.3	4,793.6	133.8	172.1
1988	12,167.6	47.5	8,638.0	80.2	140.9
1989	13,680.2	12.4	12,650.9	46.5	108.1
1990	15,989.3	16.9	18,470.9	46.0	86.6
1991	18,591.6	16.3	22,563.3	22.2	82.4
1992	20,290.5	9.1	26,059.4	15.5	77.9
1993	21,453.9	5.7	28,858.2	10.7	74.3

Source: Secretaría de Hacienda y Crédito Público de México.

In 1993 two periods may be set apart. In the first half of 1993, the important capital inflows observed in the previous year continued, although with a decreasing tendency that became clear in the second quarter. The Central Bank kept playing an active role through monetary policy, which resulted in the accumulation of international reserves and the permanence of relatively high interest rates. During the second half of the year, a clear deceleration of capital inflows set in during the period July–September, due mainly to the uncertainty stemming from the pending approval of NAFTA by the U.S. Congress. The sharp fall in those inflows, along with decreasing domestic interest rates, brought about a reduction in the fiscal impact of the sterilization policy.

Direct foreign investment. Throughout Mexico's recent economic history —since the 1950s—direct foreign investment has responded to factors such as: (1) the behavior of international corporations regarding their strategies of expansion and product development; (2) the growth potential of the recipient country's domestic market; and (3) particularly in the last two years, the expectations about NAFTA. Direct foreign investment has also responded to basic determinants such as the cost of capital, wage costs, and legislative and administrative regulations. Nevertheless, it is important to point out that direct foreign investment flows have responded, to a great extent, to companies' marketing strategies and not only to rates for profitability, as is the case for portfolio investment.

Reviewing the behavior of direct foreign investment in Mexico from a long-term perspective, it can be concluded that until the 1970s it responded mainly to the rate of economic growth and the expansion of the domestic market. The high protectionism of that period offered direct foreign investors oligopolistic earnings. Its scant contribution to the improvement of the economy's competitiveness, rooted in the excessive protectionist structure, generated pressures of a nationalistic character to impose stricter regulations on direct foreign investment.

It is possible to distinguish four stages in the inflow of direct foreign investment in the 1980s. In the first stage, from 1980 to 1981, the domestic market's great dynamism and GDP growth were the most important factors in attracting direct foreign investment, despite the deep structural imbalances of the economy. In the second stage, from 1982 to 1984, an excessive external indebtedness prevailed, which caused a severe contraction in economic activity and also in FDI. In 1985 there was a slight upturn, which consolidated in 1986–1987, when direct foreign investment once again increased as a result of the implementation of the debt-for-equity swaps program. Through this program, direct foreign investment benefited from an implicit subsidy coming from the spread between the price at which investors purchased Mexican debt paper in the secondary market and the price at which they sold it to the Mexican government.[8] These years constitute what would be the third stage.

The fourth stage began in 1989, when direct foreign investment flows have responded mostly to investment opportunities associated with NAFTA (Figure 6.3 and Table 6.6). The rules of origin negotiated within the agreement afford enough flexibility to enable the participation of investors from other parts of the world.

Foreign investment flows are linked to some of the changes that have taken place in the real sector of the economy. From 1989 to 1993, there is a shift in relative prices related to changes in the real exchange rate. Thus, the price index of tradables has grown at a slower pace than nontradables, because the opening of the economy that simultaneously took place cushioned the price increases of tradables by means of an enlarged imports supply. Hence, the price index of tradables in relation to nontradables dropped from 140.9 in 1988 to 74.3 in 1993 (Table 6.5).

Nevertheless, from 1989 to 1993 there was not a wide gap among the growth rates of the components of GDP, with the exception of agriculture. Gross domestic product grew at an average rate of 3.5 percent, agriculture activities grew at 0.9 percent, industry at 3.9 percent, and services at 4.5 percent.

Another interesting aspect of foreign investment is its allocation among different economic activities (Figure 6.4). From 1989 to 1993 manufactures decreased its share as recipient of foreign investment from 67 percent to 49 percent, whereas services increased its share from 32 percent to 49 percent. The primary sector is stagnant at very low levels.

Portfolio foreign investment. The Mexican securities market has shown rapid expansion accompanied by high yields from 1988 onward, placing it among the most important emerging markets of the world. In December 1990 the total portfolio of foreign investment at market value amounted to U.S.$4.5 billion. By December 1993, this total had increased to U.S.$54.6 billion (Table 6.7).

Among the factors that explain portfolio foreign investment flows to developing countries, particularly in the case of Mexico, the following may be mentioned: the relative yield of the country's assets compared to those offered by markets of industrialized countries; the country's financial solvency, measured by several indicators that reflect a more solid position; the lower risk perceived by foreign investors with regard to Mexico's domestic economic situation; the lower risk of suffering losses in the real value of assets, caused by a contingent devaluation due to a pre-established sliding of the exchange rate; and the modifications to the legislation to provide more protection to foreign investors.

Figure 6.3   Foreign Capital Flows, Mexico
(millions of U.S.$)

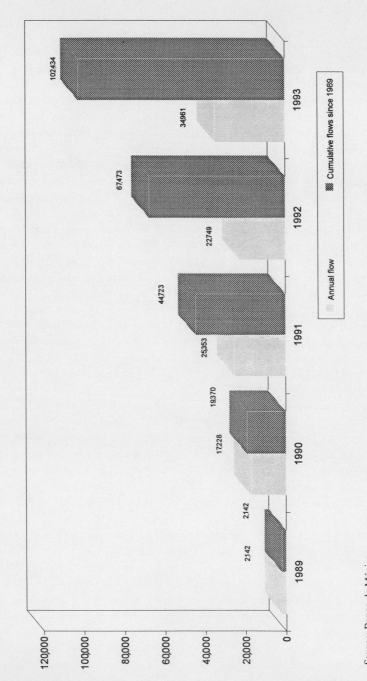

Source: Banco de México.
Note: Includes indebtedness and foreign investment

Table 6.6   Foreign Investment, Mexico, 1987–1993
(millions of U.S.$)

	1987	1988	1989	1990	1991	1992	1993[a]
Direct	2,634.6	2,880.0	3,175.5	2,633.2	4,761.5	5,365.7	3,712.1
New investments	2,318.4	2,204.9	1,660.5	2,017.5	4,605.9	5,392.8	3,195.2
Fresh investment	868.8	1,336.8	1,271.6	1,932.8	4,586.7	5,392.8	3,195.2
Debt-equity swaps	1,449.6	868.1	388.9	84.7	19.2	0.0	0.0
Reinvestments	412.5	691.9	958.3	653.6	756.6	874.0	757.5
Accounts with the head office	–96.3	–16.3	556.7	–37.9	–601.0	–901.0	–240.6
Purchase of foreign enterprises	—	—	—	0.0	0.0	0.0	0.0
Portfolio			493.3	1,994.5	9,870.3	13,553.2	11,321.9
Total	2,634.6	2,880.0	3,668.8	4,627.7	14,631.8	18,918.9	15,034.0

Source: Banco de México, *Indicadores Económicos.*
Note: [a]As of September 30.

Figure 6.4   Direct Foreign Investment by Economic Sector, Annual Flows, Mexico, 1988–1993 (millions of U.S.$)

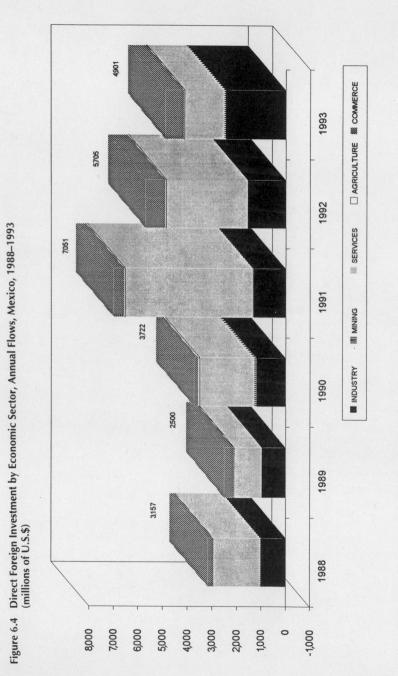

Source: Secretaría de Comercio y Fomento Industrial (Mexico) (SECOFI).
Notes: Excludes portfolio investment.

**Table 6.7   Portfolio Foreign Investment at Market Value, Mexico
(millions of U.S.$, on December 31, 1993)**

Issuing Company	ADRs/GDRs	Free Subscription Shares[a]	Nafin Fund	Mexico Fund[b]	Total	Percent of Total
TELMEX	20,781	1,238	0	99	22,119	40.5
CIFRA	2,169	1,779	133	189	4,269	7.8
CEMEX	1,178	1,507	647	92	3,424	6.3
GFB	1,311	776	153	42	2,283	4.2
TELEVISA	2,629	732	0	20	3,381	6.2
GCARSO	1,001	0	1,297	68	2,367	4.3
FEMSA	272	1,043	0	34	1,349	2.5
BANACCI	0	1,242	470	55	1,766	3.2
KIMBER	28	22	977	83	1,110	2.0
TTOLMEX	93	865	0	48	1,006	1.8
VITRO	267	0	221	24	512	0.9
ICA	695	0	118	20	833	1.5
GGEMEX	190	634	0	9	833	1.5
APASCO	25	15	647	65	751	1.4
TMM	625	24	0	5	654	1.2
OTROS	2,696	3,029	1,718	533	7,975	14.8
Total	33,960	12,906	6,381	1,386	54,632	100.0
Percent of Total	59	26	11	2	100	

Source: Comisión Nacional de Valores, Banamex, Nafinsa, and Citibank.

Notes: [a]Free subscription shares include variable income investment funds, according to the percentage invested in equities (U.S.$59 million).

[b]Total valuation of the Mexico Fund is $1,363.7 million from which $1,173.7 million (86.1 percent) is invested in variable income and $190.0 million (13.9 percent) in fixed income.

The instruments among which Mexican portfolio foreign investments are distributed is presented in Appendix 6.2.

The strategy of internationalization of the Mexican securities market has also rested on the signing of different memoranda of understanding with authorities and agencies of other countries. This has facilitated the placement of Mexican securities abroad, and several international recognitions have been received allowing Mexican issuers to have access to markets abroad.

Moreover, issuers have been favored by the enactment of Rule 144-A, approved by the Securities and Exchange Commission of the United States, thereby simplifying the procedures established by the Federal Securities Act permitting qualified institutional investors to trade privately placed securities. On October 22, 1992, amendments to Rule 144-A were approved increasing the number of qualified institutional investors, thereby opening the way for the participation of trust funds held by governments and banks, such as pension plans, and also that of separate accounts of qualified insurance companies. Some issuers have taken advantage of this flexibility to trade, initially, in private markets, and subsequently to list their stock in a public market (for example, Vitro and Transportación Marítima Mexicana).

The coordination of efforts with the U.S. regulators has also been sought to facilitate concurrent public offerings in the U.S. and Mexican markets. Such was the case of the stock issued by Teléfonos de México. Coordination was enhanced by standardizing legal and accounting practices among both markets. The high level of foreign investment in government securities can be seen in Table 6.8.

Placement of bonds. Another significant aspect of the return of Mexico to international capital markets has been the great number of bond issues placed by public sector entities and by the larger private sector firms. The importance of this source of financing, however, is still relatively modest. The total balance of Mexican public external debt in bonds rose from U.S.$4.1 billion in December 1989 to U.S.$9.4 billion in December 1993.[9]

In June 1989, a Mexican entity placed the first issue of noncollateralized bonds since the beginning of the debt crisis in 1982. This bond issue was for U.S.$100 million, with a maturity of five years, to yield 17 percent, priced at a spread of 820 basis points above the comparable yield on U.S. Treasury notes. Since then and until December 1993, public entities and private sector companies have issued 130 bond offerings for about U.S.$16.4 billion.

The acceptance of these issues has been influenced by the fact that even during the debt crisis, Mexico continued to service its bonds, since

Table 6.8   Foreign Investment in Government Securities, Mexico
             (millions of U.S.$)

	1991	1992	1993
January	—	5,520	15,203
February	3,679	6,447	16,493
March	4,226	7,266	17,527
April	5,003	7,198	18,649
May	5,480	7,790	18,872
June	5,141	8,359	19,024
July	4,157	9,436	19,789
August	3,452	11,037	21,570
September	4,238	11,926	21,921
October	4,697	12,753	22,077
November	5,121	13,633	20,879
December	5,652	14,159	21,263

Source: Banco de México.
Note: Average balances at market value.

this debt formed part of the so-called excluded debt. Moreover, particularly during the initial phase of return to voluntary capital markets, Mexico has resorted to using diverse financial credit-enhancing techniques, including the use of collateral and options with the purpose of making the issues more attractive. In time, with the increase of the country's presence and financial prestige, the number of secured issues have virtually disappeared. Thus, in 1990, roughly 50 percent of the issues involved offered some type of guarantee; in 1991–1993, however, there was not one single collateralized Mexican bond offering, and yields have decreased substantially.

The spread or premium of unenhanced paper above that of risk-free securities has narrowed from 820 basis points in the case of the Bancomext issue (June 1989) to a current level of 120 basis points, or even lower, in the case of securities offered by Mexican public sector entities.[10] While the premium of the first bond offering reflects the entry cost, it should be pointed out that recent issues by public sector entities have been priced at levels reserved for securities of well-established credit capacity.

Although the greater part of the Mexican bond offerings have been denominated in U.S. dollars, Mexico has sought to diversify markets in search of the best conditions at the moment the issue is made. Thus Mexican borrowers have placed bonds in yen, deutsche Marks, ECUs, and Spanish pesetas. Additionally, institutional investors have recognized the increasing credit quality of Mexican debt. This was demonstrated by the Yankee bond market's acceptance of a Mexican government issue, the first Latin American bond offering to be placed directly in the U.S. market and registered with the SEC, paying a yield typical of instruments with an investment-grade credit rating. In February 1994, Nacional Financiera issued U.S.$250 million in "Dragon" bonds with a spread of 100 basis points over LIBOR. It was the first issue of a Latin American country in that market and it was also the lowest yield that has paid Mexico in the international capital markets.

About 73 percent of all Mexican bond issues correspond to the private sector, for a total amount of nearly U.S.$12 billion. The issues have been priced from a maximum spread of 830 basis points in January 1990, to 290 basis points in December 1993, depending on the credit quality of the issuer (see Table 6.9 for related data).

One of the factors that has determined the lower financing costs for Mexican placements and the access to new international capital markets has been the improved credit rating given to Mexican issues by specialized international rating agencies. Currently, international investors, in making their investment decisions, pay close attention to credit ratings assigned by recognized agencies. In fact, in a great number of cases, according to their statutes and regulations, institutional investors cannot acquire issues that have not been rated or assigned an investment-grade rating.

Table 6.9   International Bond Issues, Mexico, 1989–1993

Year	Amount (millions of U.S.$)	Coupon[a]	Spread[a]	Maturity (years)[a]
1989	570	10.72	447	4.2
1990	2,311	11.11	450	4.6
1991	2,475	10.16	305	5.6
1992	3,665	9.10	322	5.4
1993	7,329	8.26	299	5.5

Sources: IMF (1991c); Comisión Nacional de Valores and Secretaría de Hacienda y Crédito Público.

Note: [a]Weighted annual average.

In December 1990, Moody's Investors Service assigned a Ba3 credit rating to the restructured debt bonds of the Mexican government. At the same time, the federal government in general as a debtor was assigned a better level, Ba2. According to that agency, both ratings ranked Mexico in the speculative-grade category.[11] Even though this rating was low, the sustained increase in the price of Mexican debt quoted in secondary markets clearly indicates that investors had a different risk perception.

Subsequently, in July 1991, Standard and Poor's (S&P) Ratings assigned a BB+ rating to Mexican long-term debt, at the high end of the speculative-grade category. According to S&P, Mexico was only one level away from the bracket recommended for investment (investment grade).

In December 1992, S&P assessed Mexico's peso-denominated, short-term public debt (Cetes), assigning it the highest classification that S&P grants to a liability that is short term and in local currency.

Finally in 1993, the rating agency Duff and Phelps assigned the investment grade to debt issued by the two leading development banks, Nacional Financiera and the Banco Nacional de Comercio Exterior.

Despite the growing acceptance of Mexican paper in international markets, Mexican borrowers have followed a cautious strategy so as not to force their entry into the markets, phasing in public offerings in order to avoid a saturation of the market. As for offerings by the private sector, legally there is no restriction that affects the amount, terms, or frequency of these issues. However, informal consultations are maintained with the Ministry of Finance regarding the performance of the markets in order to avoid placing issues under unfavorable market conditions.

Other types of indebtedness.   Mexico has also entered international short-term debt markets (with maturities between 90 and 180 days). Euro–certificates of deposit and Euro–commercial paper have been issued mainly by private sector investors since 1990.

Thus, at first Mexican banks were able to raise sizable amounts of capital through the issue of Euro–certificates of deposit. One year later, some Mexican private firms began to place Euro–commercial paper through public offerings and private placements. In April 1991, Hylsa launched the first program of Euro–commercial paper issued by the private sector. In March 1992, Pemex began to implement in the United States the first program of commercial paper issued by a public sector entity. The financing costs in these markets have also improved, to the degree that some commercial paper issues by Pemex in the United States have offered yields below the prevailing LIBOR.

Greater importance has been given to credits granted by multilateral organizations (the World Bank and the IDB) and those granted by governmental agencies for imports and exports. Multilateral loans have financed projects aimed at strengthening structural change and the modernization of the economy. Between mid-1989 and December 1993 the amount of loans granted by the World Bank and the IDB amounted to U.S.$12.1 billion. They were used to finance projects of decentralization and development, modernization of the education sector, and health-care services, as well as for agriculture and livestock, mining, and electricity. On the other hand, the bilateral export-credit lines currently finance more than 25 percent of Mexico's foreign trade flows, and there are 573 credit lines available with twenty-six countries, for a total of U.S.$15 billion, thus enabling Mexico to use more efficiently its stock of foreign exchange. During the mid-1989 to December 1993 period, bilateral credit lines were used that amounted to U.S.$22.6 billion.

Capital repatriation. Among the measures that have encouraged the return of flight capital are the liberalization and modernization of the Mexican financial system, the offering of positive real interest rates, and the so-called stamp tax facility. The latter is a fiscal incentive started in August 1989 that makes it easier to discharge tax obligations for those taxpayers with capital deposited abroad who want to bring it back. During the first months of the stamp tax facility program, the tax rate depended on the date when the deposit was made abroad. But from May 1990 onward, the government has applied a single flat rate of 1 percent. It was easier, and most important, it was anonymous. If ever a tax audit was performed, the investor simply justified his income by showing the 1 percent stamp and saying it was repatriated money.

From the time the stamp tax was instituted (August 1989) until December 1993, around U.S.$11.5 billion of capital repatriation has been recorded. Of this amount, 65 percent was channeled through Mexican brokerage firms, and banks received the remaining 35 percent. Thus, capital repatriation recorded through the stamp tax facility equaled, in just forty-two months, 40 percent of the capital flight estimated to have occurred between 1973 and 1988 (Gurría and Fadl, 1990).

The Role of the Monetary and Exchange Rate Policies

Capital inflows, while increasing the Mexican economy's import capacity, also entail the risk of expanding aggregate demand excessively and, consequently, generating inflationary pressures. For this reason, since mid-1989, when a sizable inflow of capital into Mexico began to be recorded, the government implemented a diversity of measures to absorb it: (1) privatization, (2) sterilization, (3) limiting banks' foreign currency liabilities, and (4) a more flexible management of the exchange rate policy. It should be pointed out that the surplus in public finances has played a key role in this process, inasmuch as it opened the way for debt amortizations with the Central Bank. This, in turn, has facilitated the task of implementing effective sterilization measures, while leaving room for the private sector to take advantage of the availability of financial resources.

The sterilization policy. The greater flexibility in exchange rate management is due to the adoption of a rule that allows the peso's exchange rate to fluctuate within a specified band. The upper limit of the band depreciates at a preannounced daily pace and the lower limit remains fixed. The Banco de México has agreed to intervene to maintain the peso–U.S. dollar exchange rate between both intervention points. Under these conditions, the monetary authorities are not able to totally control the nominal amount of money, which is determined by variations in domestic credit and in balance-of-payment surpluses.

The stabilization of aggregate demand and a lower inflation have been the foremost goals of economic policy. Accordingly, the Central Bank has pursued an active monetary policy to partially avoid the impact that capital inflows have on the overall liquidity of the economy and hence on the price level and aggregate demand. On the other hand, this policy has contributed to the accumulation of international reserves.

Moreover, the policy has reduced the total amount of domestic credit granted by the Central Bank with two visible results. (1) An increase in nominal interest rates brings about higher levels of public expenditure due to the interest payments on domestic public debt. High nominal interest rates coupled with the rapid decline in inflation have resulted in high real rates. (2) The permanence of high interest rates, in a scenario of favorable expectations, keeps luring capital inflows into the country, which in turn requires further efforts of sterilization.

It should be noted that the Banco de México's law, in force since January 1, 1985, has been crucial for achieving greater effectiveness in monetary

policy management; the charter empowers the Banco de México to determine the maximum domestic financing that it can grant in a year. In fact,
the above-mentioned charter has separated monetary policy from fiscal
policy, making them independent from each other, and has also constituted
a precedent for the autonomy of the Banco de México, recently approved
by the Mexican Congress.[12]

Between December 1989 and October 1993, net international assets of
the Banco de México increased by approximately U.S.$15.2 billion,
whereas domestic credit recorded a reduction of U.S.$12.2 billion (Figure
6.5). The latter was a result of the surpluses of the public sector and of the
restrictive monetary policy.

Divestiture of public enterprises has also had a sterilization effect because the government absorbs part of the excessive liquidity. The proceeds
of the divestiture have been placed in the contingency fund and subsequently used for the amortization of public debt, thus rendering a permanent benefit to public finances. This is another way in which the negative
impact of capital inflows on inflation is offset.

The sterilization policy requires careful handling because restrictive
monetary policy tends to increase the interest rate level, raising the servicing
of the domestic debt. Nonofficial figures estimate that the cost of sterilization
in Mexico was approximately, on average, 0.13 percent of GDP for the period 1990–1993, representing an additional 3 percent in interest payments on
domestic debt by the public sector over the same period (Table 6.10).

Table 6.10   Fiscal Impact of Sterilization

Year	Change in International Reserves (millions of U.S.$) (1)	Interest Rate Differentials: Mexico–U.S. (%) (2)	Fiscal Impact of Sterilization (millions of U.S.$) (3)=(2)x(1)	Fiscal Impact as a Percentage of GDP (4)
1990	3,414.3	15.48	528.5	0.22
1991	7,821.5	9.60	750.9	0.26
1992	1,161.4	6.99	81.2	0.02
1993[a]	4,030.1	2.78	112.0	0.03

Source: Banco de México.
Note: [a]January–September.

Although it is true that the high level of real interest rates has caused
several undesirable effects, it is also true that it is not the only factor that
has provoked economic slowdown or an increase in overdue bank loans.
For instance, in 1989, real interest rates grew to 17 percent while GDP

Figure 6.5   Monetary Base of Mexico
(billions of new pesos)

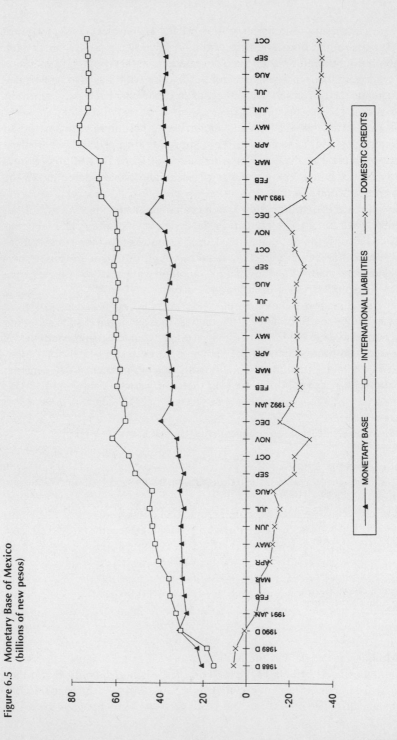

Source: Banco de México.

grew 3.3 percent; on the other hand, in 1993, real interest rates decreased to 6 percent and economic growth was 0.4 percent.

Regarding overdue bank loans, several elements explain this problem, such as, among others, an insufficiently developed mechanism for evaluating credits. Given the strengthening of public finances and the possibility of access to finance through the sale of debt in the open market, the public sector resorted less to bank credit. In such circumstances, commercial banks were forced to compete to place funds with private borrowers at a time when their capacity to assess credit risk had weakened. As a result, assets with little or no risk (public sector debt and loans to selected private borrowers) diminished their importance in the portfolio of banks. This factor, combined with the slowdown of economic activity and the high levels of interest rates, has led to an increase in the ratio of overdue to total credit portfolios. In March 1991, a new system was instituted for rating credit portfolios and creating preventive reserves. Additionally, the banks have had to strengthen their capitalization in accordance with the Base 1 concordat. This requirement was introduced even for banks that are not involved in international operations.

Foreign indebtedness by commercial banks. In the two-year period of 1990–1991, Mexican commercial banks began to issue short-term dollar-denominated certificates of deposit. Although conditions for the issues have become increasingly favorable, the rate of growth of the indebtedness and the risks inherent in the foreign currency liabilities began to generate certain concern.

Therefore, the monetary authorities decided to introduce a liquidity coefficient for liabilities in foreign currency originating in operations of commercial banks and their branches or representative offices abroad. The purpose was to moderate the capital inflows to avoid an impact on inflation.

Despite these measures, commercial bank liabilities in foreign currency increased about 10 percent in three months (December 1991–March 1992), totaling U.S.$11 billion. Therefore, a limit on foreign currency borrowing equivalent to 10 percent of the bank's total liabilities was established. Additionally, a liquidity coefficient for dollar liabilities was set at 15 percent. This coefficient must be invested in low-risk or risk-free assets, so that, in case of an eventual withdrawal of dollar deposits, affected commercial banks could readily draw on a foreign currency source other than international reserves.

The exchange rate policy. In November 1991, the exchange controls system—in force since 1982—was dismantled, in light of the change in circumstances and the virtual matching of the free and controlled exchange rates. The government introduced a widening band formula inside of which the exchange rate fluctuates, affording certainty to the exchange market in the medium term. At the same time, the new formula permits Mexico's exchange rate market to respond with greater flexibility to short-term factors, provided the band stands at an "adequate" level. The widening was achieved by permitting the band's ceiling to continue to depreciate 20 centavos daily, but the band's floor was fixed at the level quoted on that date.

Notwithstanding the widening of the band, the market exchange rate stayed well within the band (Figure 6.6). In October 1992, the daily depreciation of the ceiling was increased from 20 to 40 centavos, so that the exchange rate could fluctuate with greater flexibility. As expected, Banco de México's intervention in the exchange market was reduced. Maintaining a fixed nominal floor in the band prevents an undesirably strong appreciation of the exchange rate.

The advantages of this formula are evident, given the conditions prevailing on international financial markets and the openness of the Mexican economy, which demand that exchange rate policy be more responsive. The widening of the fluctuation band means that some problems posed by capital flows can be solved more easily. If the exchange rate is flexible, the greater supply of capital may be simply reflected in an appreciation of the currency, and an increase in the demand of foreign currency indicates a depreciation in the domestic currency.

The greater flexibility of the exchange rate also helps to discourage capital flows of a very short-term nature. As the band widens, so does the exchange risk for foreign investors, thereby discouraging capital flows that seek only very short-term speculative yields.

Conclusions[13]

Currently, most developing countries that have received sizable private capital inflows in the form of portfolio investment (mainly in highly liquid instruments such as government securities) are trying to anticipate the adverse effects stemming from a reversal of such capital flows. Mexico is not the exception; more than ever, it is necessary to persevere with the reinforcements of policies that reduce the adverse effects of renewed capital flight. Continuing with the strengthening of public finances, reducing inflation to international levels, and strengthening the productivity and competitiveness of the economy are actions in which every effort must be undertaken, thus giving financial viability to the balance of payments in the long term.

The deep changes that have taken place in the Mexican economy have opened a vast array of opportunities for foreign investors. From 1989 to

Figure 6.6 Peso/Dollar Fluctuation Band

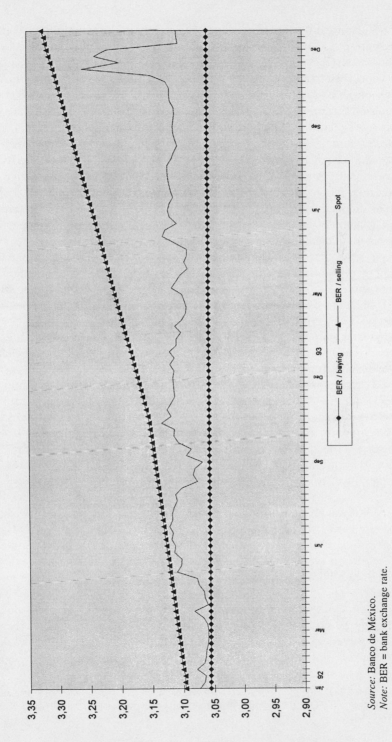

Source: Banco de México.
Note: BER = bank exchange rate.

1993, capital inflows have played a decisive role. Between 1988 and 1993, the current account deficit grew by around U.S.$20 billion (from 1.5 to 6.6 percent of GDP), and the gross fixed private investment is estimated to have increased by U.S.$32 billion (from 12.1 to 17.0 percent of GDP). The imbalance in the external sector may be attributed, in part, to private sector decisions leading to a growth of private investment above the domestic savings capacity, thus requiring increasing amounts of foreign capital. Of those inflows, portfolio investment has been the main component.

A clear change in relative prices took place in the same period between tradable and nontradable goods, making the latter an attractive opportunity for investors: the price index of tradables in relation to nontradables dropped from 140.9 in 1988 to 74.3 in 1993. Appreciation of the real exchange rate appears to be one of the results of massive capital inflows.

A restrictive monetary policy was implemented to partially offset the expansive effect that capital inflows have on the overall liquidity of the economy, and hence on aggregate demand and price level. This policy has contributed, on the one hand, to the goals of lower inflation and stable growth, and on the other hand, has led to the accumulation of international reserves. The control on the total amount of domestic credit by the Central Bank explains the persistence of high nominal interest rates that result, among other things, in high interest payments on domestic public debt. Nonofficial figures estimate that the cost of sterilization was, on average, approximately 0.13 percent of GDP for the period 1990–1993, representing an additional 3 percent in interest payments on domestic public debt by the public sector over the same period. High interest rates in real terms have prevailed due to the rapid decline of inflation and—along with favorable expectations—have lured capital inflows into the country, although during most of 1994 interest rates in the United States showed increases that influenced the rhythm of capital inflows into Mexico.

Appendix 6.1   A History of Foreign Exchange Regulation in Modern Mexico

1954 to August 1976	A fixed exchange rate at 12.50 pesos per U.S. dollar.
September 1976 to December 1976	A regulated floating exchange rate system; the peso lost 80 percent of its value.
December 1976 to August 1982	Controlled depreciation with an important devaluation in February 1982 (from 26 to 45 pesos per U.S. dollar).
August 1982	A sharp devaluation to 95 pesos per U.S. dollar, followed by a regulated floating exchange rate system (it floated briefly until it reached 120 pesos per U.S. dollar).
September 1982 to December 1982	A regulated dual exchange rate with a controlled depreciation established; rigorous foreign exchange controls imposed.

(continues)

Appendix 6.1   continued

December 1982 to December 1987	The regulated dual exchange rate system with controlled depreciation continued, but with more flexibility in the exchange controls. Discrete devaluation (the free exchange rate went from 245.42 to 347.50 pesos per U.S. dollar) and acceleration of the pace of the controlled depreciation beginning in August 1985.
December 1987 to February 1988	The dual exchange rate system continued and a managed floating exchange rate was established with the initiation of the Economic Solidarity Pact.
February 1988 to January 1989	The dual exchange rate continued, but the controlled exchange rate was fixed at 2,257 pesos per U.S. dollar.
January 1989 to November 1991	The regulated dual exchange rate system and controlled depreciation continued. From January 1989 to May 1990 a daily depreciation of one peso was observed in both exchange rates; from May 1990 to November 1990 the daily depreciation was 80 centavos; from November 1990 to November 1991 the daily depreciation was 40 centavos.
November 1991 to November 1992	Elimination of the dual system and of exchange controls; the daily depreciation was 20 centavos.
November 1992 to December 1994	Daily peso/U.S. dollar depreciation of 40 centavos; monetary reform eliminated three zeros from the Mexican currency denomination. An exchange rate band was established.

Source: Catherine Mansell Carstens (1992), "Las Nuevas Finanzas en México," Milenio, México, p. 88.

Appendix 6.2   Distribution of Portfolio Foreign Investment

Portfolio foreign investment in Mexico is distributed among the following instruments:

1. American Depositary Receipts (ADRs) or Global Deposit Receipts (GDRs). These instruments allow foreign investors to acquire stock indirectly in Mexican companies. They are negotiable receipts that are backed by securities of the issuer and are issued and administered by a foreign bank.

2. Free subscription series. This is the traditional instrument that foreign investors have used to acquire assets of Mexican companies. There are no quantitative restrictions for their acquisition and they offer foreign investors the same ownership and corporate rights as those offered to Mexican citizens.

3. Certificates of Ordinary Participation (CPOs) of a neutral trust. This instrument was included in the new Regulation for Foreign Investment. It operates through the formation of trust funds so that foreign investors can acquire shares that under other circumstances would be reserved exclusively to Mexicans.

4. International investment funds. These are funds that maintain an investment portfolio of shares representative of leading companies listed on the Mexican Stock Exchange and that are quoted on the major international markets. These funds have as a precedent the Mexican Fund, created in 1981. It should be pointed out that between 1981 and 1989 no other fund was created, but since then more than fifteen funds, which include Mexican stocks and securities, have been launched in the international markets.

5. Government securities. These investments are made by direct transactions in the money market through Mexican brokerage firms or banks.

Notes

1. This law also established the different percentages for foreign investment participation in Mexican firms, which in no case could exceed 49 percent. However, the National Commission for Foreign Investment was empowered to rule on the increase or decrease of the percentage of participation. According to the law, the following activities were reserved exclusively to the state: (1) petroleum and other hydrocarbons, (2) basic petrochemicals, (3) exploitation of radioactive minerals and generation of nuclear energy, (4) some areas of mining, (5) electricity, (6) railroads, and (7) telegraphic communications. Reserved to Mexicans were (1) radio and television; (2) passenger and cargo transportation on urban, intercity, and federal highways; (3) national air and sea transportation; (4) forestry exploitation; and (5) gas distribution.

2. Since 1973 the new strategy caused an accelerated increase in the inflation rate, averaging 23.9 percent annually between that year and 1982 (in contrast to an annual average rate of 4.7 percent between 1954 and 1970, the period of so-called stabilizing development), as well as a sharp deterioration in the current account deficit, which rose from 2.4 percent of GDP in 1971 to 6.4 percent in 1981.

3. This figure is based on the methodology developed in Gurría and Fadl (1990).

4. The appreciation of the real exchange rate (approximately 27 percent) between 1978 and the beginning of 1982 and the drop in the international price of oil in the second half of 1981 began to generate great uncertainty, which resulted in large capital flight and, subsequently, in the virtual interruption of foreign loans and direct foreign investment. These events led to the devaluations of 1982 (in February, August, and December). Besides, after the devaluation of the peso in August 1982, strict exchange controls were established, which, for the first time in the history of Mexico, restricted free capital movements and the convertibility of the peso.

5. The fixing of the exchange rate in the two markets was done by establishing an initial margin of undervaluation of the peso, sufficient to absorb the adjustment of domestic prices and to provide the necessary spread, so that the other measures of the stabilization program could induce a decrease in inflation. It is estimated that in December 1982 the margin of undervaluation for the controlled exchange rate was 28 percent, and in December 1983 it was 15 percent. The nominal exchange rate was adjusted essentially to the conditions of the market, even though on occasion the Bank of Mexico took part in both markets and the difference between the two quotations expanded considerably, such as in 1985.

6. The approval by the SEC of Rule 144-A in 1990. See IMF (1991b).

7. In the 1989–1990 debt restructuring package with the commercial banks, it was agreed to implement a debt-for-equity conversion program. Conversion rights were allocated by means of two auctions. The outcome of those auctions, held in July and October 1990, was very satisfactory. The resulting conversion prices of 47.95 and 48.0 cents per dollar, respectively, were very close to the quotation for the Mexican public sector debt in the secondary market prevailing at that time (around 43.9 cents per dollar). The conversion rights exercised during the time the swap program was in force (July 1990–April 1992) allowed the cancellation of U.S.$813 million of external public debt.

8. The implicit discount of all the authorized operations in the first swaps program was 18.7 percent.

9. This implies a semiannual growth rate of 23 percent in this period. This increase is explained in great part by the placements in 1991, when the amount of

this type of debt increased 37.5 percent, since a part of these resources were used to finance debt reduction operations.

10. For example, during the first two months of 1994, Nafin placed bonds at spreads of 100 and 112 basis points, Bancomext at 163, and Pemex at 115.

11. Ba2 is in the middle of the speculative grade.

12. It should be noted that in the period of greater economic instability in Mexico from the beginning of the decade of the 1970s to the middle of the 1980s, domestic credit of the Central Bank was the safety variable, supplementing the financing of the public deficit.

13. This chapter was finished in June 1994, six months before the controlled exchange rate scheme was suspended and left to fluctuate freely, bringing forth a devaluation of more or less 50 percent between December 19 and December 30, 1994. Notwithstanding the benefits of the previous plan, various phenomena pressed the exchange rate further than sustainable. Some of the phenomena specifically are: an increase of the current account deficit in 1994 to approximately U.S.$28,000 million (8 percent of GDP); the increase of international interest rates; and investors' uncertainty, due to both economic and political factors, which motivated a considerable reduction of the international reserves to U.S.$6,148 million at the end of 1994.

References

Banco de México, *Indicadores Económicos*, México, D.F., various issues.

————, *Informe Anual*, México, D.F., various issues.

Calvo, G., L. Leiderman, and C. Reinhart (1993), "Afluencia de capital y apreciación del tipo de cambio," *IMF Staff Papers*, vol. 40, no. 1, IMF, Washington, D.C., March.

Cumby, R. E., and M. Obstfeld (1983), "Capital mobility and the scope for sterilization: Mexico in the 70s," in P. Aspe, R. Dornbusch, and M. Obstfeld (eds.), *Financial policies and the world capital market*, NBER, University of Chicago Press, Chicago.

Díaz-Alejandro, C. (1983), "Stories of the 1930s for the 1980s," in P. Aspe, R. Dornbusch, and M. Obstfeld (eds.), *Financial policies and the world capital market*, NBER, University of Chicago Press, Chicago.

Gurría, J. A. (1992), "La política de deuda externa de México, 1982–1990," in C. Bazdresch, N. Bucay, S. Loaeza, and N. Lustig (eds.), *México: Auge, crisis y ajuste*, Serie de Lecturas del Trimestre Económico, vol. 2, no. 73, Fondo de Cultura Económica, México.

——— (1993), "La nueva política de deuda externa de México," in M.E. Vázquez Nava (ed.), *La administración pública contemporánea en México*, Secretaría de la Contraloría General de la Federación and Fondo de Cultura Económica, México.

Gurría, J. A., and S. Fadl (1990), "Estimates on the capital flight in Mexico, 1970–1990," *A Series of Monographs*, no. 4, IDB, Washington, D.C.

International Monetary Fund (IMF) (1991a), "Determinants and systemic consequences of international capital flows," *World Economic and Financial Surveys*, March.

——— (1991b), "International capital markets: Developments and prospects," *World Economic and Financial Surveys*, May.

——— (1991c), "Private market financing for developing countries," *World Economic and Financial Surveys*, December.

Mancera, M. (1993), "La política monetaria en México," in *Testimonios sobre la actuación de la banca central*, vol. 1, Centro de Estudios Monetarios Latinoamericanos, México.

Rodríguez, M. A. (1988), "Consequences of capital flight for Latin America," in D. Lessard and J. Williamson (eds.), *Capital flight: The problem and policy responses*, Institute for International Economics, Washington, D.C.

7

Surges in Capital Flows and Development: An Overview of Policy Issues

ROBERT DEVLIN, RICARDO FFRENCH-DAVIS
& STEPHANY GRIFFITH-JONES

International capital markets have grown dramatically since the mid-1960s. Although international capital movements partly reflect expanding economies, increasing world trade, and the globalization of production, they also involve purely financial factors that rise notably faster. In the 1960s, the growing presence of little-regulated international offshore financial centers stimulated capital movements by evading national financial regulations, capital controls, and taxes. Then, in the 1970s and 1980s, many countries began to deregulate their domestic financial sectors and to relax or abandon the regulation of foreign exchange transactions. These actions, combined with revolutionary technological advances in the handling of information and telecommunications and the emergence of increasingly sophisticated financial engineering, contributed to a boom in both national and international financial flows.

It is premature to speak of integrated financial markets because international capital mobility is clearly far from perfect. Nevertheless, there is no doubt that capital flows and global financial integration are increasing sizably. These developments have aroused controversy. At one extreme, there are those who see rising integration as a sign of greater efficiency; according to this interpretation, markets are overcoming the financial repression characteristic of inefficient government regulation. At the other extreme, there are those who see the boom in capital flows as high-risk speculation that threatens national sovereignty. Of course, between these two extremes there are various intermediate positions that recognize the significant potential advantages of greater international capital mobility, but are also concerned about issues such as the sustainability, composition, and terms of capital flows, and the need to ensure that they are consistent with macroeconomic stability, international competitiveness, growth, and social equity.

Recently, this controversy has assumed greater importance for Latin America. In the 1980s, the links with international capital markets were largely severed as a result of the debt crisis.[1] However, the region has enjoyed a booming expansion of capital flows during 1991–1994. These inflows were most welcome because they overcame a binding external constraint that was contributing to low investment levels and to a severe economic recession in the region. Nevertheless, these inflows have also had an unwelcome effect on the evolution of exchange rates, the degree of control over the money supply, external liabilities, and, probably, future vulnerability to new external shocks.

There is a common overarching theme that emerges in this chapter. Capital flows are clearly an extremely valuable instrument in economic development, as well as in the process of integration of the world economy. However, the intertemporal character of financial transactions and incompleteness of available instruments contribute to making finance markets some of the most imperfectly functioning in the market economy. Hence, improved information, financial sector regulation, and broad prudential macromanagement (direct and indirect) of financial flows constitutes a public good for which there is a shared role for governments—on the supply side for industrialized-country officials and on the demand side for developing-country authorities, coordinated, where relevant, by international organizations. If such precautions are not taken, risks for stability are quite high.

Open Capital Accounts and External Savings

External Capital and Development

In recent years there has been increasing attention to the positive contributions of capital mobility generally, which has given rise to policy recommendations for capital account opening. The arguments in favor of freely mobile capital are backed by powerful theoretical arguments. However, unfortunately, the real second-best world in which we live can seriously condition many of the textbook appreciations. This in turn gives rise to concern about interpreting fashionable theories too literally and applying them to policy without attention to the important caveats that can arise out of a more empirically rooted evaluation of the role of capital mobility in the development process. This can be illustrated by reviewing some of the most commonly cited reasons to promote capital mobility. Among the main ones are the channeling of external savings toward countries with insufficient capital and the compensatory financing of external shocks, which helps stabilize domestic spending.

At the aggregate level, capital movements from developed to developing countries are said to improve the efficiency of world resource allocation (Mathieson and Rojas-Suárez, 1993) because real returns on marginal investment in capital-rich countries are typically lower than those in capital-scarce countries. Like many theoretical arguments, the predicted outcomes depend on compliance with some conditions. Among these is the condition that financial markets, which intermediate most international movements of capital, must have what Tobin (1984) has termed fundamental valuation efficiency. That is, market valuations must accurately reflect the present value of the dividends that the assets in question can be reasonably expected to generate over time.

Accurate pricing is extremely important because prices are the main signal for the market's reallocation of capital. Unfortunately, price movements in financial markets are known often not to reflect fundamentals (Tobin, 1984; Stiglitz, 1993; Kenen, 1993). Thus, empirical studies (summarized in Tobin, 1984; Akyüz, 1993; Lessard, 1991) as well as historical analyses (Kindleberger, 1978) suggest that serious inefficiencies can arise from the allocative mechanisms of capital markets.

In the short term, the imperfections in question can cause financial markets to allocate too much or too little capital (vis-à-vis the underlying returns) to some recipients at a given moment. When the short-term misallocation is very large, it can induce a crisis and have devastating consequences for firms, economic sectors, and nations.

These short-term disturbances in finance, which seriously disrupt output and distort returns to capital, can obviously impart arbitrary advantages and disadvantages on different economic agents, which in themselves can become determinants of returns and thus of international resource allocation trends. It is evident that the phenomenon of hysteresis is extremely relevant in financial matters and their interrelationship with the real economy (Reisen, 1994, chapter 10).

Mobilization of external savings is the classic role for capital flows to a developing country. This has been perhaps the most traditional, and certainly the strongest, argument in favor of international capital mobility and flows to LDCs. Indeed, net inflows of external savings can supplement domestic savings, raise investment, and boost growth. In turn, expansion of aggregate income can further raise domestic savings and investment, thereby creating a virtuous circle in which there is sustained economic expansion, eventual elimination of net foreign debt, and transformation of the country into a capital exporter (see ECLAC, 1994, chapter 10).

Although obviously highly stylized, this traditional framework has some powerful messages. First, external capital flows should consistently go to augment aggregate investment and not be diverted to consumption. Second, an aggressive domestic savings effort is called for: from the outset of a debt cycle, the marginal savings rate must be kept at a level that is much higher than the country's average savings rate and also considerably greater than the investment rate, thus eventually permitting a savings surplus to emerge for repayment of debt. Third, the investment must be efficient. Fourth, the country must aggressively invest in tradable goods in order to be able to create a trade surplus large enough to transform domestic savings into convertible currency, so as to service the debt. Fifth, creditors must be willing to provide stable and predictable flows of finance on reasonable terms.

These conditions may not all be complied with in practice. Countries may experience an ongoing substitution of domestic savings by foreign savings; investments may not always be efficient or channeled sufficiently into tradable goods, and creditor behavior may differ from the desired pattern. Indeed, as convincing as the traditional argument for the transfer of international savings to relatively poorer countries is, the above problems and ensuing payments crises have often caused this valuable developmental mechanism to operate only feebly. Notwithstanding these serious difficulties, foreign savings have historically played a significant role in the development of many countries, with some emerging as industrialized nations and subsequently evolving into major capital exporters.

Capital mobility also can help to spread out over time the costs of intertemporal differences between output and expenditure. However, this process may not always evolve smoothly in practice. If the transitory swings in external variables are reasonably predictable, free capital markets could provide the desired finance without much difficulty. But in developing countries it is not always easy to ascertain whether a downturn in the external sector is transitory and, if so, for how long. This uncertainty, coupled with imperfections in international capital markets (especially informational asymmetries and enforcement problems; see Stiglitz and Weiss, 1981), represents obstacles to the arrival of adequate amounts of external finance.

When this valuable role of international capital mobility is played only imperfectly, the costs of adjustment for developing countries can be enormous. That is because in the face of a negative external shock (and easily exhaustible domestic international reserves), any shortfalls in capital inflows will require immediate cutbacks in domestic expenditure to restore the external balance. Output will almost certainly fall because of the natural rigidities standing in the way of resource reallocation, and there also tends to be a disproportionate cutback in investment. Latin America's external adjustment in the 1980s illustrates these points very well (ECLAC, 1984; Ramos, 1985; Devlin and Ffrench-Davis, 1994).

If finance is treated analytically analogously to goods, social benefits could be perceived in a two-way international trade in financial assets because capital mobility would allow individuals to satisfy their risk preferences more fully through greater asset diversification. This microbenefit is presently the most common argument in favor of capital mobility (Mathieson and Rojas-Suárez, 1993),[2] and has been a widely used argument for justifying a full opening of the capital account of developed and developing countries alike.

The analogy between free trade in goods and free trade in financial assets may be mistaken. Trading in international financial assets is not identical to, for example, cross-border trade of wheat for textiles (Díaz-Alejandro, 1985; Devlin, 1989). The latter transaction is complete and instantaneous, whereas trade in financial instruments is inherently incomplete and of uncertain value because it is based on a promise to pay in the future. In a world of uncertainty, incomplete insurance markets, informational costs, and other distortions, ex ante and ex post valuations of financial assets may be radically different. Moreover, the gap in time between a financial transaction and payment for it, coupled with informational barriers, generates externalities in market transactions that can magnify and multiply errors in subjective valuations to the point where finally the market corrections may be very abrupt and destabilizing. It is precisely because of this that social well-being may decline with deregulation of trade in financial assets and actually rise with a certain degree of increased public intervention (Stiglitz, 1993). Thus, some forms of regulation of trade in certain financial assets not only make markets function better but improve the overall performance of the economy through the enhancement of macroeconomic stability and better long-term investment performance.

Liberalization of the Capital Account: The Evolution of Policy

There is a broad consensus that international capital mobility is a necessary component of the development process. However, most general equilibrium frameworks analyze capital as a whole and take no account of important real-world conditions such as informational bottlenecks, the institutional peculiarities of investors, the structure of the market within which investors operate, the volume and timing of financing, and its costs and volatility. These and other factors do not always mix in ways that permit countries to tap the full potential benefits of external capital movements. Indeed, systemic market failure can and does occur. Frequent reminders of this problem are the major financial crises, accompanied by macroeconomic collapse, that have repeatedly appeared in economic history, including the recent debt crisis in Latin America.

Because the real world can condition the merits of even the most attractive theoretical arguments, it is not surprising that lively debates have arisen over the functioning of international financial markets and capital mobility. For many years, the number of proponents of open capital accounts in developing countries has steadily grown, to the point where many consider that full openness should be a central objective of economic policy. More recently, there seems to be a growing trend toward more pragmatic thinking regarding capital account opening; this view counsels caution and gradualism, to the point of severely questioning the urgency of a perfectly open capital account. There has been some sympathy for the idea of permanently monitoring flows, with regulation being used if necessary to protect domestic macroeconomic balances. A review of trends is given below.

From closed to open economies. During the 1950s and 1960s mainstream professional thinking on development predominantly focused on real economic activity rather than questions of money and financial markets. Moreover, the analysis of capital inflows concentrated on a limited number of channels of funding, basically bilateral aid, multilateral lending, and foreign direct investment. Most developed and developing countries had comprehensive controls on capital movements.

This situation had its roots in the concrete historical circumstance of the Great Depression and the sluggish activity of international private finance in particular, up through the early 1960s. This policy orientation did not have a monopoly of ideas, however. Indeed, it was confronted by competing paradigms, particularly variants of classical laissez faire economics. Moreover, these latter ideas enjoyed a growing international following toward the end of the 1960s, due partly to the increasing difficulties that governments were encountering in bringing their regulation in line with the realities of domestic and international market activity.

The new trends also contributed to a decisive change in the direction of development policy. Major studies emerged that focused on the need to reduce government intervention and to liberalize markets, with special emphasis on domestic finance.

It was also held that an open capital account was needed as a way to raise national savings, deepen domestic financial markets, reduce the costs of financial intermediation through enhanced competition, satisfy individuals' demand for risk diversification, and optimize resource allocation. In short, most of the benefits of capital mobility outlined above were invoked.

Opening up and sequencing. Those attracted to this approach were in broad agreement on the diagnosis and general policy prescription, but there were big differences of opinion regarding implementation. Some argued that basic reforms were part of a "seamless web" and should ideally be undertaken simultaneously in a type of "big bang" (Shaw, 1973). Others favored the sequencing of reforms, with the capital account being opened up only after consolidation of the other liberalization measures, with domestic financial reform and trade liberalization being given the highest priority (McKinnon, 1973).

The capital account was deemed an especially sensitive area because if it were opened up in conjunction with other reforms, it could induce a surge of capital inflows that could bring premature exchange rate appreciation, with negative consequences for trade liberalization and resource allocation. According to this view, a competitive exchange rate was crucial to trade reform. Hence, the regulation of capital flows could be justified as a way to temporarily reduce pressures for exchange rate appreciation.

The different policy approaches began to have real implications for Latin America in the mid-1970s when three Southern Cone countries underwent radical economic liberalization processes, inspired partly by the financial repression hypothesis and the theoretical simplicity of the monetary approach to the balance of payments (see Ffrench-Davis, 1983).

There was an additional incentive for encouraging capital account opening. Many analysts viewed the worldwide boom in international bank lending of the 1970s as an inherently benign event for development. On the supply side, private financial markets—and especially the unregulated Eurocurrency market—were considered to be highly efficient and capable of imposing "market discipline" on borrowers, in contrast to the allegedly inefficient and permissive lending of official agencies (Friedman, 1977). Furthermore, it was felt that portfolio and direct investment decisions were based on the long-term key variables ("fundamentals") of the countries concerned, and were therefore inherently favorable to greater order and discipline. On the demand side, there was also a popular notion that if the borrowers were from the private sector—in contrast to public sector agencies—the resources would be deployed efficiently (Robichek, 1981).

As is well known, the Southern Cone experiment ended in failure, as the economies collapsed under large price disequilibria and speculative bubbles on asset prices, low domestic savings and investment, a huge external debt, and domestic insolvencies. The most popular explanations of the bad experience were the failure of international financial markets and/or flawed sequencing of the liberalization reforms.

As far as market failure is concerned, it was concluded that the so-called discipline of the private financial market had simply not materialized, for instead of facing an upward supply curve for loans, with credit rationing—as would be assumed for a market with efficient lenders—many developing countries in the 1970s apparently faced a horizontal supply curve (with decreasing spreads charged by lenders and appreciating exchange rates in borrower markets), which gave perverse price signals for the savings and investment process. The reasons for the horizontal supply curve and market failure have been cited by some as the existence of direct or indirect public guarantees for lenders and borrowers (McKinnon, 1991); others have stressed flaws in the structure of financial markets and institutional lending practices, as well as permissiveness in national and international regulatory frameworks (Devlin, 1989).

Concerning sequencing, there is now some consensus in support of the idea that the capital account opening was premature and should have been postponed until other major reforms had been consolidated and equilibrium prices established. The lesson is that during adjustment, open capital accounts (especially in periods of elastic supply of international finance) can induce surges of capital inflows with destabilizing macroeconomic and sectoral effects.

First, if domestic financial markets are still shallow and uncompetitive, they will not be able to efficiently intermediate a surge in capital flows, thereby threatening the sustainability of the flows themselves. Second, fiscal parameters must be consolidated and policy must be flexible, for without a solid tax base and flexible fiscal instruments, authorities must rely too much on monetary policy to regulate the domestic economy. Furthermore, the tax base must be strong enough to sustain adequate levels of public spending consistent with long-term development needs.

Last, because part of the capital flows are inevitably spent on non-tradables, the relative price of the latter tends to rise, with consequent real exchange rate appreciation. This, in turn, is reflected in widening of the current account deficit. The real appreciation of the exchange rate can obviously distort resource allocation and investment, seriously weakening a country's medium-term structural objective of penetrating external markets with new exports. Real appreciation also tends to bring unnecessary social costs, as domestic resources most probably will later have to be switched back to production of more tradable goods through real exchange rate depreciation (Edwards, 1984; Park and Park, 1993; World Bank, 1993). This is because the counterpart of the current account deficit is an accumulation of external liabilities, which must eventually be serviced in foreign exchange.

A considerable body of expert opinion has thus emerged that urges that several segments of the capital account should be opened only after the consolidation of other major liberalization programs, especially in the areas of trade and domestic finance; indeed, according to McKinnon (1991, p. 117), "during liberalization, stringent controls on suddenly increased inflows (or outflows) of short-term capital are warranted" (see also World Bank, 1993).

Where there has been perhaps most divergence of opinion is with respect to the speed of capital account opening once the decision is taken. Some have advocated rapid and ambitious opening up, whereas others counsel a gradual approach. The former position is favored by those who distrust government intervention in foreign exchange and capital markets and/or fear that vested interests will paralyze liberalization programs. The latter approach stems from the belief that macroeconomic stability also requires a certain sequence in capital account opening itself.

At a more general level, a clear distinction is drawn between inflows and outflows, and it is suggested that countries should liberalize the former before the latter, partly because the benefits that can be derived from outflows are more evident for a country that has accumulated substantial net foreign assets (Williamson, 1991, 1993). There could also be sequencing within the components of inflows and outflows; for instance, long-term inflows could be liberalized before short-term transactions, whereas in the case of outflows, priority might be given to direct export-oriented investments and trade credit.

The gradualist approach is more consistent with the insights gained from the international discussion on the sequencing of reforms. Thus, even though developing countries may have made radical reforms, it may take many years before conditions emerge (such as a deep and institutionally diversified domestic financial market; a broad, consolidated tax base; a diversified, internationally competitive export sector; or a wide range of available macroeconomic policy instruments) that will allow their economies to absorb unregulated movements of external capital in ways that are consistent with sustained growth and social equity.

The proponents of sequencing question only the order and timing of liberalization, not the ultimate objective of an open capital account. Yet the overriding importance of macroeconomic stability, coupled with the overwhelming size of international capital markets compared with the much smaller Latin American economies and the serious imperfections existing in such markets, may make an inflexible commitment in all circumstances to an across-the-board open capital account undesirable. Indeed, the increasing volatility of international capital flows, and their size, has already given rise to renewed discussion in the industrialized countries on the potentially destabilizing behavior of capital markets and the possible need for their regulation, especially under certain circumstances.

The Surge of Private Capital Flows in the 1990s:
Policy Implications From the Supply Side

Broad Supply Trends

Massive increase in scale of flows. The first point that needs stressing here is the massive scale of private capital flows to Latin America in the early 1990s, as well as the fact that such massive inflows were unexpected. As can be seen in Table 7.1, the net capital inflow into Latin America reached an overall record in 1992–1994, climbing to an average of U.S.$61 billion. Furthermore, net capital inflows reached 5 percent of GDP, which exceeds the ratio of the previous historical peak of 4.5 percent in 1977–1981.

Particularly dramatic has been the sharp increase in flows to Mexico (see Table 7.1), where net capital inflows were nearly zero in the 1983–1990 period, and in 1992–1994 they exceeded 8 percent of GDP, a ratio well above that in 1977–1981. As can also be seen in Table 7.1, both Argentina and Chile recorded large increases in their capital inflows in the early 1990s, but these were less dramatic than those of Mexico.[3]

Change in type of flows. A second important trend of these capital inflows into Latin America is the significant diversification of sources and, above all, the change in their composition. As can be seen in Table 7.2, the share of FDI more than doubled between 1977–1981 and 1991–1992, portfolio equity emerged as a new source of finance for the LAC region (and increased its importance further in 1993 and 1994), and bonds also notably increased their participation, whereas the share of commercial bank lending fell quite dramatically.

These changes in the structure of finance seemed rather positive, as they favor apparently more sustainable flows, and flows with variable interest rates (particularly badly suited for funding long-term development, as shown by the debt crisis of the 1980s) represent a small proportion of total inflows. However, there are some important caveats to this overall positive evaluation of the composition of flows, most of which we will discuss below. Nevertheless, it seems worthwhile to stress here that a source of potential concern is that a fairly high proportion of net capital inflows in the early 1990s (and a higher one than in previous decades) corresponds to short-term flows, where the risk of volatility is both intuitively and empirically higher (ECLAC, 1994).

Finally, it is important to emphasize—as this is often forgotten—that the changes in composition of flows follow overall very similar trends to global ones, especially regarding the declining importance of commercial bank lending and the rapid rise of securities (both bonds and equities). The

Table 7.1 Net Capital Flows to Latin America (annual averages)

	Total Net Flows (billions of U.S.$)				Percentage of GDP[a]			
	1977–1981	1983–1990	1990–1991	1992–1994[b]	1977–1981	1983–1990	1990–1991	1992–1994[b]
Latin America and the Caribbean	29.4	9.6	27.8	61.1	4.5	1.3	2.6	5.0
Argentina	1.9	1.4	1.1	10.6	2.0	2.1	0.6	5.1
Chile	2.6	1.5	2.3	3.1	12.7	7.0	7.3	7.8
Mexico	8.2	0.8	16.3	25.2	5.1	0.2	6.3	8.5

Source: ECLAC (1994, chapter 9).

Notes: Includes long- and short-term capital, unrequited official transfers, and errors and omissions.

[a]These are rough estimates that are extremely sensitive to the exchange rate used to convert GDP in domestic currency into U.S. dollars. For 1990–1994 an average of two estimates was used: one derived from the real parity in 1990 and one based on current rates in each year.

[b]Preliminary figures.

Table 7.2   Capital Flows, Western Hemisphere
             (annual averages as % of total)

	1977–1981	1991–1992
Foreign direct investment	10.7	23.7
Portfolio equity	—	9.9
Bonds	4.5	17.0
Commercial bank loans	66.7	10.4
Suppliers and export credits	6.2	7.3
Official loans	11.1	26.9
Grants	0.8	4.8
Totals		
percentage	100.0	100.0
billions of U.S.$	(49.7)	(56.0)

Source: Based on IMF, World Economic Outlook, October 1993.
Note: This table presents gross flows (excluding short-term loans).

trend toward more short-term flows also seems to be a global one, although it is more true for the LAC region than for East Asia.

The regional composition of the supply flows. The United States is a major source of the private capital flows that come to LACs. Indeed, for the 1987–1990 period, around 35 percent of FDI flows originated in the United States, spurred subsequently by the prospects of NAFTA and broader hemispheric integration. In 1987–1990, around 25 percent of total FDI to the region came from Europe (see Chapter 2). Japan provided a far smaller share of the total, only around 5 percent. It is also interesting that, as Chuhan and Jun point out in Chapter 3, the dominant share of Japanese investment in the LAC region is in tax haven countries; indeed, tax havens such as the Cayman Islands, Bahamas, Bermuda, Virgin Islands, Netherlands Antilles, and Panama received nearly three-quarters of Japanese FDI to the region in 1991.

Equity flows, especially initially, were predominantly from U.S.-based sources (including return of Latin American flight capital). Indeed, as Culpeper reports in Chapter 1, U.S. investors have provided a significant proportion of flows to stock markets of major Latin American countries, especially Mexico, Brazil, and Argentina, with the share for Mexico being particularly large. On the other hand, Japanese investors have clearly and consistently favored East Asian markets. In contrast, European-based sources initially focused on the Pacific Basin but later increased the share of their equity flows going to Latin America; in 1991, European investors were estimated to have reached a peak of 40 percent of total secondary flows to Latin American emerging markets, with this share declining somewhat in later years.

In 1993, bonds became the largest source of private flows going to LACs. It is extremely difficult, however, to distinguish the regional sources of bond financing, especially in the international (or Eurobond) markets, which during the 1990s absorbed from three to five times the volume of foreign bond issues offered in the main domestic markets of the United States, Japan, and Europe. However, it seems worth stressing that an extremely high share of Latin American bonds are raised in U.S. dollars, which does give some indication that U.S.-based investors (including Latin American flight capital based in the United States) are a major source of such funding. The high share of dollar-denominated bonds would seem to reflect both the currency preference of investors and the currency composition of Latin American companies' receipts. Also, very low U.S. interest rates in 1991–1993 encouraged U.S.-based investors to buy Latin American equities. It should be mentioned that, although a vast proportion of LAC bonds are dollar denominated, they are practically all listed in Europe (mainly in Luxembourg); this is due to the greater regulatory freedom and possible tax advantages of European-based transactions in dollar-denominated paper.

As in the case of FDI and equities, Japanese sources have played a minor role in funding LAC bonds. The near absence of Latin American borrowers from the Japanese bond market contrasts with the fairly important presence of some other emerging market countries, especially in the Samurai sector; some of these issuers have been attracted to the Japanese bond market by a cost differential vis-à-vis the Eurodollar market.

Regarding the much smaller domestic bond markets, Latin American borrowers have been mainly active in the U.S. private placement market, where the easing of regulations (and especially Rule 144-A) has greatly facilitated borrowing. In contrast, both European and Japanese domestic bond markets have hardly been tapped by Latin American borrowers.

We can therefore conclude that U.S.-based lenders and investors emerge in the early 1990s as the main source of flows to LAC; this seems linked to a number of factors, including traditional factors, such as geographical proximity, strong political links, and greater knowledge of the area, as well as fairly new factors, such as hemispheric integration (particularly NAFTA and its likely extension southwards) and the large yield differential between investments in the United States and in the LAC region. European flows, although second to those of the United States, are more important than is generally perceived in the region. Furthermore, they seem to have certain features that make them particularly interesting. For example, European foreign direct investors have behaved as "bad weather friends": in 1983–1988, when FDI flows from Japan fell and U.S. flows became negative (due to the debt crisis), European funding fell far less and became the largest source of FDI flows to LACs (see Chapter 2). Also, European FDI in LACs is especially active in manufacturing, in contrast with the United States and Japan, which are reported to be especially active in primary sectors. It may therefore be worthwhile for Latin American companies to make greater efforts than are being done at present to tap European markets as sources of funds, both in securities and in FDI.

An area that has emerged as having likely great future potential for LAC borrowers is that of U.S. and Continental European institutional investors, as both the value of their assets and the proportion of those assets invested internationally are likely to rise quite significantly in coming years.

The main feature of Japanese sources for funding the LAC region has been rather low level. This is disappointing because Japan offers special advantages, not only in potentially better financial terms in some cases (e.g., bonds), but possibly of more importance, because of collateral benefits. For example, the high quality of Japanese technological and managerial know-how may make Japanese FDI particularly valuable in certain sectors. The reasons for low Japanese flows to the LAC region (and declining Japanese investment abroad) are partly transitory, including the wealth effects related to the decline of the Japanese stock market, the decline in the property market, as well as the appreciation of the yen in relation to the dollar. Interestingly, weak Japanese economic growth is reported by Chuhan and Jun in Chapter 3 to be another transitory factor that depresses outward investment. This is in contrast with the U.S. situation, where most analysts have argued that recession and/or slow growth have encouraged outflows in search of more profitable opportunities.

Special efforts by LAC governments and companies may be particularly necessary to overcome the more institutional factors that limit Japanese outflows to LAC, such as fairly stringent regulatory requirements, which imply, for example, that non–investment-grade borrowers are not afforded access to the Japanese bond market. It is to be noted that some of these restrictions have begun to be eased. However, a more binding constraint for Japanese institutional investors to place funds in emerging markets is their preference for highly creditworthy investments. In relation to LAC borrowers, memories of the debt crisis of the 1980s seem to lead to prudence among Japanese lenders and investors to a far greater extent than those from the United States or Europe. As a result, special efforts may be required to persuade Japanese investors and lenders, as well as government officials, that investing in Latin America is profitable in the medium-term.

Some similarities and differences of flows from diverse regions. There are some important similarities and differences between flows originating in the United States, Europe, and Japan. Although such comparisons are useful for a better and deeper understanding of the different markets, it is necessary to stress that there are limits to the distinction, due to a significant movement toward the globalization of such markets. Furthermore, although we stress in our analysis the United States, Europe, and Japan, it is important to mention two caveats. First, there are other, new geographical sources of funds, such as Taiwan. Second, it may be useful for some purposes to disaggregate European flows, distinguishing, for example, between the United Kingdom and the Continent, as traditions and regulations imply significant differences among them, even though the single European market has begun to erode such diversities.

A broad similarity in the three large markets analyzed is that in all of them institutional investors, and especially pension funds and insurance companies, have seen their total assets increase dramatically in the last decade (see Table 7.3). This is particularly the case of U.S. pension funds and insurance companies, whose U.S.$5–6 trillion in assets at end 1992 accounted for nearly 15 percent of all U.S. financial assets and more than 30 percent of assets of financial institutions. Japanese and European (especially U.K.) assets of institutional investors are also very large, and have grown rapidly (see Chapter 3).

There has been a clear trend, in some institutional investors, toward an increase of foreign assets as a percentage of total assets (see Chapter 2, Table 2.12). Particularly sharp has been the increase of this ratio in the U.K. pension funds, where by 1990 it reached around 20 percent, and in the Dutch pension funds, where it reached 15 percent. This is in sharp contrast to German pension funds, where by 1990 only 1 percent of total assets were foreign. The U.S. pension funds are in an intermediate position, as their share of foreign assets was still fairly low in 1990 (at 4 percent of the total), but this share is likely to increase sharply as experts have recommended that these funds should rapidly increase their investment abroad. As a result of these trends, there is a large effective and potential supply of funds available for investing in developing countries, and in particular in the LAC region.

A second similar trend in the major countries is that regulatory changes have taken place that improve access by developing countries to their equities and bond markets. Perhaps particularly important have been measures that facilitate access to the U.S. stock exchange and the private placement segment of the U.S. bond market (see Chapter 1). However, there have also been regulatory changes that facilitate access to the Japanese market, such as the relaxation of quality guidelines for Samurai bond issues and of rules relating to the private placement market for non-Japanese issues (see Chapter 3). To a lesser extent there has been liberalization of regulations in some European countries. For example, the U.K. Securities Investment Board is proposing that the concept of approved markets for authorized unit trusts be abolished. Changes at the European Community

Table 7.3   Total Assets of Institutional Investors
             (billions of U.S.$)

	1980	1988	1990	1991	1992
Pension funds					
Canada	43.3	131.3	171.8	188.4	
Germany[a]	17.2	41.6	55.2	58.6	67.5[b]
Japan	24.3	134.1	158.8	182.3	191.9
United Kingdom[c]	151.3	483.9	583.5	642.7	
United States	667.7	1,919.2	2,257.3	3,070.9	3,334.3
Life insurance companies					
Canada[d]	36.8	85.5	106.1	118.1	
Germany	88.4	213.6	299.5	325.7	375.3[b]
Japan	124.6	734.7	946.9	1,113.7	1,214.9
United Kingdom[c]	145.7	358.9	447.9	516.7	
United States	464.2	1,132.7	1,367.4	1,505.3	
1.624.5					
Insurance companies					
Canada[d]	46.0	108.2	132.9	141.4	
Germany	125.1	301.1	425.8	453.1	529.3[b]
Japan	159.2	890.7	1,137.2	1,329.2	1,433.3
United Kingdom[c]	177.0	431.1	533.2	606.3	
United States	646.3	1,586.6	1,896.6	2,096.9	2,253.2

Sources: Statistics Canada, *Quarterly Estimates of Trusteed Pension Funds & Financial Statistics; Bank of Canada Review;* Statistics Canada, *Financial Institutions' Financial Statistics; Geschaftsberichs des Bundesaufsichtsemtes;* Bank of Japan, *Economic Statistics Monthly;* Board of Governors of the Federal Reserve System, *Flow of Funds Accounts;* Central Statistical Office, *Financial Statistics.*

Notes: [a]Pension and burial funds for 1980 and 1988.
[b]September.
[c]Figures in the first column are for 1981.
[d]Assets held in Canada.

level, linked to the single financial market, also tend to liberalize regulations (see Chapter 2).

Indeed, broad regulations do not seem to be the major constraint for access by Latin America borrowers to bonds and equities markets in the industrial countries, even though regulations of institutional investors in some cases do pose important restrictions. Further study is required to ascertain whether this is the case, and to detect the remaining regulations that unduly restrict such access. Indeed, the main reason institutional investors in the major industrial countries—investors who are attractive from the perspective of the borrowers, given their long-term horizon—are only slowly beginning to invest in or lend to Latin America is not due to regulations; it is because, although conscious of important improvements in Latin American economies and higher returns, they still see LACs as potentially volatile, both economically and politically. Japanese institutional investors are especially prudent because they tend to purchase only high-investment-grade securities and also because memories of the Latin American debt crisis are stronger in Japan due to the closer integration between different segments of investors and lenders. In contrast, U.S. institutional investors have invested relatively more than their European or Japanese counterparts in Latin American paper, and especially in Mexico. As said, the relatively stronger interest of such investors is explained by geographical proximity as well as growing business links with the region, further stimulated by the prospects of broader hemispheric integration.

Issues of Data

Because the mechanisms through which capital flows in the 1990s to the LAC region are on the whole new ones, data on these flows tend to be incomplete. Especially incomplete is information on portfolio flows, in particular on secondary market and derivative transactions. Information on how much institutional investors from the major countries are investing in LACs is also particularly incomplete and tentative. It is difficult for policymakers and regulators to take correct decisions if they have very incomplete data on the magnitude of different types of flows; this was demonstrated in the late 1970s, when poor and incomplete information on bank lending to the LAC region became an important factor influencing incorrect decisions by both market actors and regulators (ECLAC, 1994).

Although important efforts have been made to improve data, additional work is urgently required in this field. At a global level, and for developing countries as a whole, the IMF and the World Bank need to improve data. At a regional level, institutions such as ECLAC and/or the IDB can further improve their reporting of these flows. Last but not least, major source countries need to improve information on outflows to different emerging markets. More complete, consistent, and prompt reporting of private flows will be beneficial to all participants, source and recipient countries, savers, investors, and borrowers alike.

A second area in which data are insufficient and incomplete is the information available to brokers, investment managers, and particularly institutional investors' managers on Latin American economies and on individual companies. When lenders feel that they know less about credit risk than borrowers, they may choose to ration credit rather than raise interest rates, particularly to borrowers whose credit quality is more difficult to ascertain (Stiglitz and Weiss, 1981). This will tend to occur in a context where uncertainty increases, which can cause financial instability (Mishkin, 1991).

Therefore, there are strong practical and theoretical reasons to significantly improve the quality of information about Latin American borrowers that reaches different investors and/or lenders. In particular, the depth of contact should be improved, to channel information toward, for example, large pension fund and insurance managers directly. Culpeper reports in Chapter 1 that the chief constraint on issuers of equity or bonds in the key U.S. market now appears to be the transparency of their financial reporting. For this reason, the implementation across the region of standardized generally accepted accounting principles would apparently be a powerful way to give LAC companies greater access to the U.S. market. Similar efforts need to be made to help tap the European, Japanese, and other markets.

A third area in which information and analysis is very incomplete relates to the ultimate use of the private flows in the different recipient countries. To what extent are these flows being channeled to investment, how efficient is such investment, and what proportion is being channeled to tradables? Answers to such questions would be crucial to help establish that inflows will effectively contribute to long-term growth and development, and that the danger of a future serious debt problem is minimized. The primary responsibility for monitoring the use of such flows would seem to lie with the central banks and regulators of the recipient countries, even though lenders and investors (as well as central banks and regulatory authorities of source countries) would also be expected to take a keen interest in the subject. Systematic monitoring on this topic, as well as more in-depth research where feasible, seems very crucial.

The Financial Risks of the New Capital Flows

The benefits of interaction with private capital flows for the development of recipient economies is partly dependent on stable and predictable access to financial markets. The risk of abrupt restrictions in supply and/or inordinately sharp increases in cost and shortening of the maturity terms of external liabilities are partly determined by perceptions of risk and hence host-country policies. But from the standpoint of LDCs, access also can be heavily conditioned by exogenously determined supply-side dynamics, related to industrialized-country policies in the areas of macroeconomics and prudential regulation.

From this latter perspective, Latin America may be confronting considerable risks of volatility regarding the new financial flows of the 1990s. First, there is a degree of consensus that one driving force behind the new inflow of capital has been exogenously based in a conjunctural relaxation of monetary policy in the OECD area and a consequent dramatic decline in international interest rates, especially U.S. rates (Calvo, Leiderman, and Reinhart, 1993). The increased differential yields on investments in the region have attracted investors that had become accustomed to a decade of relatively high real interest rates in the low-risk OECD area. Moreover, given the special conjunctural setting in Latin America—recovery from a deep and protracted recession—investors were able to capture high returns, with low informational costs, as the need to discriminate among countries and firms was not great. Any significant rise in international interest rates, coupled with higher informational costs for locating high yields, could induce a reversal in the flow of some of the less-committed investors. The negative impact on flows into the LAC region of the 1994 increase in U.S. interest rates further illustrates this point.

The international financial markets may be also more structurally vulnerable than in the past to volatile swings in pricing and volume. For example, many new financial instruments are complex and sometimes not completely understood by all participants, or even by the brokers that put the deals together. There is a growing potential for market instability as derivatives become increasingly important in financial activity. On the one hand, these transactions are unregulated with no margin or capital standards; on the other, the marketing of these instruments is driven by the up-front fees the seller accrues immediately without risk. Finally, information on derivative transactions is extremely incomplete.

In addition to more systemic risks, countries should also be aware of the potential specific risks of the particular modalities through which capital flows to Latin America in the 1990s. This would allow them to maximize benefits and minimize potential costs of private flows.

A major source of the new flows to Latin America is bonds. These have the advantage of being mainly at fixed interest rates. However, as discussed in Chapter 2, the average maturity for bonds in the 1990s is very short (around four years). This implies that a high share of the stock could be rapidly withdrawn, should bonds not be renewed. Less dramatic, but also a cause of concern, is the risk that if renewal of bonds is possible pari passu with higher interest rates, the average cost of borrowing would significantly increase fairly soon, as maturities are so short.

A new form of external private funding for Latin America is equity investment. This has the advantage of a cyclical sensitivity of dividends. However, equity flows also carry important risks for recipient countries. Foreign financiers could, for different reasons, stop investing in equities, and even try to sell their stocks quickly if they feared a worsening prospect in the country. This could either lead to pressure on the exchange rate and/or lead to price falls in the domestic stock exchange. Although the latter effect would diminish the risk of a large foreign exchange outflow, it could have a negative impact on aggregate demand, via a wealth effect, and on the domestic financial system, especially if banks and securities activities are closely integrated either through cross-holdings or investor leveraging. To the extent that a growing part of investment in Latin American shares originates in institutional investors, who seem to allocate their assets using more long-term criteria, the risk of large reversals of flows is smaller. But as long as markets are moved in an important proportion by players who specialize in short-term yields, and as long as equity markets remain relatively thin, the risks of great volatility are inherent to this new modality of external financing.

On the whole, FDI flows seem to be more stable and long-term. It is therefore desirable that a far higher proportion of capital inflows to Latin America come in the form of foreign direct investment than was the case in the 1970s.

Less encouraging is the fairly high proportion of short-term capital flows. (Exact figures are not available—here again an important issue of data improvement arises.) Such short-term flows, by their very nature, pose higher threats of volatility. Indeed, statistical analysis in ECLAC (1994, chapter 9) confirms that short-term flows have been quite volatile in the 1950–1992 period.

Policy Initiatives on the Supply Side

From the perspective of supply, a number of policy issues arise as a result of the greater availability of private flows.

Move to eliminate existing discriminatory regulatory barriers. Understanding regulations and their changes allows borrowing countries to detect noneconomic barriers in source countries that implicitly discriminate against Latin American borrowers. Very strict restrictions on institutional investors' ability to diversify in some source countries toward developing areas would seem to be only one of several possible examples.

In those cases, recipient countries' governments—either on their own or, more effectively, jointly—should lobby for such regulatory barriers to be lowered or eliminated. Here regional institutions such as the IDB and ECLAC could play a valuable supportive role, as could more global organizations such as the IMF and the World Bank.

Participate in global discussions of regulation. There are a number of fora, either global ones such as IOSCO (International Organization of Securities Commissions), or industrial-country ones such as the BIS, where issues of systemic risk of international flows are analyzed, and regulations are suggested or implemented geared to reduce systemic risk and/or to protect investors.

Latin American central banks and governments should actively seek to participate in such regulatory fora; within them, they should support regulatory changes that imply a reduction of systemic risk. Indeed, less systemic risk internationally benefits Latin American countries, which historically have been particularly vulnerable to instability in world financial markets. The types of global regulatory issues that are of crucial interest to LACs seem to include:

1. A coordinated supervision globally of securities markets. Although important efforts have been made to deal with the difficult issues of regulating capital adequacy for bank securities activities, no equivalent basis yet exists for nonbank securities. Indeed, achieving a more closely integrated system of supervision of internationally active intermediaries in securities markets seems to require regulators to develop their equivalent of the Basle concordat for bank supervisors. This is an important regulatory gap that needs filling.
2. More broadly, a serious effort needs to be made to extend regulatory coverage to financial institutions that are now effectively unregulated, such as financial conglomerates.
3. Although agreements on capital requirements for banks reached in the context of the Basle agreement provide a key regulatory step forward, there also needs to be a large effort to reach agreement on standards, such as those for accounting and disclosure, in the different sectors of the financial industry.
4. Also in other aspects, the task of supervisors and regulators goes beyond examination of appropriate capitalization of financial institutions (the area best developed until now) to include more difficult aspects such as concentration of risk, implications of innovations, and potential liquidity of intermediaries' assets and liabilities in crisis situations.
5. There seems to be an increasing need for far better global integration of contract law, so contracts can be internationally challenged and regulators can carry out liquidation proceedings that are internationally equitable and effective.
6. As Lamfalussy (1992), president of the embryonic European Central Bank, has suggested, increasing exposure by banks to off-balance-sheet risks (via swaps, forward agreements, and so forth) aggravates problems of information on bank portfolios, thus increasing the risk of runs. Because derivatives have increased linkages between market segments, disruption in one segment may more easily feed into others, generating systemic risk.

The potential threats posed by derivatives to systemic stability are difficult for regulators to handle, particularly as most trades occur privately between dealers and their customers and are therefore not listed on the exchanges (see Chapter 1). Nevertheless, this is an important challenge for regulators that needs tackling.

Participation in global macroeconomic policy discussions. As mentioned above, the sustainability of private capital flows and the avoidance of rapid withdrawal, potentially leading to crisis, does not depend just on the structure and regulation of international capital markets; it also crucially depends on global macroeconomic conditions.

For this reason, it seems important for Latin American governments to be given the opportunity to participate in discussions of global macroeconomic coordination (such as those dealt with by the G-7), particularly in the case of variables such as interest rates and exchange rates, which so directly affect them. Latin American countries should also put forward their concerns and views to the authorities in individual major industrial countries, regarding the potential impact of those countries' macroeconomic policies on Latin American economies. Again here the IDB and ECLAC may be particularly effective.

An important step toward regional macroeconomic coordination was taken in April 1994 when the governments of Canada, Mexico, and the United States (parties to NAFTA) reached an agreement to establish an exchange stabilization fund of U.S.$8.8 billion.[4] The agreement came after the Mexican peso had experienced several weeks of volatility and uncertainty in foreign exchange markets, threatening to undermine the Mexican government's economic program.

It was not envisaged that this facility would often be drawn upon to defend the currencies in question; rather, the fund was designed to be large enough to discourage speculation and thereby reduce short-term exchange rate volatility. In addition, however, the three countries established a consultative group (the North American Financial Group), involving the finance ministers and central bank governors of the NAFTA parties. This group will engage in regular consultations on economic and financial policy arrangements. This consultative mechanism could provide a vital channel of communication and coordination in the event that exchange rate adjustment is precipitated by the domestic policies of one of the partners (for example, increases in interest rates by the U.S. Federal Reserve Board).

As regional trade liberalization and economic integration spread throughout the Western Hemisphere, it is crucial that such mechanisms of economic and financial coordination be broadened. The establishment of the NAFTA stabilization fund is an acknowledgment of the rapidly growing interdependence among countries, and of the fact that individual countries (particularly the larger ones) should not make macroeconomic policy decisions based on domestic considerations alone without taking into account their impact on trading partners.

Greater prudence by market participants. Market participants need to frequently examine market conditions as well as the consequent appropriateness of their pricing of risk. They need to understand, for example, how assured their credit lines are, how strong their asset backing is, and how much their exposure to different types of risk has been increasing. This refers to both domestic and foreign liabilities. As regards the latter and their risks, interactions among participants from different countries (e.g., via international associations) seem very valuable.

The Surge of Capital Flows in the 1990s: Policy Issues from the Demand Side

Capital Inflows and Their Macroeconomic Effects

The sudden surge in capital inflows has provided the financing needed to continue, in a more socially efficient way, the structural adjustment programs initiated by several countries in the 1980s. However, they have posed challenges concerning the introduction of safeguards designed to prevent them from triggering financial crises, guarantee the stability and sustainability of macroeconomic equilibria, and promote investment. An increasingly relevant issue is that of appreciation-led reduction of inflation. Concern about these challenges has re-emerged as a key element in policy design.

For the region as a whole, the entry of capital has had positive Keynesian-like effects in that it has removed the binding foreign exchange constraint and enabled existing productive capacity to be used more fully and production, incomes, and employment to pick up as a result. The lifting of the external constraint since the beginning of the 1990s has contributed to the recovery of economic growth, whose annual rate increased from 1.6 percent in 1983–1990 to 3.4 percent in 1991–1993 (Table 7.4, line 17) and 3.7 percent in 1994.

The recovery is based largely on the fact that the greater availability of foreign savings has made it possible to finance the larger imports associated with an increased use of existing productive capacity; this, through its effect on output and income, has reactivated aggregate demand. The expansive effect has been general throughout the region, and particularly strong for some countries (for example Argentina, Chile, and Venezuela); nevertheless, there are exceptions. Thus Mexico, although experiencing a particularly large influx of private capital, has not seen such a recovery of growth during the period. The extent to which capital inflows lead to growth is greatly influenced by the existing gap between actual GDP and productive capacity; the nature of domestic economic policies, particularly macroeconomic ones; expectations of economic agents; political developments; and external factors such as the terms of trade.

Table 7.4   Macroeconomic Indicators for Latin America

	Amount (billions of 1980 U.S.$)						Shares of GDP (percent)					
	1976–1981	1983–1990	1991–1993	1991	1992	1993	1976–1981	1983–1990	1991–1993	1991	1992	1993
1. Net capital inflows	32.7	8.9	46.3	32.3	51.8	54.7	4.9	1.1	5.2	3.8	5.9	6.0
2. Change in reserves	6.6	1.3	18.2	16.0	21.9	16.8	1.0	0.2	2.1	1.9	2.5	1.8
3. External savings (1–2)=8	26.1	7.6	28.0	16.2	29.9	37.9	3.9	1.0	3.1	1.9	3.4	4.2
4. Terms-of-trade effect[a]	5.5	30.3	54.2	48.6	53.9	60.2	0.8	3.9	6.1	5.7	6.1	6.6
5. Trade deficit	4.3	–54.9	–47.8	–54.7	–43.8	–45.0	0.6	–7.0	–5.4	–6.4	–5.0	–4.9
6. Factor services	16.9	34.4	28.3	28.8	27.3	28.9	2.5	4.4	3.2	3.4	3.1	3.2
7. Unrequited transfers[b]	0.6	2.3	6.7	6.5	7.4	6.2	0.1	0.3	0.8	0.8	0.8	0.7
8. Deficit on current account (4+5+6–7)=3	26.1	7.6	28.0	16.2	29.9	37.9	3.9	1.0	3.1	1.9	3.4	4.2
9. GDP	671.3	784.9	885.2	858.5	884.3	912.9	100.0	100.0	100.0	100.0	100.0	100.0
10. GNI[c] (9–4–6+7)	649.5	722.4	809.3	787.5	810.5	830.0	96.8	92.1	91.4	91.7	91.7	90.9
11. Consumption	513.5	599.7	684.0	664.1	683.9	704.0	76.4	76.4	77.3	77.4	77.3	77.1
12. Investment	162.2	130.3	115.0	139.6	156.6	163.9	24.2	16.6	17.3	16.3	17.7	18.0
13. Excess of expenditure over output (11+12–9)=5	4.3	–54.9	–86.2	–54.7	–43.8	–45.0	0.6	–7.0	–5.4	–6.4	–5.0	–4.9
14. Excess of expenditure over income (11+12–10)=3	26.1	7.6	28.0	16.2	29.9	37.9	3.9	1.0	3.1	1.9	3.4	4.2

(continues)

Table 7.4   continued

	Amount (billions of 1980 U.S.$)						Shares of GDP (percent)					
	1976–1981	1983–1990	1991–1993	1991	1992	1993	1976–1981	1983–1990	1991–1993	1991	1992	1993
15. Per capita GDP (1980 U.S.$)	2,044	2,013	2,036	2,013	2,034	2,061						
16. Per capita GNI (1980 U.S.$)	1,978	1,853	1,861	1,823	1,847	1,864						
17. Rate of growth of GDP (%)	4.6	1.6	3.3	3.5	3.0	3.2						
18. Rate of growth of exports (goods)	4.2^d	5.6	6.5	4.9	8.1	6.4						
19. Rate of growth of imports (goods)	5.1^d	2.4	14.8	16.1	19.8	8.7						
20. Goods exports	81.8	124.1	167.5	155.5	168.1	178.9	12.2	15.8	18.9	18.1	19.0	19.6
21. Goods imports	79.5	72.7	121.6	104.2	124.8	135.8	11.8	9.2	13.7	12.1	14.1	14.9

Source: ECLAC, on the basis of figures from the balance of payments and national accounts of nineteen countries.

[a] Resources necessary to cover the loss resulting from the increased price of imports as compared with exports by the region, measured at 1980 prices.

[b] Corresponds to private flows in the form of donations and other nonofficial operations.

[c] GNI = gross national income.

[d] Corresponds to the annual rates of growth between 1981 and the averages of 1973–1975.

Since 1990, net capital inflows surged, reaching an annual average of U.S.$61 billion in 1992–1994 (see Table 7.1). About half of net inflows in 1991 went to build up the Latin American depleted international reserves; this share has steadily decreased to one-third in 1993 and to one-eighth in 1994 (before the Mexican devaluation), pari passu with the increased absorptive capacity of the region. Obviously, this capacity has been enhanced by the significant exchange rate appreciations allowed or pushed by several LACs.

Since the terms of trade have worsened significantly during the 1990s (see table 7.4, line 4), there still prevails a sizable gap between GDP and gross national income (GNI) (see Table 7.4, lines 15 and 16).

The investment rate only in 1992 achieved a level above the average of 1983–1990. Furthermore, for only a few of the countries in the region that have received large capital inflows, such as Chile, this increase in capital inflows has been accompanied by a comparatively high investment rate. In all, if we compare 1983–1990 with 1993, net external savings (capital flows minus the increase in reserves) have risen by about three percentage points of GDP, and the investment ratio increased by only one point. The remainder has gone to consumption or to compensate worsening terms of trade, with a crowding-out of domestic savings.

Together with economic recovery, the speed with which capital inflows have closed the external gap and generated a surplus of foreign funds has been reflected in a tendency toward exchange rate appreciation, a rapid reduction in trade surpluses, and an increase in the current account deficit (see ECLAC, 1994). These trends initially reflected the recovery of "normal" levels of aggregate demand, imports, and the real exchange rate, all of which were conditioned by external constraints during the previous period. However, the continuing abundance of capital is tending to maintain these trends over time and has confronted the economic authorities with a dilemma crucial to future stability in that, if capital inflows fall, the levels of aggregate demand and imports and the exchange rate will not be sustainable in the medium term. In their equilibrium values, these variables should reflect the conditions of the domestic goods and money markets as well as the availability of external savings, which depends on the permanent or transitory nature of capital flows.

Three major effects occurred during 1991–1993. (1) A larger proportion of capital inflows was devoted to the accumulation of reserves than in the 1970s, thereby moderating the impact of these resources on the region's economies. (2) Domestic expenditure rose faster than domestic output and national income, with the surplus in the nonfinancial current account at constant prices being reduced and a deficit at current prices appearing, for the first time since 1981, by 1992. (3) National savings were (moderately) crowded out by external savings, as reflected in the fact that the increase in total investment was lower than that in external savings (see Table 7.4).

The effects of the new inflows of capital have not been the same in every country. This is associated with the access to such resources, but particularly with the use the region's economies have made of international financing. The capacity to absorb these flows, and the policies pursued by countries, have been affected by the point reached by each country in the process of economic adjustment. Indeed, the renewed links with international financial markets caught countries at different stages of their adjustment programs.

Policy Approaches

When the authorities are faced with an unexpected abundance of external financing, which they consider to be partly transitory or as flowing too fast for the economy to absorb it efficiently, they can intervene at three levels. At the first level, they can act to moderate the impact on the exchange rate through purchasing foreign currency (i.e., accumulating reserves) by the central bank. At a second, deeper level, they can adopt sterilization policies (e.g., open domestic market operations) to mitigate the monetary impact of the accumulation of reserves at the first level of intervention. At the third level, they can adopt policies on incentives, surcharges, or quantitative controls to regulate capital inflows, thereby influencing the latter's composition and volume. The aim is to encourage flows whose volume is consistent with the economy's domestic absorptive capacity, channeling them into productive investment projects, and, conversely, to discourage the entry of short-term capital.

In general, within a context of financial liberalization, the instruments adopted have been directed primarily at the so-called first and second levels of intervention. Depending on the importance attached to mitigating trends toward appreciation, the authorities of several LACs have carried out different interventions in the foreign exchange market. Moreover, according to whether they have chosen to pursue an active or a passive monetary policy, they have introduced different degrees of intervention to regulate aggregate demand. Some countries have also directly regulated capital flows in order to influence their composition and bring them more into line with their development objectives.

The possible combinations between the first and second levels yield different mixes of exchange rate and monetary policies, which distinguish two major intervention alternatives, nonsterilized and sterilized.

Nonsterilized intervention. The first level, nonsterilized intervention, has been frequently adopted by countries that especially target price stability as the main objective, anchoring it to a fixed nominal exchange rate, and are willing to accept a passive monetary policy. In fact, the central bank must accumulate substantial international reserves as it buys foreign currency brought in by the capital inflows, without sterilizing the monetary effect of these operations. The bet is that national interest rates and inflation rates will converge rapidly with international rates.

An important part of the success of this strategy will ultimately depend on the confidence of economic agents in the capacity of monetary authorities to maintain the nominal exchange rate. Success also depends on the relationship between the nominal exchange rate and inflation. In the face of inertial components of inflation and/or lags in adjustment of imports (which can cause the monetary base to expand beyond desirable levels or the prices of importables to remain high), the use of the exchange rate as an anchor to stabilize prices can cause marked real exchange rate appreciation, a growing excess of aggregate expenditure, and a change in the composition of output biased against tradables. An extreme reliance on this approach to attack inflation is clearly a high-risk strategy. Should important disequilibria emerge, the policy options often narrow down to a severe recession or abrupt and destabilizing corrective measures. Indeed, some would counsel the alternative of direct action on inflation through active fiscal, income, and monetary policies. As Peter Kenen (1993) has commented: "no sensible sailor throws out the anchor before the boat stops moving."

While in practice the countries of the region have used different policy mixes, one can single out Chile in 1979–1982 and Argentina in the 1990s as countries that have come the closest to the pure form of this alternative. The trade-offs in Argentina recently, at least for the medium term, have been relatively large (see Chapter 5). Inflation has come down sharply and the economy has experienced a sizable recovery in investment and economic activity. However, exchange rate appreciation, coupled with import liberalization, has contributed to a marked deterioration of the trade balance, and the current account deficit has been expanding while domestic and national savings have shown a downward trend. Because domestic activity is being fueled disproportionately by external savings, the trajectory of the economy is heavily reliant on the sustainability of capital flows.

Sterilized intervention. This intervention approach involves a sterilization of the monetary effects of accumulating reserves during surges of capital inflows. The purpose is to isolate the money stock from large fluctuations stemming from the mobility of foreign capital (Reisen, 1993). This type of sterilization, if effective, prevents domestic real interest rates from falling and limits the expansion of aggregate demand. This second level of intervention has been preferred by countries that have left behind a recessive conjuncture, maintain an active monetary policy, and, at the same time, maintain a more cautious position regarding capital inflows. It reflects a concern for the sustained development of the tradables sector, and the channeling of foreign capital toward savings and investment (preferably in that sector).

In economies that are making full use of their productive capacity, sterilization has the advantage of helping to control aggregate spending and preventing further appreciation of the real exchange rate. However, if interest rate differentials persist, capital inflows continue to be stimulated, generating further needs for sterilization. At the same time, this intervention may be a source of quasi-fiscal deficits, since the central bank is placing commercial paper in the domestic market at higher interest rates than those it obtains on its international reserves.[5]

Thus, sterilized intervention is not problem-free. Conflicts arise more strongly when there is too little flexibility in the tax system for national economic authorities to be able to use this policy to offset domestic or external shocks. What happens in these cases is that the other policy instruments are overcommitted; in effect, authorities must rely solely on monetary and exchange rate instruments to moderate aggregate spending or to stimulate the economy. A more flexible tax system would permit a better policy mix and more stable interest and exchange rates.

In the absence of a flexible fiscal policy, the problems of sterilized intervention are heightened, enhancing the dilemma confronting the economic authorities when they try to control, simultaneously, the real interest rate (as a monetary instrument for implementing stabilization policies) and the real exchange rate (as an instrument of trade policy for promoting the growth of tradable production). If an interest rate consistent with the objective of curbing inflation (by sterilizing the monetary effects of accumulating reserves) is higher than the international rate adjusted for expectations of devaluation, capital inflows will continue to exert pressure toward real exchange rate appreciation, thereby jeopardizing the objective of competitivity of the tradables sector. Conversely, if the domestic interest rate is allowed to fall, both objectives are thwarted because the higher expenditure induced by lower interest rates will put pressure on prices and will also lead to a real appreciation (Zahler, 1992).

It is for this reason that, in practice, the alternative of sterilized intervention has been combined with other policy measures: (1) at the first level of intervention, to influence the foreign exchange market; (2) at the second level, to regulate aggregate demand through mechanisms other than the interest rate; and (3) at the third level, to modify the volume and composition of capital flows, either directly, through restrictions and charges aimed particularly at short-term capital, or indirectly, by generating exchange rate uncertainty for short-run dealers (see Chapter 4). Within each of these interventions, there exist possible measures, elaborated below.

At the first level of intervention, designed to influence the effects on the foreign exchange market, possible measures include: (1) Increase the demand for foreign exchange through incentives for the outflow of capital during periods of surplus. This can be done by relaxing the rules governing investment by nationals abroad and the repatriation of FDI and by authorizing various debtors to make advance payments. (2) Encourage increased investment intensive in imported capital goods and inputs. (3) Foster mechanisms that encourage productivity increases in keeping with exchange rate appreciation.

At the second level of intervention, the purpose of which is to control the impact on aggregate demand, possible measures include: (1) Introduce mechanisms to regulate financial systems in order to avoid distortions and market incompleteness in the sector, and remove weaknesses in the prudential regulation of the financial system (see ECLAC, 1994, chapters 7 and 12). (2) Impose fiscal discipline to avoid excessive pressures on demand. (3) Supplement the exchange rate policy with social contracts related to prices and wages (as in Mexico).

At the third level of intervention, designed to alter the composition of capital flows, possible measures include: (1) Apply indirect exchange rate measures aimed at reducing the entry (and fostering outflows) of short-term capital by introducing uncertainty as to the short-run evolution of the exchange rate, through intervention by the respective central bank in the determination of this rate. (2) Adopt direct measures to impose restrictions on capital inflows, which can take the form of reserve requirements, without interest, on bank deposits or other credits from abroad, and various kinds of quantitative controls (requirements as to minimum maturity periods, minimum volumes for bond issues, and regulations on the participation of foreign capital in the stock market).

Among the countries that have opted for active intervention, Chile has done so most persistently, but others, such as Colombia, Costa Rica, and Mexico, also deserve mention (see ECLAC, 1994, table 11.4).

Chile is an example of a country deploying a battery of policies at the three levels, so far with excellent results regarding growth, increased domestic savings, and investment (see Chapter 4). The Chilean authorities opted for intervention because they wanted to regulate domestic activity via an active monetary policy, and also to support the country's hard-won export drive by influencing the determination of the real exchange rate in the short term, on the basis of two assumptions: (1) the monetary authority has a better idea of future macroeconomic trends in the balance of payments and their long-term effects on the economy; and (2) more fundamentally, its objectives are longer-term than those of agents operating in short-term markets (Zahler, 1992). Hence, in the face of intense capital inflows, the authorities, interpreting part of this to have a permanent character, allowed for some appreciation. However, they significantly moderated the size of the change, with an active and rather comprehensive intervention, including a number of regulations on short-term capital. Naturally, in order to moderate appreciation of the exchange rate, the country had to be more flexible in its goal of arriving at one-digit inflation. But at 13 percent in 1993, inflation is quite manageable and low by historical standards. As a consequence, Chilean management of capital flows seems particularly effective up to early 1994.

Mexico is an intermediate case between Chile and Argentina. On the one hand, it has given primary attention to convergence of domestic inflation (with that in the United States). However, it has not gone to the extreme of fixing the nominal exchange rate, as has Argentina. There has been considerable real appreciation of the exchange rate, but this has been moderated by some small degrees of levels two and three types of intervention (see Chapter 6), although less comprehensively than Chile. The result has indeed been the achievement of one-digit inflation. However, very tight monetary and fiscal policies, along with political problems in 1994, have kept growth down. It could be said that Mexico introduced elements of heterodox management of foreign capital flows (such as a band in the exchange rate) too late.[6]

It is a cause of concern that even with an extremely low growth rate (0.5 percent of GDP in 1993), the Mexican current account deficit was very high that year, and rose further in 1994. Although the approval of NAFTA opens new possibilities for Mexico, the high level of the current account deficit makes it very dependent on capital inflows; it is consequently vulnerable to any major decline in such inflows. To help avoid such a decline, the economic authorities need to use high interest rates, which have negative effects on the domestic economy.

A Policy Prescription for Stability and Sustained Growth

From a public-policy standpoint, the ideal way to evaluate a response to a surge of capital inflows would be to separate the permanent components from the temporary ones. If there is a permanent additional flow, such related phenomena as real exchange rate appreciation, growth of the current account deficit, and increased consumption could be interpreted as stabilizing adjustments and, therefore, economically healthy. If capital flows are temporary, the aforesaid movements in key variables would be distortionary because they would create economic imbalances and the likelihood of disruptive future adjustments with potentially high costs. This distinction is, of course, very difficult to make in practice. However, there are economic policy measures that can have a differentiated impact on short- and long-term flows or on flows of productive as opposed to purely financial investment (see Chapter 4).

The externalities and other major imperfections of international capital markets give rise to, among other things, frequent cycles of abundance and scarcity of resources, and systemic crises, with the result that even potentially permanent flows can disappear overnight (Guttentag and Herring, 1984). Accordingly, it is always advisable for governments to exercise a degree of caution where capital inflows are concerned, in order to promote a situation where their aggregate amount and main components are consistent with macroeconomic stability, investment, and growth based on international competitiveness. Particularly if the size and composition of capital flows are inconsistent with these parameters, sooner or later their sustainability could be threatened, making it necessary to resort to socially costly national adjustments. This problem of the level and quality of domestic absorptive capacity is compounded by the inherent risks of short-term external shocks in international financial markets.

Since capital flows can affect, and are affected by, national macroeconomic variables, governments should exercise caution on two fronts. First, they should avoid a situation in which capital inflows create atypical values (outliers) or major distortions in key domestic macroeconomic indicators, such as real interest and exchange rates, sectoral and national indebtedness, inflation (including asset prices), consumption, investment, and the production of tradables.

Second, governments should guard against using capital inflows as their main instrument for achieving a rigid or extreme target for a single domestic economic variable (such as reducing inflation with appreciation), especially over a prolonged period of time. Doing so usually throws other important variables out of balance, thereby affecting the very instrument they used in the first place, namely, capital inflows.

Capital flows clearly are not always consistent with the objectives of macroeconomic stability in its broad sense, sustained economic growth, and social equity; a degree of direct or indirect public "management" in order to influence the volume and composition of these flows is therefore justified. There have been numerous past experiences, successful and unsuccessful, in applying this approach. What constitutes an appropriate degree of liberalization of the capital account could vary over time, depending on short-term domestic and international conditions and the level and needs of national development.

With respect to the speed at which the capital account should be liberalized, the process must be tailored also to the economy's capacity to absorb and efficiently allocate external resources. For instance, as discussed previously, a distinction could be made between capital inflows and outflows and different components of each (Williamson, 1991).

Capital account liberalization in the industrialized countries has been fairly slow and gradual, accelerating only in the past ten years as capital markets have become globalized. It is interesting to note that Spain, Portugal, and Ireland introduced certain restrictions on capital movements in 1992 to combat exchange rate instability. Once the objectives of stability were achieved, the restrictions were lifted. This highlights the importance of flexible instruments that, according to circumstances, allow some temporary constraints to be imposed on capital movements to support efforts toward macroeconomic stability.

In periods when resources are scarce, there would be justification for seeking specific and more general ways of attracting capital inflows and erecting certain barriers to capital outflows. The situation in the first half of 1994, of diminished flows to much of Latin America, illustrates clearly how rapidly external flows can dry up and how, in these circumstances, it is important for governments to make special efforts to attract capital inflows. The reverse would apply when there was an obvious abundance of capital in the markets, as in the 1990–1993 period for many Latin American countries. It seems desirable in such circumstances that certain kinds of inflows were restricted and some channels for capital outflows were promoted.

There are a number of ways to manage capital flows. The more pressing the need for management, and the more underdeveloped the fiscal and monetary policies are, the more likely it is that the use of direct regulations on certain types of capital flows will be warranted, even if only temporarily. Of course, controls of any type are often considered inefficient and capable of being circumvented by ever more sophisticated capital market operations. But, as Williamson (1991, p. 139) has pointed out, "assertions about the ineffectiveness of capital controls are vastly exaggerated." As mentioned earlier, there are obviously costs involved in the use of these instruments. However, these must be measured against the global social benefits in terms of macroeconomic stability, investment, and growth as well as against the feasibility and reliability of possible alternative ways to achieve the same goal. As Zahler (1992) had argued, the possible microeconomic costs of regulating capital movements may be more than offset by the benefits resulting from greater macroeconomic stability. Naturally, the net result will depend on the nature of the economic climate and the quality of the regulation policies applied.

Managing capital flows entails some costs. However, experience has shown that always leaving the market to determine the volume and composition of such flows may also entail costs, and these may be notably larger. There is no instrument, or set of instruments, that can operate with complete efficiency; in an imperfect world, they must be judged by their overall results. Pragmatic use must be made of the policy instruments that offer the greatest net benefits in terms of macroeconomic stability and growth while minimizing costs.

The reorganization of financial systems, including the opening of the capital account, should give priority to channeling resources into savings and investment. Thus the relationship between the financial system and national savings and investment processes, and between the domestic financial system and external markets, also must be considered carefully.

Where the relationship between financial markets and capital formation for development is concerned, an institutional framework is needed to complete or perfect markets according to two criteria. The first is that a dynamic long-term segment of the financial market must be developed in order to finance productive projects. This involves discouraging short-term segments and concentrating on long-term international capital accompanied by access to technology and to export markets. This is particularly relevant for small and medium-sized firms discouraged by the segmentation of the capital market. To that end, credit institutions and guarantee mechanisms are needed to do what capital markets have failed to do spontaneously. Second, it must be recognized that in countries with "emerging" stock markets, financial liberalization of the capital account, by opening it to international portfolio investment, runs the risk of creating external debt overhang and excessive stock market and exchange rate fluctuations. Large-scale foreign capital inflows to domestic markets can trigger both "stock market bubbles" and appreciation of the local currency at the same time. The subsequent decline in stock market prices can, in turn, cause capital outflows, currency depreciation, and overall instability.

Concern about risks associated with financial markets, such as the generation of speculative bubbles, implies the need to introduce regulatory and supervisory mechanisms to ensure the stability of financial institutions operating in capital markets. Such mechanisms are particularly essential in open, free-market economies. Strengthening prudential regulation can soften the above risks and contribute to a more orderly, stable process of attracting portfolio investments from abroad. Of course, effective regulation will require countries to improve their monitoring systems for external capital flows. This must be done not only at the microlevel for individual financial institutions, but also at the macrolevel to ensure that the volume and composition of flows are consistent with economic stability.

Notes

We are grateful for the valuable comments at seminars in the Brookings Institution, the Institute for Latin American Studies of the University of London, the IDB, the OECD Development Centre, the Secretariat of the United Nations in New York, and at ECLAC in Santiago. In particular, we are indebted to Guillermo Calvo, Sebastian Edwards, Helmut Reisen, and Peter West.

1. For an extensive analysis of the region's insertion into capital markets during the 1970s and the emergence of the debt crisis, see Devlin (1989), Feinberg

and Ffrench-Davis (1988), Griffith-Jones and Rodríguez (1992), World Bank (1993), and Devlin and Ffrench-Davis (1994).

2. For diverse theoretical views of the microeffects of freely mobile external capital, see ECLAC (1994).

3. Note that Chile adopted effective policies to moderate short-run capital inflows. See Chapter 4.

4. The authors thank Roy Culpeper for suggesting and developing this point.

5. If the net inflows are only transitorily large, this eventual cost would tend to be compensated by subsequent sales by the central bank of foreign currency at prices above those at which it made purchases. See discussion of the issue in Reisen (1993) and Chapter 4 in this volume.

6. Nevertheless, the band, together with the exchange stabilization fund, turned out to be extremely effective in the emergency faced by Mexico in early 1994.

References

Akyüz, Y. (1993), "Financial liberalization: The key issues," *Discussion Papers*, no. 56, UNCTAD, Geneva.

Calvo, G., L. Leiderman, and C. Reinhart (1993), "Capital inflows and real exchange rate appreciation in Latin America: The role of external factors," *IMF Staff Papers*, vol. 40, no. 1, March.

Devlin, R. (1989), *Debt and crisis in Latin America: The supply side of the story*, Princeton University Press, Princeton, N.J.

Devlin, R., and R. Ffrench-Davis (1994), "The great Latin American debt crisis: A decade of asymmetric adjustment," in G. Helleiner, ed., *Poverty, prosperity and the world economy*, MacMillan, London.

Díaz-Alejandro, C. (1985), "Good-bye financial repression, hello financial crash," *Journal of Development Economics*, vol. 19, no. 1/2, September.

ECLAC (1984), "Políticas de ajuste y renegociación de la deuda externa en América Latina," *Cuadernos de la CEPAL*, no. 48, United Nations, Santiago, Sales No. S.84.II.G.18.

———— (1994), *Policies to improve linkages with the global economy* (LC/G.1800 (SES.25/3), United Nations, Santiago.

Edwards, S. (1984), "The order of liberalization of the balance of payments. Should the current account be opened first?" *Staff Working Papers*, no. 710, World Bank, Washington, D.C., December.

Feinberg, R., and R. Ffrench-Davis (1988), eds., *Development and external debt in Latin America*, University of Notre Dame Press, Notre Dame, Indiana.

Ffrench-Davis, R. (1983), ed., *Relaciones financieras externas: Su efecto en la economía latinoamericana*, Fondo de Cultura Económica, México.

Friedman, I. (1977), *The emerging role of private banks in the developing world*, Citicorp, New York.

Griffith-Jones, S., and E. Rodríguez (1992), eds., *Cross conditionality, banking regulation and Third World debt*, MacMillan, London.

Guttentag, J., and R. Herring (1984), "Credit rationing and financial disorder," *Journal of Finance*, vol. 39, December.

Kenen, P. (1993), "Financial opening and the exchange rate regime," in H. Reisen and B. Fischer (eds.), *Financial opening*, OECD, Paris.

Kindleberger, Ch. (1978), *Manias, panics and crashes*, Basic Books, New York.

Lamfalussy, A. (1992), "The restructuring of the financial industry: A central banking perspective," lecture at City University, mimeo, London, March.

Lessard, D. (1991), "The international efficiency of world capital markets," in H. Siebert (ed.), *Capital flows in the world economy: Symposium 1990*, J.C.B. Mohr, Tubingen.

McKinnon, R. (1973), *Money and capital*, Brookings Institution, Washington, D.C.

——— (1984), "The international capital market and economic liberalization in LDCs," *The Developing Economies*, vol. 22, December.

——— (1991), *The order of economic liberalization: Financial control in the transition to a market economy*, Johns Hopkins University Press, Baltimore.

Mathieson, D., and L. Rojas-Suárez (1993), "Liberalization of the capital account," *Occasional Papers*, no. 103, International Monetary Fund, Washington, D.C., March.

Mishkin, F. S. (1991), "Assymetric information and financial crises: An historical perspective," in R. G. Hubbard (ed.), *Financial markets and financial crises*, University of Chicago Press, Chicago.

Park, Y. Ch., and W. A. Park (1993), "Capital movement, real asset speculation, and macroeconomic adjustment in Korea," in H. Reisen and B. Fischer (eds.), *Financial opening*, OECD, Paris.

Ramos, J. (1985), "Stabilization and adjustment policies in the Southern Cone, 1974–1983," *CEPAL Review*, no. 25, Santiago, April.

Reisen, H. (1993), "Capital flows and their effect on the monetary base," *CEPAL Review*, no. 51, December.

——— (1994), *Debt, deficits and exchange rates*, OECD Development Centre/ Edward Elgar Publishing Company, Hants, England.

Robichek, W. (1981), "Some reflections about external public debt management," *Estudios Monetarios VII*, Banco Central de Chile, Santiago.

Shaw, E. (1973), *Financial deepening in economic development*, Oxford University Press, New York.

Stiglitz, J. (1993), "The role of the state in financial markets," *Proceedings of the World Bank Annual Conference on Development Economics*, vol. 2, World Bank, Washington, D.C., May.

Stiglitz, J., and A. Weiss (1981), "Credit returning in markets with imperfect information," *American Economic Review*, vol. 71, June.

Tobin, J. (1984), "On the efficiency of the financial system," *Lloyds Bank Review*, no. 153, July.

Williamson, J. (1991), "On liberalizing the capital account," in R. O'Brien (ed.), *Finance and the international economy*, no. 5, Amex Bank, London.

——— (1993), "A cost-benefit analysis of capital account liberalization," in H. Reisen and B. Fischer (eds.), *Financial opening*, OECD, Paris.

World Bank (1993), *A decade after the debt crisis*, Latin America and the Caribbean Region, Washington, D.C., September.

Zahler, R. (1992), "Monetary policy and an open capital account," *CEPAL Review*, no. 48 (LC/G.1748-P), Santiago.

Index

ADRs. *See* American Depositary
  Receipts
American Depositary Receipts, 37*n11,*
  70, 82, 97*n10,* 101, 102*tab,* 108–109,
  110*tab,* 115*tab,* 221*app;* secondary,
  109, 137
Amnesty Tax Law (Argentina), 157
Arbitrage, 111, 122, 123; incentives for,
  126; interest rate, 116, 136;
  profitability of, 126
Argendollars, 157, 166, 167, 168*tab,*
  170, 174, 180
Argentina: access to markets, 2; Amnesty
  Tax Law, 157; balance of payments,
  146, 153, 159, 164, 166, 167, 185*n12;*
  bond issues, 11*tab,* 12, 14*tab,* 68*tab;*
  Bonex Plan, 169, 170, 171*tab,* 184*n8,*
  184*n10,* 186*n25,* 186*n26;* capital
  flows in, xii–xiii, 145–183, 234,
  235*tab;* capital markets, 167,
  169–172, 174–176; *Carta Orgánica,*
  174, 176; Central Bank, 148, 149, 150,
  157, 174; Convertibility Plan, 153,
  156, 157, 158, 159–161, 165, 169,
  171, 176, 185*n15;* current accounts in,
  148, 151, 152*tab,* 159; debt
  conversions in, 8; Deregulation
  Decree, 157–158; Economic
  Emergency Law, 156; economic
  growth, 183; economic policy, 176;
  equity issues, 15*tab,* 18, 19*tab,* 81;
  European investment in, 47, 48*tab,* 56;
  exchange rate policies, 146–153;
  financial policies, 146–153; gross
  domestic product, 180, 181, 182*tab;*
  inflation in, 150, 153, 158, 159, 169,
  177; interest rates in, 146, 147, 148,

170, 171*tab,* 180, 181; investible
  returns, 17*tab;* Law for the Reform of
  the State, 158; liberalization program,
  29, 146–150; London Inter-Bank Offer
  Rate, 170, 171*tab,* 184*n8;*
  macroeconomic stability in, 176–183;
  monetary policy in, 149, 156; private
  sector, 149, 151, 159, 160, 165–167,
  178, 180; privatization in, 8, 114,
  154*tab,* 156, 158, 160, 161, 162*tab,*
  163*tab,* 164, 175, 180, 185*n15;* public
  sector, 148, 151, 153, 156, 158, 161,
  164–165, 181; relative prices, 178,
  178*tab;* savings rate, 181; stock
  market in, 19*tab,* 87*tab,* 156, 157,
  174–176; trade accounts, 185*n16;*
  U.S. bank claims in, 23*tab;* U.S.
  investment in, 24, 25*tab,* 26, 26*tab,*
  27*tab,* 36*tab*
Asia: bank credits to, 23; capital flows,
  44*tab;* Japanese investment in, 77, 94,
  95, 236
Aylwin, Patricio, 120

Bahamas, 14, 37*n5,* 37*n8,* 84, 236
Balance of payments, 5, 6, 68, 70, 101,
  105*tab,* 125, 132, 139*n6,* 146, 153,
  159, 164, 166, 167, 185*n12,* 196, 214,
  231
Bank for International Settlements, 23
Bank(s): capital adequacy, 9; capital-
  asset ratios, 9; capital reserves, 97*n15;*
  central, 3; certificates of deposit, 5;
  collateralized credit, 6; commercial, 1,
  4, 45, 81, 190, 191, 192, 193, 217,
  234; competition in, 6, 77, 172;
  confidence in, 3, 33, 49; cooperative,

Organization of Petroleum Exporting
Countries, 57
Overseas Private Investment
Corporation, 31

Pacto de Solidaridad, ("Pacto")
(Mexico), 158, 194, 200
Panama, 84, 236
Paraguay, 28, 48*tab*
Pemex Oil Company (Mexico), 37*n10*,
72*n10*, 213, 223*n10*
Pension funds, 9, 33, 77, 78*tab*, 140*n24*,
141*n30*, 209, 239; assets, 15; British
Rail, 56; defined-benefit, 10; defined-
contribution, 10; foreign assets in, 50,
50*tab*, 53, 54, 55; investment decisions
by, 58; investment regulations, 62;
private, 54, 108, 114, 123; public, 22,
54; reform, 131, 137; regulation of, 20,
22; structure of, 10
Perot, Ross, 58
Peru, 48*tab*, 56
Petrobas (Brazil), 81
Petrodollars, 5, 190
Pinochet, Augusto, 119
Policy: compensatory, 115*tab;* demand-
reducing, 116; demand side issues,
247, 250–258; development, 230;
domestic, 3; economic, 3, 16, 66, 84,
100, 179, 191, 192–194; exchange
rate, 100, 119–125, 122, 124, 189,
214–218; fiscal, 58, 125–131;
flexibility, 232; incentives, 100;
interest rate, 35; intervention, 115*tab;*
issues in capital flows, 225–258;
macroeconomic, 116–119; market-
friendly, 145; monetary, 38*n19*, 116,
120, 125–131,.149, 156, 176, 187*n32*,
190, 192, 193, 204, 214–218, 242,
251; promotional, 31–32; regulatory,
30–32, 121; relaxation of, 242;
responses to capital inflows, xiii;
restrictive, 38*n19*, 190, 194, 220;
stability, 58; supply side, 234,
236–247; tax, 31
Political: stability, 60, 61; uncertainty,
153
Price(s): adjustments, 202; controlled,
193; correction, 196; deflation, 6;
deregulation, 202; distortions, 187*n32;*
domestic, 193; freezing of, 185*n14;*

misalignment of, 183; public sector,
194; relative, 187*n32;* stabilization,
202
Privatization, 8, 18, 58, 76, 81, 84, 108,
114, 156, 158, 160, 161, 162*tab*,
163*tab*, 164, 175, 180, 185*n15*, 196,
202, 214
Production: development of, 129;
expansion of facilities, 183;
globalization, 225; rationalization of,
30; specialization in, 30
Protectionism, 61, 191, 204

Real estate, 6, 7, 36*n4*, 89, 89*fig*, 91,
97*n16*, 149, 180, 238
Recession, 6, 10, 149, 166, 167, 179,
190, 194, 226, 243
Reform: banking, 3; domestic, 146;
economic, 10, 16, 28, 190, 196, 200,
202; financial, 147, 149, 231; New
Deal, 4; pension system, 131, 137;
public sector, 158; sequencing, 231,
233; social security, 131; structural,
58, 145, 156–158, 196, 200, 202; tax,
129, 179, 193, 196; trade, 231
Regime, democratic, 120, 129
Regime, military, 101, 119
Regulation, 41, 237; administrative, 204;
banking, 5, 101, 157; capital market,
194; changes in, 239; collateral
requirements, 92; domestic, 60–61;
environmental, 35; financial, 145;
global issues, 245; insurance company
funds in, 37*n12;* international, 6;
investment, 30–31, 61–66; lack of, 6;
legislative, 20, 204; liberalization, 239,
240; market, 118; of money supply,
131; relaxation of, 244; Rule 144-A,
20–23, 21, 82, 97*n10*, 209, 237; Rule
17f-5, 20–23; of Securities and
Exchange Commission, 20; of
securities trading, 4; social, 35
Regulation Q, 3, 6
Regulation S, 21
Resources: allocation of, 100, 119, 134,
180, 227, 231; investment, 118;
reallocation, 229; transfer of, 182
Risk: associated with lending, 66–71;
capital, 106, 242–244; credit, 97*n8;*
decreasing, 16; devaluation, 166, 167;
and diversification, 17; investment,

About the Contributors

Manuel Agosin is director of the Graduate School of Economics and Business, Universidad de Chile. He has worked in various agencies of the United Nations dealing with international economics and economic development issues. In recent years, he has been a consultant for ECLAC, UNCTAD, and the Inter-American Development Bank. He has also been adviser to Chile's Ministry of Foreign Affairs on international economic relations. He is coeditor of the recently published book *Trade and Growth: New Dilemmas in Trade Policy*.

Punam Chuhan is an economist in the International Economics Department of the World Bank. She is currently working with major issues pertaining to private financial flows to developing countries. Ms. Chuhan is responsible for producing the World Bank publication *Financial Flows and the Developing Countries*. Prior to joining the Bank, Ms. Chuhan was an economist in the International Finance Department of the Federal Reserve Bank of New York.

Roy Culpeper has worked for the Cabinet Planning Secretariat of the Manitoba government, the federal department of finance, the federal department of external affairs, and the World Bank, where he was adviser to the Canadian executive director. Since 1986 he has been at the North-South Institute directing the institute's research on international debt and finance. In 1991 he was named the institute's vice president. Among his recent publications are *The Debt Matrix, Canada and the Global Governors*, and *High Stakes and Low Incomes: Canada and the Development Banks* (coauthored with Andrew Clark).

Robert Devlin is chief of the Integration, Trade and Hemispheric Issues Division of the Inter-American Development Bank in Washington, D.C. Prior to that he was deputy director of the International Trade and Finance Division of UN ECLAC in Santiago, Chile. He has written extensively on international economics. His most recent book is *Debt and Crisis in Latin America: The Supply Side of the Story*.

José María Fanelli, an Argentinean economist, is currently director of the Economics Department at the University of Buenos Aires. Since 1984 he has been senior researcher at the Center for the Study of State and Society (CEDES) and Conicet (the national research council) in Buenos Aires. He is a specialist in macroeconomics and monetary economics and has published several books and articles on stabilization, structural reform, and the financial system in Latin America. He has also worked as a consultant for ECLAC, UNCTAD, OECD, and IDRC.

Ricardo Ffrench-Davis, a Chilean economist, is postgraduate professor of international economics at the University of Chile. He was director of research of the Central Bank of Chile from 1964 to 1970 and from 1990 to 1992. He held the post of director and vice president of the Center for Economic Research on Latin America (CIEPLAN) from 1976 to 1990. He has also worked as a consultant for the United Nations, the Inter-American Development Bank, and the OECD. He is currently principal regional adviser of ECLAC. His publications include *Políticas económicas en Chile, 1952–70, Economía internacional: teorías y políticas para el desarrollo,* and *Capital Formation and the Macroeconomic Framework.*

Stephany Griffith-Jones is a senior fellow at the Institute of Development Studies, Sussex University. Previously she worked at the Central Bank of Chile. She has acted as senior consultant to many international agencies, including the World Bank, the Inter-American Development Bank, the EEC, and UNCTAD. She has written widely on international finance, especially, but not only, in relation to Latin America. She has also written recently on financial sector reform in transitional economies.

José Angel Gurría has led the negotiating team restructuring Mexico's foreign debt since 1982 and is currently minister of foreign affairs of Mexico. From 1989 to 1993 he served as undersecretary for international financial affairs at the Mexican Ministry of Finance. He has held other key financial posts, including executive president of the National Bank of Foreign Trade (Bancomext) and executive president of Nacional Financiera (Nafin). He served as a consultant for the United Nations Center on Transnational Corporations and has lectured on debt management and negotiations in Asia, Africa, Europe, and Latin America. He is also secretary for international affairs for the Institutional Revolutionary Party (PRI).

Kwang W. Jun is currently a senior financial economist in the International Finance Division of the World Bank. His interests cover a broad range of issues on international capital markets and investment flows. He is the author of numerous major policy and research papers in these fields. Prior to joining the World Bank in 1986, Dr. Jun was a finance faculty member at Michigan State University and Indiana University and did extensive consultant work for major investment banks.

José Luis Machinea, an Argentinean economist, is currently a private consultant and adviser of the Argentine Industrial Union (Unión Industrial). He was president of the Central Bank of Argentina from 1986 to 1989, and previously he was undersecretary of economic policy and undersecretary of planning. He has written numerous articles and has participated in several national and international conferences on stabilization policies and topics related to the financial system. He has also worked as a consultant for ECLAC, IDB, and the World Bank.

Andras Uthoff is a Chilean economist and commercial engineer. He was regional adviser to PREALC, ILO, and is presently regional adviser to ECLAC and a professor at the University of Chile and ILADES/Georgetown.

About the Book and Editors

Private capital flows to Latin America have increased dramatically since 1989, approximately doubling in volume each year. This book examines the possible causes and consequences of the new—and unforeseen—wave of investment, from both the borrower and the lender perspectives.

The authors first analyze direct investment, securities, and bank lending, considering the motivations of investors in the United States, Europe, and Japan, as well as the regulations affecting them. They then turn to the features of capital flows, their macroeconomic impact, and policy responses in three recipient countries: Argentina, Chile, and Mexico.

An important theme of the book is that, while the return of private capital flows to Latin America is to be welcomed, the mutual benefits will be sustainable only if governments in both source and recipient countries more effectively monitor and supervise the flows and, equally important, adequate macroeconomic measures are undertaken in the recipient countries.

Ricardo Ffrench-Davis is principal regional adviser of ECLAC (Santiago, Chile). He previously served as deputy manager and later director of research (1990–1992) at the Central Bank of Chile, and in 1976–1990 was vice president and researcher at the Center for Economic Research on Latin America (CIEPLAN). He has published extensively in international economics, development strategies, foreign debt, and Latin American economies. **Stephany Griffith-Jones** is a senior fellow of the Institute of Development Studies, Sussex University. Formerly head of Credit at the Central Bank of Chile and adviser on Latin America to Barclays Bank International (U.K.), she is author or editor of eleven books and has published numerous articles on finance, macroeconomic policies, and Latin American and East European economies.

A o ππ

Roswll D ππ

4   Nπw

30 - 80

0ιυ ι/ι0 ππ